MANLY STATES

*Columbia University Press*
*New York*

# manly states

## Masculinities, International Relations, and Gender Politics

CHARLOTTE HOOPER

Columbia University Press
Publishers Since 1893
New York    Chichester, West Sussex
Copyright © 2001 Columbia University Press
All rights reserved

Library of Congress Cataloging-in-Publication Data

Hooper, Charlotte.
   Manly states : masculinities, international relations, and
   gender politics / Charlotte Hooper.
      p. cm.
   Includes bibliographical references and index.
   ISBN 0-231-12074-5 (cloth : alk. paper) — ISBN
   0-231-12075-3 (pbk. : alk. paper)
      1. Masculinity—Political aspects. 2. International
   relations—Psychological aspects. 3. Economist
   (London, England : 1843) I. Title.

   HQ1090 .H66 2001
   305.31—dc21

                                        00-060142

CIP
Casebound editions of Columbia University Press books are
printed on permanent and durable acid-free paper.

Printed in the United States of America

c 10 9 8 7 6 5 4 3 2 1
p 10 9 8 7 6 5 4 3 2 1

# Contents

*v*

*Illustrations*

*Acknowledgments*

I WOULD LIKE to thank the British Economic and Social Science Research Council for funding the research that formed the basis for this book. I am also grateful to the editor and staff of *The Economist* for their assistance, not least in helping trace advertising sources. I am grateful to the following companies, who have kindly given permission for their advertisements to be reproduced: AEtna; Alcatel Alsthom; Canon; $EMC^2$; Ernst & Young; J. P. Morgan; Morgan Stanley; Unibanco; Unisys; Vacheron Constantin.

I would also like to thank Cynthia Enloe, and the British International Studies Association doctoral dissertation prize panel (1998), without whose encouragement this book would probably never have been published; and Eric Herring, Celia Hodes, Esme Hodes, Richard Little, Xanthe Ponsford, Penny Starns, Hannah Thomson, and Zachary Thomson for their various contributions of support, encouragement, and endurance along the way.

Most of all I would like to thank Judith Squires, for her invaluable critical input, and David Hodes, for doing much of the administrative work involved in preparing the manuscript for publication, as well as offering general support and encouragement throughout the whole project.

AN EARLIER, condensed version of some of the discussion from chapters 1, 2, and 3 was previously published as "Masculinist Practices and Gender Politics: Multiple Masculinities in International Relations," in *The Man Question in International Relations*, edited by Marysia Zalewski and Jane Parpart (Boulder, Colorado: Westview Press, 1997). Part of chapter 3 has also previously appeared as "Masculinities, IR, and the 'Gender Variable': A Cost-Benefit Analysis for Sympathetic Gender Skeptics," *Review of International Studies* 25, no. 3 (Cambridge University Press, 1999). An earlier version of chapter 5 was published as "Hegemonic Masculinities in Transition: The Case of Globalization," in *Gender and Global Restructuring*, edited by Marianne Marchand and Anne Sisson Runyan (London: Routledge, 2000).

MANLY STATES

# Introduction

ONE of the achievements of feminist contributions to international relations has been to reveal the extent to which the whole field is gendered.[1] The range of subjects studied, the boundaries of the discipline, its central concerns and motifs, the content of empirical research, the assumptions of theoretical models, and the corresponding lack of female practitioners both in academic and elite political and economic circles all combine and reinforce each other to marginalize and often make invisible women's roles and women's concerns in the international arena (Enloe 1990; Grant and Newland 1991; Tickner 1992; Peterson and Runyan 1993, 1998; Sylvester 1994; Pettman 1996). The world of international relations appears to be truly a man's world, both through the predominance of men in practice and through the "masculinist underpinnings" (Tickner 1992, xi) of the discipline, whereby success is measured in terms of the "masculine" virtues of power, autonomy, and self-reliance.

Having established that international relations is a male-dominated and masculinist field, feminist contributors have rightly gone on to focus most of their energy on reclaiming women and "femininity" from the margins. This is not to say that men and masculinity have been entirely neglected,[2] but the relationship between masculinity and international relations has not yet been fully articulated. More might be said about how masculinity or masculinities shape both the theory and practice of international relations. But one could also ask, what place does international relations (both theory and practice) have in the shaping, defining, and legitimating of masculinity or masculinities? Might causality, or at least the interplay of complex influences, run in both directions, in mutually reinforcing patterns? Might international relations discipline men as much as men shape international relations?[3]

My starting point for thinking about the relationship between masculinity and international relations was Ann Tickner's (1992) book *Gender in International Relations*. First, Tickner traced the masculinism and misogyny of realism, where the ideal of the glorified male warrior has been projected onto the behavior of states. In realist discourse, security is seen to rest on a false division between a civil(ized) domestic political order and the "natural" violence of international anarchy. This division is traced back to Hobbes's view of the state of nature as a state of war—a dangerous and wild place where men had to rely on their own resources to survive. The international realm, outside the jurisdiction of a single government, was deemed to be anarchic and, as such, like a state of nature. As Tickner argued, women were largely absent in Hobbes's picture. She went on to discuss Machiavelli, who, although in the context of a very different tradition, characterized the disordered and "natural" realm of anarchy itself as feminine. If Hobbes's men were in a state of nature, then Machiavelli's men wished to have dominion over it. Given that Hobbes and Machiavelli are often (in spite of their differences) quoted in the same breath, these "founding fathers" of the discipline have between them contributed to a vision of international relations in which women are virtually absent and where heroic men struggle to tame a wild, dangerous, and essentially feminine anarchy.

Second, after examining the realist approach to security, Tickner looked at the masculine assumptions underpinning the models used in international political economy under the heading "Three Models of Man" (67). These were the abstract rational-actor model favored by liberal economists; game-theoretic models applied by economic nationalists; and the capitalist production model used by Marxists. As Tickner pointed out, all three models have been criticized by feminist theorists for offering only a partial, and masculinized, account of human agency and production. Third, she explored the role of nature in international politics and argued that the control and domination of nature has played a crucial part in the development of modern international relations, which cannot be divorced from men's control and domination of women, who are generally more closely associated with nature than men, through their reproductive role. In the final chapter, Tickner considered feminist alternatives to masculinist theorizing and mentioned alternative conceptions of masculinity, as well as possibilities for there being a nongendered model of human action.

Tickner's analysis suggests that masculinist perspectives in IR do not apply a uniform understanding of masculinity, but rather make use of a number of different "models of man" (Tickner 1992, 67). She also warned against the essentializing tendency of separating women from men as undifferentiated categories. However, as I shall argue in chapter 2, the suggestion that there may be a number of masculinities operating in IR theory is rather overshadowed by the main thrust and structure of her book, which tends to oppose a monolithic "masculinism" against an equally monolithic "feminism." This is a pity because the structure thus serves to essentialize both masculinity and feminism. Clearly not all feminisms are compatible, and neither are all models of masculinity. For example, men cannot be both in a state of nature (the Hobbesian, realist view), and yet have control and domination over it (the neorealist view) at the same time. Thus the historical eclipse of realism by neorealism in the postwar period represents a reversal of the relationship between man and nature as conceptualized in international-relations (IR) theory.

The relationship between masculinity and international relations appears to be more complex than a straightforward masculinist/feminist dichotomy would allow. If there are a number of different and perhaps incompatible masculinities at play in the discipline, then this raises new questions: What is the relationship between them? How do they fit in with feminist understandings of masculinism? What is their significance for the gendered identities of men who participate in international relations?

These questions made me turn to the emerging literature on multiple masculinities that is being produced by feminists and theorists of men's studies outside the discipline of IR. Here I found useful approaches with which to think through such questions (see chapters 1, 2, and 3). It has been established that neither masculinity nor femininity are monolithic and unchanging categories (Brod 1987; Riley 1988; Nicholson 1990). Indeed, there are a variety of masculinities and femininities at large in Western culture, as well as variations historically (Roper and Tosh 1991) and between cultures (Brod and Kaufman 1994; Cornwall and Lindisfarne 1994). Which attributes count as masculine or feminine depends on circumstances and is subject to change and struggle. Recent literature in the field of gender studies points to a global hierarchy of masculinities dominated by a loosely coherent and evolving hegemonic form (Connell 1987; Brittan 1989). This current, Western (largely Anglo-American) hegemonic masculinity is being reforged and reframed in the light of redefinitions of the feminine and other challenges posed by both feminism and the feminized, exoticized, non-European world (Chapman and Rutherford 1988; Segal 1990). It is also being undermined, perhaps more seriously, by the internationalization of the economy, deindustrialization, and the rise of the woman worker, which has more to do with the requirements of capitalism than with feminism. Indeed, the "crisis" and possible transformation of hegemonic masculinity triggered by globalization, and wrought through multiple gendered struggles and rivalries, is a major preoccupation in the literature (Kimmell 1987a; McDowell 1991; Hanke 1992; Connell 1993, 1995; Pfeil 1995).

Reading this literature, I became convinced that both IR and international relations on the ground must be playing an important part in these contemporary struggles over the future shape of gender relations. No account of the transformation of a hitherto globally dominant Anglo-American hegemonic masculinity can afford to ignore the influence of an Anglo-American masculinist discipline that reflects the outlook of the hitherto (at least for the last few hundred years) globally hegemonic powers of the West.[4] Putting together all three of my concerns—that international relations might influence men and masculinity as well as be influenced by them; that there are a number of different masculinities at play in the field; and that an important contemporary issue is the challenge to hegemonic forms of masculinity in connection with globalization—has brought me to the central issue that this book will address. My main question is: What role does international relations play in the shaping, defining, or legitimating of masculinity or masculinities? My supplementary question is: What is the relationship between this role and the process of globalization that offers challenges to the existing gender order? Such questions cannot be answered comprehensively in the space of a single volume. While making some observations that I believe to be pertinent to the questions in general, this book will concentrate not on the practices of international relations, but rather on the role that the discipline of IR plays in such matters. This role will be explored through an analysis of the discipline itself, together with an examination of its relationship to changing gender symbolism and the discourse of globalization in the wider culture.

These questions are relevant for a number of reasons. First, the field of international relations has been dominated by (often elite) men, and—in the division of modernity into private life/domestic politics/international politics—it is conceptually situated at the furthest extreme from the private life of families, where women are positioned. It thus seems a particularly appropriate site for an investigation into masculinities, and particularly into their dominant, or "hegemonic," forms. In this book, the focus will remain on the relationship between IR and the construction of hegemonic Anglo-American masculinities. I argue that these masculinities have strong historic links with the notion of the international—links that have been forged through "foreign adventure" and colonialism. The connections between Anglo-American hegemonic masculinities and Anglo-American notions of the international realm beyond the state's borders are such that one cannot regard such masculinities as purely "domestic" constructions. It is therefore my view that a study that wants to make sense of the contemporary challenges and changes in Anglo-American masculinities must take account of the international dimension. This book will, hopefully, thus provide insights that are useful to both students of international relations, and to those interested in masculinities more generally.

Second, if both the discipline and practices of international relations are heavily implicated in the construction of hegemonic masculinities, and if both the "content" of international politics and the "fixing" of masculine identities are simultaneously "achieved" when men engage in activities in the "international arena," then strategies aimed at dismantling the field's inherent masculinism, if at all successful, are likely to prove personally challenging to large numbers of men. Removing masculinism would involve a drastic reformulation of models of masculinity and alternative understandings of what it means to be a man and where men belong. For many men, it would involve no less than a revolutionary change of identity. In this case, revealing the mechanisms by which such identities are constantly being produced and reproduced might help reveal opportunities for change that can be exploited by feminists and their sympathizers.

Third, the salience of questions of culture and identity in international politics has been highlighted recently. This can be seen in both in the post-cold war resurgence of ethnic rivalry and of identity politics in domestic, international, and transnational situations (e.g., Smith 1992; Waever et al 1993; Huntington 1993; Joffe 1993; Davis and Moore 1997) and in the writings of postpositivist academics (Ashley 1989; Rengger 1989; Connolly 1991; Campbell 1992; Weber 1995; Lapid and Kratochwil 1996; Doty 1996; Linklater 1996). As Yosef Lapid argues, "a swing of the pendulum toward culture and identity is . . . strikingly evident in post-Cold War theorizing" (Lapid 1996, 3). This is in response to an awareness among IR scholars of their mounting theoretical difficulties with apparently "exponential increases in global heterogeneity and diversity" (Lapid 1996, 7).

In the more mainstream analysis, the significance of resurgent identity politics for the practices of international relations has been examined—for example, in relation to potential East-West conflict (Huntington 1993), to European Community integration (Waever et al 1993), to transnational ethnic groups (Davis and Moore 1997), and not least in relation to ethnic conflicts that have flared up in the aftermath of the cold war (Brown 1993; McDermott 1994; Gagnon 1994). Postpositivists, in contrast, have tended to view the question from the opposite direction, asking rather how both the practices and the theories of international relations might be implicated in the construction of politicized identities. For example, David Campbell (1992) has shown how U.S. foreign policy has been used to construct a U.S. identity; Roxanne Doty (1996) has argued that British postwar Commonwealth and immigration policy helped to reconstruct British identity; and Cynthia Weber (1995) has explored the performative nature of apparently stable sovereign identities. That theories, too, might be implicated in identity construction follows from the observation that the production and circulation of theories is a power- and culture-laden set of practices in itself. Thus Richard Ashley (1989) has been able to show how realism uses dualistic language and the notion of "anarchy" to construct a "sovereign" identity, and William Connolly (1991) has discussed how the notion of identity has always, in one way or another, been predicated on difference.[5]

The approach to identities taken by postpositivists runs counter to the tradition of regarding identities as biological, sociological, or psychological givens. In the postpositivist view, identities are seen as mutable and as constituted through political, social, and discursive processes, rather than as foundational or fixed. Examining the politics of identity construction forms part of the expansion of "the political" out of formal politics and international relations and into other areas of life that were perhaps previously assigned to sociology (Rowe 1995). However, what counts as political is itself a political question. Politics has no natural borders but is defined and contested differently in each age. Different things get politicized, and identity is politicized right now—as is testified by contemporary controversies over multiculturalism, feminism, race, and religious and ethnic identities. Traditional political conceptions of the self that pay no attention to the politics of identity but merely take identities as the foundation of politics are not adequate to the task of mapping such contemporary struggles (Emmett and Llewellyn 1995). Nor can they account for the ways in which the politics of identity construction might intersect with and inform other, more conventional forms of politics.

Feminist contributors to international relations share this interest in the politics of identity construction with other postpositivist approaches. The politics of identities is, after all, heavily gendered, and has long been at the core of feminist concerns (Nicholson 1990). Virtually all feminist international-relations scholarship that examines gender constructions, divisions, and exclusions deals with, implicitly if not explicitly, the oppositional construction of masculine and feminine gender identities. However, recently some feminist IR scholars have given more explicit attention to the production and reinforcement of a range of particular hierarchical gender identities—those created, for example, through colonialism and nationalism (Pettman 1996; Tickner 1996a). Others have examined more fluid forms of identification and the role of discourse in their construction (Weber 1990; 1993; Sylvester 1994). These trends follow developments in mainstream feminist theory that have moved away from dualistic and toward multiple and fluid analyses of gender that emphasize difference (Nicholson 1990). This book will contribute to this new stream of feminist IR scholarship that is beginning to examine the multiple and changing intersections of identity construction.

The feminist concern with identities also has wider relevance. Indeed, because of the attention that has been given to the politics of identity construction in feminist scholarship, this is an ideal place to begin looking for more general theoretical insights into the subject. In their essay "Questions about Identity in International Relations," Marysia Zalewski and Cynthia

Enloe (1995) used examples drawn from feminist research to make more general claims about the relationships between international relations and identities.[6] They argued both that the processes of international relations help to construct particular (gendered) identities and that processes of identity formation affect international politics. These influences take place in ways that realism, pluralism, and structuralism/globalism are all "too restricted ontologically, methodologically and epistemologically to consider" (Zalewski and Enloe 1995, 297).

Contemporary interest in questions of identity is not confined to international relations but goes right across the social sciences, relating to three forms of identity crisis that we appear to be experiencing all at once, and on a global scale. These include a crisis of identity within modernity, with disillusion over modern notions of progress and universalism; a continuing crisis between modernity and what is left of nonmodern and premodern forms of life; and a crisis relating to the need to reorient and reinvent ourselves in relation to rapid globalization. As the process of globalization is itself also challenging the traditional boundaries and subject matter of IR, it is particularly important to be able to make connections across a wide range of disciplines at this juncture, "to tease out important points of convergence between international relations and cognate fields" (Linklater and MacMillan 1995, 11).

In combining feminist theory, men's studies, IR theory, and cultural studies approaches in order to examine the contemporary relationship between IR, globalization, and hegemonic masculinity, this book attempts to do just that. My questions about the relationship between international relations and the shaping of masculinities, while specifically addressing an issue of relevance to gender politics and making use of feminist insights, can hopefully further the general development of postpositivist enquiries into contemporary questions of identity in international relations and in politics in general.

Before outlining the structure of the text in more detail, I would like to make two more points. First, in my discussion of "hegemonic masculinity" I have by and large confined myself to the Anglo-American case. I justify this on the grounds that through the British Empire in the nineteenth century and the superpower status of the United States in the twentieth, Anglo-American culture is itself in a hegemonic position within international relations, and thus, globally, Anglo-American hegemonic masculinity is likely to exert a disproportionate influence. Meanwhile, in disciplinary terms the Anglo-American influence is also very strong, and the theoretical underpinnings of the discipline largely reflect the Anglo-American philosophical tradition. On the other hand, to restrict the bulk of my analysis to a discussion of Anglo-American hegemonic masculinity may run the risk of dealing only with the stereotyped and the trite—not to mention giving yet more attention to the powerful and overprivileged at the expense of the marginalized, a strategy that goes against the grain in feminist circles. However, the observation that this construction of masculinity has become so easily identified as a stereotype is not a good reason for assuming that it no longer has any power. The intention here is not to reproduce such stereotypes but to unpack them and reveal the power moves that keep them influential. It is always wise to "know thine enemy." As a white, middle-class, educated English-woman I am already intimately acquainted with the kinds of masculinity that I investigate here. To critics who would prefer to see my efforts expended on those who are rendered invisible by mainstream IR, I reply that as a relatively privileged woman, I am not personally well placed to speak for the majority of marginalized Others—nor do they necessarily wish to be "spoken for" by such as myself. Better that my efforts be concentrated on an aspect of the gender order that impinges on my own daily life, and of which I can claim to have personal knowledge.

Second, this intimate knowledge, while extremely useful as a background to investigating hegemonic forms of masculinity, may also to some extent compromise my own position as a feminist; I may be too close to it, having unconsciously absorbed aspects of hegemonic masculinity into my own identity and work. For example, this book discusses masculinist codes of representation and masculinist rhetoric at length, and is critical of such language in both *The Economist* newspaper and in IR theory; however, the reader may notice that my own writing style is at times not dissimilar and that it can reproduce the very rhetorical strategies that I criticize. After years of education in the British university system and of reading academic books and papers, not to mention ten years of reading *The Economist* every week, virtually from cover to cover, it is hardly surprising that some of it has rubbed off on me. I have unconsciously learned to reproduce the codes of hegemonic masculinity in my writing because these are the codes that have met with credibility and academic success. Carol Cohn had a similar experience when she immersed herself in a U.S. center for defence intellectuals.

In spite of her criticisms of the highly gendered, abstracted, and euphemistic language that was used to cloak U.S. nuclear-defence thinking, she soon found herself talking the talk. This was the only way to be taken seriously: "What I found was that no matter how well-informed or complex my questions were, if I spoke English rather than expert jargon, the men responded to me as though I were ignorant, simpleminded or both. . . . A strong distaste for being patronized and dismissed made my experiment in English short-lived" (Cohn 1987, 718).

There is a dilemma here for feminists, of whether to try and avoid masculinist language but risk not being taken seriously, as Christine Sylvester (1994) has done, or whether to make strategic use of it to gain credibility for feminist arguments (or otherwise subvert it for feminist ends), and perhaps risk compromising one's own feminist message. In my own case, the thought of trying to change the style in which I write is daunting, although my own attitude to academic language is fairly irreverent: I sometimes use an ironic tone and frequently lapse into colloquialisms. While a playful approach to academic language could be seen as subversive, unfortunately, this too can have masculinist connotations. Thus my own use of language can at times mirror the ironic, journalistic tone characteristic of *The Economist*, which I criticize. To some extent complicity is the lot of us all, as poststructuralist feminists, following Foucault, have argued. As long as we engage in social interaction, there is no "innocent" position, even for the oppressed (Haraway 1991; Bordo 1993; Sylvester 1994). I can only hope that the ideas expressed in this book challenge the status quo rather more than the language they are written in might help to support it.

## Mapping the Text

The book is organized into two parts. Part 1 (chapters 1 and 2) will concentrate on theoretical issues connected with the construction of identity; theorizing masculinities; and feminist critiques of masculinism. Chapter 1 surveys different theories of gender-identity construction—drawing on feminist social psychology, sociology/social anthropology, cultural studies, and political theory—to develop a model that demonstrates the "embeddedness" of gender identities. The chapter reveals the processes of identity construction through the dimensions of embodiment, institutional practices, and symbolic or discursive constructions. The argument here is that we should move away from static or unilinear conceptions of gender identity (whether essentialist or otherwise) toward an understanding of gender identification as a more multiple and fluid process, without losing sight of the historical and cultural contexts and the material and corporeal constraints that nonetheless have to be negotiated.

Chapter 2 moves on to an examination of the gender politics of masculinity and explores how masculinist practices (as identified by feminists) influence the relationships between different groups of men as well as the relationships between men and women. This involves theorizing and historically situating masculinities and includes an explanation of the notion of "hegemonic masculinity," its qualities, and its relationship to other masculinities. Some of the historical connections between manhood and hegemonic masculinity in the Anglo-American tradition are then traced, and some ideal types identified. The involvement of masculinist practices in policing male behavior and in the competition between different masculinities is also examined.

Part 2 (chapters 3 to 6) examines the relationship between international relations and the gender politics of masculinity from the point of view of the theoretical perspective developed in part 1. In order to do this, I found it necessary to consider the cultural context in which the discipline of IR is situated. It is through the sharing of ideas and perspectives on the world between the discipline and popular culture that the effects of the discipline (as opposed to the practices of international relations) in shaping masculinities can be most clearly seen. The channels through which such ideas are shared are represented, in this instance, by *The Economist* newspaper, which as I shall argue below is an important and influential site for the cross-fertilization of ideas between popular culture, practitioners, and academics in the field. This is the case not only with regard to the overt subject matter of international affairs, but also, as I hope to demonstrate, with regard to the historic and contemporary gender politics of masculinities—not least in relation to the challenges of globalization.

The relationships between international relations, masculine identities, and popular culture (as represented here) are summed up in figure 1. These relationships all involve influences running in both directions. In the figure, the arrow running from masculine identities toward international relations is the one more usually considered, whereby international relations is said to reflect the interests and identities of men and masculinity.

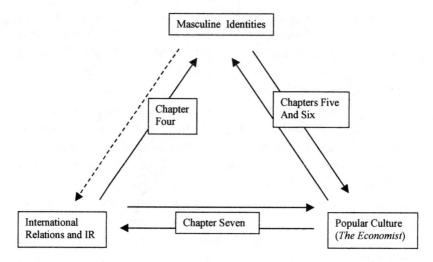

FIGURE 1. Mapping the text of part 2, by chapter. This diagram shows the relationships between international relations, masculine identities, and popular culture. The common observation that international relations reflects the world of men and masculine interests is represented by the broken arrow. The more complex, two-way relationships that are discussed in this book are shown by the solid arrows, with the relevant chapters indicated alongside.

To mention just a few of these connections: international relations is a world of traditionally masculine pursuits—in which women have been, and by and large continue to be, invisible (Enloe 1990; Halliday 1991; Peterson and Runyan 1993, 1988). The focus on war, diplomacy, states, statesmen, and high-level economic negotiations has overwhelmingly represented the lives and identities of men. This is because of the institutionalization of gender differences in society at large and the consequent paucity of women in high office. Between 1970 and 1990, for example, women worldwide represented under 5 percent of heads of state, cabinet ministers, senior national policymakers, and senior persons in intergovernmental organizations (Peterson and Runyan 1993, 6). States have historically been oppressive to women, who have often been denied full citizenship. Rights and duties of citizenship have depended on the bearing of arms, a duty by and large confined to men (Stiehm 1982). Men form not only the decision makers, but also the law enforcers, backed by the threat of violence (Enloe 1987). In fact, masculine violence has become thoroughly embedded, institutionalized, and legitimized in the modern state (Connell 1990). Meanwhile, the rhetoric of nationalism has been found to be heavily gendered (Parker et al 1992), with national identity often being articulated through control over women (Kandiyoti 1992). Although many women have been active in national-liberation movements, nonetheless, nationalism has been found to have "a special affinity for male society [which] legitimizes the dominance of men over women" (Steans 1998, 69).

By default, then, if international relations are deemed to be about the very public world of high office at state, interstate, and multinational business level, they have reflected the interests and activities of men. In addition, as mentioned above, much of IR theory is itself infused with gender bias, in that it reflects and celebrates interests and values that are associated with masculinity. The principles of realism are drawn from classical and renaissance theories that similarly ignore or downgrade both women and femininity in favor of masculine qualities (Grant 1991; Tickner 1992). The twentieth-century search for a science of IR has exacerbated this historic bias toward masculinity. For example, Morgenthau privileged masculine conceptions of objectivity, rational interests, power as control, and the separation of instrumental political goals from morality over more feminine conceptions such as interdependence and power as mutual enablement (Tickner 1991). The same goals of scientific objectivity, emotional distance, and instrumentality have infused postwar international-relations practices, especially in the United States, where academics and political appointees tend to have close links.

The now-well-documented ways in which international relations are said to reflect the interests and identities of men and masculinity are not followed up in any detail in part 2 of the book. Instead, chapter 3 explores the much-less-examined line of influence running in the opposite direction, from international relations to masculine identities. It gives examples of how such influences work through the dimensions of embodiment, institutional practices, and symbolic or discursive constructions (as introduced in chapter 1).[7] Examining the symbolic dimension in more detail, the chapter then takes a particular interest in the way the discipline of IR has been constructed, and also in the gender politics of masculinity that operate through internal rivalries between alternative perspectives and that appear to make use of the ideal types of Anglo-American hegemonic masculinity identified in chapter 2. Chapter 3 ends with a question about the relationship between postpositivist contributions to the discipline, new forms of hegemonic masculinity, and globalization.

The remainder of the book takes up the argument that there is a relationship between globalization and challenges to hegemonic masculinities that may involve a reformulation of the relationship between masculinities and the international. Examining the cultural context within which IR operates, chapters 4, 5, and 6 form a case study of *The Economist* newspaper during the period 1989–96 and its involvement in the politics of masculinity.[8] Because of its influential position in international current affairs, the paper has strong links both to changing masculine identities on the ground and to the construction of masculinities in the discipline of IR (see fig. 1).

The case study is intended to perform three functions. First, it provides a concrete illustration of the argument that there is a jostling for position between would-be hegemonic masculinities in which strategies of masculinization and feminization are deployed. Second, it illuminates how models of hegemonic masculinity that inform and construct gendered identities are (re)produced and circulated between popular culture, the conduct of international relations, and the academic study of IR. The focus is on the contemporary cultural environment within which IR operates, a culture in which academic IR represents the more codified end of the production of and commentary on politics and current affairs. Third, it illuminates and further develops the argument, first suggested at the end of chapter 3, that new perspectives within academic IR are linked to and implicated in changes to hegemonic masculinity being wrought in connection with globalization.

In terms of the arrows of influence in figure 1, chapters 4 and 5 explore the two-way relationships between hegemonic Anglo-American masculine identities on the ground and popular culture, as represented by *The Economist*. In chapter 4, the discussion is focused on the representation and construction of Anglo-American models of hegemonic masculinity; in chapter 5, the focus is on changing constructions of masculinity and globalization. Chapter 4 starts with an overview of the arguments that are put forward in the case study and then seeks to justify the choice of *The Economist* newspaper as an important site for the cross-fertilization of ideas between the academic world of IR and the wider cultural milieu. There is a brief explanation of the type of study that is made of *The Economist* and of the conceptual tools deployed. The remainder of the chapter demonstrates *The Economist*'s elite masculine credentials. It shows how the newspaper is saturated with the imagery of well-established constructions of hegemonic masculinity, which form a generally mutually reinforcing masculinist framework or "lens" through which readers of *The Economist* are invited to view both the world and themselves. Thus the act of reading the paper can help construct readers' own gendered identities. For this discussion, I make further use of the ideal types of hegemonic masculinity first introduced in chapter 2 and used in chapter 3 when discussing competing perspectives in IR.

Chapter 5 moves on to discuss how, within the overall masculinist framework of *The Economist*, rival models of hegemonic masculinity are in competition with each other and how masculinist strategies are deployed in the jostling for position that takes place between them. The chapter discusses how this competitive masculine imagery is mobilized in the construction of "globalization" as a masculine space. Tracing the changing mix of gender imagery that has accompanied the rise of rhetoric on globalization, I argue, with references to concurrent changes on the ground, that this change suggests new developments in the ongoing struggles over the construction of Anglo-American hegemonic masculinities.

Chapter 6 explores the third leg of the triangle in figure 1—a leg formed by the two-way influences between international relations and popular culture as represented by *The Economist*. Explicit connections are made between the rival models of masculinity on offer in *The Economist* and those embodied by various approaches to IR. Thus I illuminate the gendered moves that form a subtext to new developments in the discipline. I find a close match between the constructions of masculinity in the paper and in the discipline—including an affinity between those constructions of masculinity that in the newspaper are associated with a glamorized and masculinist discourse of globalization, and the contents of some postpositivist scholarship, which as a consequence is implicated in the transformation and reinvention of hegemonic masculinity.

All these arguments are pulled together at the end of *Manly States*. Reflecting, in my conclusion, I further discuss the particular perspective on gender politics that I have adopted throughout. Some conclusions are drawn as to the development of Anglo-American models of hegemonic masculinity in the 1990s and their relationship to developments in the discipline of IR. Finally, some comments are made about the implications of these findings for both feminist theory and feminist praxis.

In this book I seek to demonstrate that international relations plays a significant role in the creation and maintenance of masculine identities. This is an important aspect of gender relations that deserves more attention because it generates new insights into the gendered processes of international relations. These insights are not confined to refining feminist critiques of masculinism in IR—which is worthwhile in itself—but have potentially far wider relevance. One aspect is the establishment of a new agenda for applied research, which can generate knowledge about the construction of particular masculine identities through particular international processes, and how these identities and the relationships between them then feed back into international decision making. Such research may be conducted from within a postpositivist perspective; indeed, it may require it. Consequently, this book, while postpositivist in outlook, is an example of constructive, rather than merely critical, theorizing. Hopefully it will help persuade some skeptics of postpositivism of the practical value of postpositivist research. In addition, the book shows that postpositivist theorizing has not yet been freed from implicit gender constructions. I hope, therefore, that my arguments will convince some postpositivist fellow travelers who are sympathetic to feminism but still skeptical of the importance of gender to their own research efforts, to think again.

PART ONE  *Theorizing Masculinities*

# CHAPTER ONE

# The Construction of Gender Identity

R ECENT debates about identity in political philosophy have centered around the adequacy of the Enlightenment concept of the au-tonomous rational individual as a universal model of selfhood and starting point for political action, a concept that has long been central in Western thinking.[1] In the analytical philosophical tradition, mind and body have of-ten been treated separately, and abstract narratives of the mind dominate discussions of the human subject—at least in the case of the male subject, who stands in for the universal. The female subject, "woman," where men-tioned in modern political philosophy, has usually been constructed in rather a different way, as an opposite pole to "man." If man is all mind, then woman is all body. For example, whereas men were seen by Hegel as push-ing forward the dialectic of history, women were seen as incapable of the re-quired self-consciousness of conceptual thought. Mired as they were in the concrete world, they would be condemned merely to repeat the cycles of life.[2]

Critics of this concept have drawn on feminist, communitarian, and postmodern thinking to argue that a redrafting of our philosophical under-standing of the political agent would require more adequate recognition of the consequences of our physical embodiment, regardless of sex; of the way in which we are also embedded in social processes; and of the degree of indeterminacy and multiplicity in life situations. The concept of the embedded self would recognize that apparently strongly autonomous selves are themselves social products—products that emerge through interactive dialogue with others within a political and cultural framework that provides for their development—rather than individual starting points.[3]

Unlike the approaches to political identity taken by analytical philosophy, which focus on the rational mind, theoretical approaches to gender identity have, since their inception, grappled with both physical embodiment and social and institutional processes as important elements. The belated recognition by some political philosophers that men, too, are socially embedded and physically embodied, and that this could be of philosophical and political importance, shows a partial convergence of interest between what were two very different fields. This convergence might perhaps lead to a wider recognition of some of the more generally relevant insights that sophisticated and imaginative feminist approaches to gender identity have provided.

This chapter draws on feminist thinking about sex, gender, and identities to examine some theoretical accounts of the process of gender-identity formation. The literature on gender covers a wide field, with contributions from a number of disparate disciplines, representing a variety of interests and methodologies. There is no consensus on either the nature or significance of gender identities, how they are produced, or whether they should be reinforced, modified, or abolished, even among feminists, who by no means have a monopoly on gender theory. Nevertheless, in spite of their considerable differences and the complexity of the debate between them, this chapter will argue that the theories all tend to revolve around three dimensions of analysis; namely, (1) physical embodiment, including the body and the role of reproductive biology; (2) institutions and the gendered social processes that they encompass, including the family, the economy, the state; and (3) the discursive dimension of the gendered construction of language and its constitutive role in the gender order.

Some approaches have tended to emphasize the primary importance of one dimension, ignoring the others or demoting them to the status of effects. Others have discussed the relationship between two of the dimensions to the virtual exclusion of the third. During the 1990s, the center of the debate moved away from disputes both among feminists and between feminists and their critics over the relative contributions to gender identity of nature (listed above as 1) and nurture (2) toward a cleavage between both these groups and those who argue that the key to gender identity lies with discourse (3). Any adequate account of the construction of gender identity, however, needs to pay attention to all three dimensions simultaneously. It is important to trace out more of the complex interactions between these multiple factors, rather than trying to locate gender identity as being founded in any one of them.

The recognition of this need to take a more complex view of gender identity has been gaining ground among feminist academics. For example, Ramazanoglu and Holland (1993) discuss the development of feminist theorizing with reference to questions thrown up by their own research on teenage sexuality. During the discussion, they move from a position of identifying two poles of power that need to be reconciled—namely, the material and the discursive—to a final position where they argue that "there is a complex interaction between grounded embodiment, the discourses of sexuality and institutionalized power. Understanding this interaction is critical for targeting political struggles, but it remains an elusive area" (Ramazanoglu and Holland 1993, 260).

It is this move toward embracing all three dimensions of analysis as significant, while recognizing that none is entirely autonomous, that allows for the complexity of gender identifications to be analytically unraveled. Gender identity is not the product of a single cause or factor that then becomes fixed, but rather is negotiated in a lifelong process. The three dimensions and their interactions constitute a constraining or limiting field within which, or against which, such negotiations take place, whether at the individual or group level. Each dimension in turn is influenced by the power of the others, so there is a degree of indeterminacy in their relations. In particular historical periods, in different cultures or under varying circumstances, the configuration of power relations between bodies, institutions, and discourses will vary, such that the influence of each may construed as greater or lesser, and thus both the content and significance of gendered identities will also vary.

What follows is a personal and, of necessity, partial reconstruction of a more or less chronological development of feminist theorizing on the construction of gender identity, highlighting the way that the focus of theory has moved from the body, through the social, to the discursive, and back to the body again.[4] Much of the discussion is conducted in terms of women and femininity. This reflects both the concerns of feminists and the fact that the female sex has been problematized as different from the male norm in Western thinking and practice. Nevertheless, the theories considered would apply equally to men, in structure if not in content, and are therefore potentially useful for understanding the relationship between men and masculinity.

### "The Problem of Biology"

Given the importance that Western discourse has given to women's biology as a basis for their identity as women, it is hardly surprising that the role of biology has loomed large in many accounts of gender identity, and to this day remains a contested area within feminism.

The second wave of feminism, at the beginning of the 1960s and into the early 1970s, was launched against the background of a fierce nature/nurture debate between psychologists, sociologists, and sociobiologists over the relative contributions of biology and social factors to "sex roles" and gender identities. From the newly popularized postwar discipline of primatology came various biological explanations for the existence of widespread disparities between the roles and publicly recorded achievements of men and women in modern societies. Psychobiologists sought to explain the contemporary sexual division of labor and male dominance in terms of aggression, submission, and dominance hierarchies among males and their supposed significance in the development of social behavior in prehistoric times.[5] Sociobiologists, on the other hand, concentrated on genetic differences between the sexes and on genetic investment strategies. Both groups used animal behavior, especially primate behavior, as evidence of human developmental history or genetic heritage.

Many feminists regarded these theories as reductionist and conservative justifications of the status quo. They pointed out that biologically reductionist arguments have a pedigree that can be traced back for centuries in Western culture, culminating in the now discredited social Darwinism of the late nineteenth century. Psycho- and sociobiological arguments were seen as part of this tradition of "bad science" (Haraway 1991, 134) in which leaps from one period of history or level of analysis to another were made without explanation; in which human social categories were projected onto other animals and then used as a basis for explaining human behavior in the most crudely anthropomorphic fashion; and in which objectivity was never achieved due to the unacknowledged cultural biases of the researchers themselves (Sahlins 1977; Sayers 1982).

Meanwhile, a parallel line of inquiry, sex-difference research, sought to measure inherent differences between the sexes in the laboratory. In this kind of analysis, sexual character was also seen as unitary: "men" and "women" were assumed to be distinct personality types embodying stereotypically "masculine" and "feminine" traits and characteristics en mass. The research looked at "block" sex differences in such characteristics as aggression levels, tactile sensitivity, and spatial and linguistic skills. Such research has been beset by the methodological problems that all positivistic science encounters when trying to measure socially meaningful behavior. For example, how does one measure aggression? By personality testing? By hormone levels? What exactly is being measured when one measures aggression? Which behaviors count as aggressive varies according to social and cultural context; hence, it is impossible to measure objectively.[6] Even when sex-difference research has confined itself to testing things that can be measured, the results have not shown many significant differences, but rather a huge overlap in traits and abilities between the sexes (Maccoby and Jacklin 1975). Eighty years of research focused on sex differences have revealed "a massive psychological *similarity* between women and men in the populations studied" (Connell 1987, 170). Meanwhile, cross-cultural studies suggested that few sex differences in social behavior seemed inevitable, and that "the plasticity of the sexes seems quite enough to allow for a gender revolution of any sort" (Rosenblatt and Cunningham 1976, 89).

Although the feminist critique of sex-difference research and some of the cruder reductionisms in sociobiology were undoubtedly justified, it was nonetheless true that socialist-feminist hostility to biological explanations was partly motivated by a conviction that biological explanations were either conservative or fascistic. If widespread gender differences were to have a biological rather than social foundation, then women were oppressed either by their own biology or by the biology of men. The only hope of emancipation would be through the technology of artificial reproduction, a conclusion reached by the early second-wave feminist Shulamith Firestone (1971). Indeed, some feminist "maternalists" have since gone down this road, pursuing separatism, artificial insemination, and asserting women's "natural" superiority over men, but the rest preferred to look for social explanations of gender that might provide a better basis for social and political change.

### Sex and Gender

While the debate over sex differences and sex roles rumbled on, one way around "the problem of biology" was to separate it from the social by making an analytical distinction between biological sex and socially constructed gender. Popularized by Ann Oakley (1972) in the early 1970s and rapidly becoming an accepted norm in much feminist theory and gender studies literature, this distinction allowed gender differences encompassing the formation of gender identities and the qualities of masculinity and femininity to be treated as aspects of social and psychological development, separate from questions about biological sex differences (Bailey 1993, 100).[7] This sociosexual division then enabled the analysis of gender identity to move squarely into the realm of social and institutional processes.

A great deal of feminist energy has always been focused around the institutional dimension of analysis on the subject of gender inequalities, ranging from liberal feminist campaigns on women's equality in the public sphere, through socialist-feminist analysis of the relations of production and reproduction and their contribution to women's economic subordination, to radical feminist theories of patriarchy as a linchpin of social organization.[8] While these discussions have been of tremendous importance in detailing and accounting for the subordination of women, and have provided fuel for feminist campaigns, the category of "women" has been used as the relatively unproblematic basis of analysis. Because women themselves were not theorized, such accounts dealt only tangentially with gender identity as such.

Meanwhile, gender-sensitive studies of socialization have provided abundant evidence of just how differential the treatment of boys and girls is from the moment of birth, and how they are expected, encouraged, and coerced into thinking and behaving differently and into developing different skills and priorities.[9] As well as socialization through the family, education, and the workplace, the role of consumption in promoting gender identities was also beginning to be examined in feminist cultural and media-studies literature.[10]

But even supplemented by evidence of differential socialization, feminist institutional theory still tended to leave gender identity itself undertheorized. Such things as the complexity of sexuality; the degree to which the innermost sense of self is gendered; the insecurities and contradictions of masculinity and femininity; and last but not least the continuing complicity of women in their own subordination even after feminist enlightenment— none of these were fully explained by accounts of institutional structures, conditioning, and coercion.

## Psychology and Gender Identity

This deficit was made up for by a turn to psychoanalytic theory that, by introducing the unconscious, would provide a depth model of the links between male and female bodies, the institutional arrangement of the family, and the complexities of masculine and feminine character and identity. Unsurprisingly, classic Freudian analysis, which gives the penis a central role in the development of both sexes and supports the view that women are predominantly passive,[11] has gained little support from feminists;[12] instead, two revisionist psychoanalytic schools have been used by feminist scholars. These are, first, feminist object-relations theory, which developed largely in the United States; and second, British and French feminist uses of the Lacanian synthesis of Freud with Saussurean linguistics. While object-relations theory locates the formation of gender identity in a relationship between the institutional and the embodiment dimensions, Lacanian and post-Lacanian scholarship shifts the emphasis away from embodiment altogether and emphasizes the role of language, instead.

In a key move to develop a non-Freudian psychoanalytic perspective, object-relations theory shifted attention away from the penis and focused instead on the role of the maternal bond. In the pre-Oedipal phase, love and identification are undifferentiated. This presents no problem for girls, who may continue to love and identify with their mothers long after they have become aware of their own sex. But boys, in order to develop their sense of maleness, are forced to abandon their attachment to and identification with their mothers. In Nancy Chodorow's account (1978), the absence of a close bond with the father at this stage means that masculinity is defined in reaction to the mother, is defined as that which is not feminine. The more powerful his mother's influence, the more the growing boy struggles to separate from her to establish his own gender identity, the more exaggerated and aggressive his style of masculinity becomes, and the more he fears and abhors the feminine, whether within himself or in relationships with women. Thus while masculinity is overvalued in society, it remains fragile, precarious, and neurotic. This is exactly the right formula for the aggressive psychology needed for male domination and success in a competitive, capitalist world. And thus female power over male children is transformed into male power over adult women.

Arguing in a similar vein, Dorothy Dinnerstein (1976) concludes that the exclusive involvement of women in the care of young children and the psychological dynamics that this produces are leading us toward global destruction. The involvement of men in child care, however, would profoundly alter this dynamic, and such involvement is seen as the key to unraveling the oppression of women as well as providing more emotionally satisfactory experiences for antisexist men who see male power as not worth having, given the psychological (or environmental) price to be paid.

Critics of object-relations theory note that it tends to beg rather large questions about the supposed fragility of male gender identities, about the influence of outside power relations on the family, about what happens in nonnuclear families, and about the conventionality and uniformity of mothering and fathering practices. However, perhaps its biggest drawback is that by placing the weight of analysis on mother-child relations, it ignores the wider symbolic power attached to men and masculinity and treats phallocentrism as a product of neurotic male imagination rather than as a cultural reality (Segal 1990, 82). Analysis of gender identity in the object-relations school remains squarely at the institutional pole, and the only institution that is deemed to be relevant is the family.

*Language and Psychology*

An approach that attempted to introduce symbolic meaning into feminist psychoanalysis was built on the Lacanian synthesis of Freud with Saussure, and was introduced to an English-speaking audience by Juliet Mitchell (1974). Lacan reinterpreted Freudian psychoanalysis as an account of symbolic rather than physical development. The primary processes operating in the unconscious are indistinguishable from linguistic mechanisms because it is language that structures meaning; hence, Lacan saw the Oedipal phase as the negotiation of the child's entry into the symbolic order of language. In

Mitchell's formulation, the development of the unconscious becomes the method through which social and cultural laws are transmitted from generation to generation and by which the paternalistic "law of the father" is reproduced. Following Lévi-Strauss, Mitchell argues that the incest taboo is a universal cultural taboo connected to the (hitherto) universal patriarchal social arrangement whereby women are exchanged between families. Kinship ties and sexual relations both structure society and women's subordinate position in it. The physical significance of the penis is replaced by the linguistic significance of the phallus, a key signifier in patriarchal discourse representing power and desire, which is then encountered by boys and girls in different ways. Metaphor replaces biology as the key element structuring the unconscious, and language is phallocentric. While boys and men have a precarious relationship with the symbolic phallus, which they can never completely embody because it is larger than life, the female sex fares even worse. It exists in Lacanian theory only as a not-whole, a lack, an Other.

Critics of both object-relations and Lacanian psychoanalytic approaches argue that biological essentialism has merely been replaced by psychic or cultural essentialism (e.g., Brennan 1989; Butler 1990a; Cornwall and Lindisfarne 1994). In Chodorow's case, this is because of her ahistorical and ethnocentric assumption of the universality of mothering, and uniform patterns of child care in nuclear families; in Mitchell's case it is because, although culture is embraced as an important influence, it is reduced to a monolithic and universal structure of language and kinship; it is simply inaccurate to assume, for example, that the incest taboo is universal.[13] While accounts such as these may indeed illuminate typical childhood development processes in some specific cultural and historical contexts, they cannot act as general theories because they say little about the development of children's identities outside stereotypically twentieth-century, Western, middle-class nuclear families.

Nor can they explain the development of homosexuality. In this respect Lacanian and object-relations analyses are even more rigid than Freud's original theory. The formation of a gender identity as boy or girl occurs at the same time and through the same processes as sexual orientation is fixed. While heterosexuality is seen as a developmental accomplishment rather than a biological fixture, it is nonetheless a compulsory one. To quote Butler:

Although the story of sexual development is complicated and quite different for the girl than the boy, it appeals in both contexts to an operative dis-
junction that remains stable throughout: one identifies with one sex and,
in so doing, desires the other, that desire being the elaboration of that
identity, the mode by which it creates its opposite and defines itself in that
opposition. (Butler 1990b, 332)

Butler argues that this insistence on a singular narrative of development,
however complex and contradictory the unconscious is seen to be, makes
modern feminist psychoanalytic theories complicit in circumscribing gender meanings, and shoring up compulsory heterosexuality.

Ultimately, in these Anglo-American psychoanalytic models, just as in
the earlier sex-role theory, gender identities are constrained by unchanging
biology, as the dichotomous division at the level of sex is retained in unitary
conceptions of gender. A truly radical separation between the notions of sex
and gender would mean that "*man* and *masculine* might just as easily signify a female body as a male one, and *woman* and *feminine* a male body as easily as a female one" (Butler 1990a, 6). In practice, however, "once children
are given a gender label as either "male" or "female," it is presumed that this
monolithic identity adheres through their lives . . . [and] relations between
men and women are seen in terms of fixed, polarized identities" (Cornwall
and Lindisfarne 1994, 33–34).

In attempts to transcend both the pessimism and universalism of Lacanian analysis, some French post-Lacanian feminists, such as Luce Irigaray
and Julia Kristeva, have moved beyond the linguistic structuralism of Lacan
to reconsider the place of the feminine in phallocentric language. They explore ways in which alternative languages based on the logic of the female
body (Irigaray 1985) or of the pre-phallocentric, pre-Oedipal experience
with (the) mother (Kristeva 1984) might be deployed or recuperated to artic-
ulate positive feminine identities. In Kristeva's account, the masculine language of repressive phallocentric symbolism (Lacan's law of the father) and
the feminine language of semiotic heterogeneity and joy (the language of
pre-Oedipal poetry) are not necessarily attached to male and female bodies
at all. However, in spite of their attempts to transcend the straitjacket of
structuralism, critics see the writings of Irigaray as reinforcing the ideology
of biological essentialism (Butler 1990a, 30), while Kristeva is accused of virtually ignoring both the bodily and institutional dimensions altogether (Segal 1987, 133).

Meanwhile, the analytical distinction between biological sex and socially constructed gender has itself come under fire. Although this distinction was useful in combating pervasive biological determinisms, it was the result of an uncritical acceptance of the nature/culture dichotomy of Western philosophy (Harding 1986; Haraway 1991; Bailey 1993). It is important to recognize that nature is itself a man-made category (using both senses of the word *man*) and that science, including biology, is of necessity a cultural activity, with its own cultural history. As Donna Haraway argues, good science is just as embedded in culture as is bad science, and while it may avoid crude reductionism and anthropomorphism, its explanations cannot help but be couched in available metaphor, which is laden with social meanings: "Biology has intrinsically been a branch of political discourse, not a compendium of objective truth. Further, simply noting such a connection between biological and political/economic discourse is *not* a good argument for dismissing such biological argument as bad science or mere ideology" (Haraway 1991, 98).

Haraway charts the parallel and interconnected history of metaphors used in both social science and biology over the course of this century, from the functionalist concept of the body politic, with its parts and pathologies, through the economistic language of scarcity, competition, and natural selection, to the current language of information systems, boundaries, and networks, relating them to developments within capitalism. But while feminists, too, may be trapped within the prevailing metaphors of our age, feminist interventions that produce alternative scientific stories about our bodies can and have been made, and Haraway pleads for more: "To ignore, to fail to engage in the social process of making science, and to attend only to the use and abuse of scientific work is irresponsible. . . . Scientific stories have too much power as public myth to effect meanings in our lives. Besides, scientific stories are interesting" (Haraway 1991, 107).

Recently, feminists have begun to argue that, just as nature is a social category with a history of discursive construction, so are sex, gender, and even the body itself.

## Discursive (De)Constructions of Sex and Gender

The feminist literature on the discursive construction of sexed bodies draws heavily on the work of Michel Foucault, who argues that modern power (as opposed to force) is primarily productive and relational rather than oppressive or repressive, that power operates through the construction of particular knowledges, or discourses, and that humans are produced as subjects through the power of discourse.[14] Categorization inevitably proceeds through a process of exclusion, so that the norm is established by defining what it is not, what is Other. Some identities are then marginalized and denied subject status, but marginalization is not the same as oppression.[15] Our bodies are disciplined and normalized by the biopolitics of categorization, normalization, and surveillance (Foucault 1980; Ramazonoglu 1993).

Judith Butler (1990a; 1990b; 1995) uses Foucault as a resource to provide a discursive account of the construction of gender identities that include the body in a nonessentialist way. According to Butler, gender identities are neither true expressions of some ontologically prior self nor the distorted results of a repressed and molded "sex drive." The term *sex* itself is a conflation of chromosomes, anatomy, hormones, and sexual orientation and has no stable meaning. After all, the body itself has no intrinsic meaning outside of our cultural interpretation of its parts. She asks where exactly does sex reside? Is it in our genitals, our chromosomes, our hormones, our brains? Is it possible to have female genitals, male chromosomes, and bisexual desires? What sex does that make you? Perhaps sex does not lie in the body at all, but is the result of the inscription of arbitrary cultural meanings on the body. Sex, as a category—like the categories of male, female, man, woman, masculinity, and femininity—is imbued with power, and inscription is the process by which such categories achieve their solidity, where unstable meanings are "written" on the body. These categories then become naturalized through endless repetition, or "sedimentation," of discursively constituted actions. Thus our understanding of biology itself is merely a set of cultural meanings, but meanings that are literally embodied by us. Our sexed bodies, our gender identities, and our inner sense of self are all material effects of repeated actions within the power/knowledge nexus of discourse. Butler argues that sex is a kind of performance conducted by and on our bodies. It is not an inauthentic performance, however, as there is no such thing as an authentic self inside, no "doer" behind the deed, as it were (Butler 1990a, 25). Our gender identity is not first fixed internally and then manifested externally later, because "a performative act is one which brings into being or enacts that which it names, and so marks the constitutive or productive power of discourse" (Butler 1995, 134). The performance itself constructs us as gendered beings, constructs our sexuality and gendered identities. The notion of a psychological core to gender identity is a fantasy or fabrication that serves to hide the regulatory nature of discursive power and preclude an analysis of the political constitution of the gendered subject.

The performative nature of gender and sexuality can be demonstrated through an analysis of gender parody. Butler argues that parody is subversive because it disrupts the normalization of gender divisions, highlights the arbitrary nature of sex and gender, exposes the political constitution of identities, and celebrates discontinuity. It shows that gender coherence is a fabrication and that gender does not follow from sex, nor sex from gender. Drag is a clear example of the power of parody to disrupt apparent gender coherence. In the performance of drag, there is a double inversion. At one and the same time, drag can be seen as a man with the outward appearance of femininity or as a woman trapped in a man's body, and vice versa. This play on the dissonance between anatomical sex, gender identity, and gender performance

> fully subverts the distinction between inner and outer psychic space and effectively mocks both the expressive model of gender and the notion of a true gender identity. . . . Gender parody reveals that the original identity after which gender fashions itself is itself an imitation without an origin. To be more precise, it is a production, which, in effect, that is, in its effect, postures as an imitation. This perpetual displacement constitutes a fluidity of identities that suggests an openness to resignification and recontextualization, and it deprives hegemonic culture and its critics of the claim to essentialist accounts of gender identity. (Butler 1990b, 337–38)

Butler's assertion that there is no clear-cut biological basis for sex can be illustrated by looking at the legal quagmire that surrounds the qualifying terms *male* and *female*. In Britain, sex is usually designated by the midwife, on the basis of presence or absence of a penis at birth. This anatomical designation of sex need not be matched by chromosomes, which form the basis of the current tests for sex in international sporting events such as the Olympics. So one might be legally female and yet be designated male in sporting terms. The possession of a penis is not a consistent marker of maleness—even in Britain, never mind universally across all cultures.

While Butler's approach successfully brings the body back in and articulates a nonessentialist relationship between language and bodies, it suffers from a number of drawbacks. It is far from clear that everything can or should be reduced to an abstract discussion of discourse. First, Butler replicates Foucault's indifference to the relative power of men over women, so that she cannot specify the processes by which gender *inequalities,* as opposed to neutral and arbitrary constructions, are naturalized (Cornwall and Lindisfarne 1994, 40). Second, in spite of her claim that "the difficult labour of deriving agency from the very power regimes which constitute us . . . [is] *historical* work, reworking the historicity of the signifier" (Butler 1995, 136), Butler's own rendering of discourse is so abstract as to be devoid of cultural or historical context, so that, in the end, her account becomes as monolithic as the Lacanian structuralism she criticizes. She has ignored the institutional dimension of analysis completely. As Bordo suggests, Butler adopts a linguistic foundationalism that reduces the body to a textual surface, and "biology" to the discursive "product" of sexism and heterosexism. Moreover,

> In this linguistic foundationalism, Butler is very much more the Derridean than the Foucauldian, even though Foucauldian language and ideas dominate the book. Within Foucault's understandings of the ways in which the body is "produced" through specific historical practices, "discourse" is not foundational but is, rather, one of the many interrelated modes by which power is made manifest. Equally, if not more important for him are the institutional and everyday *practices* by means of which our experience of the body is organized. (Bordo 1993b, 291)

The problem of lack of context in Butler's work can be illustrated by examining the subversive potential of parody. Jean Grimshaw argues that obsessive and compulsive housecleaning is a parody of housewifery, but a destructive one in which the sufferer's oppression is increased rather than reduced, so that "parody can sometimes be little more than a defensive structure bred of powerlessness" (Grimshaw 1991, 7). Apart from the importance of context, Grimshaw argues that there is also a narrative element involved, through which the performer makes sense of her performance.

In a more successful use of the discursive approach, paying more attention to context, Denise Riley also deconstructs the unity of "women." Her starting point is that no woman totally identifies with being a woman. A woman's consciousness of being a woman as opposed to some other identity that is ascribed to or claimed by her or will otherwise "take her weight" (such as being a black, a person, a computer operator, or whatever) waxes and wanes, according to circumstances. In Riley's view, people are inclined to inhabit whichever of the multiple identities proves most applicable to the situation, or useful for the purposes of the moment. Being a woman is a state that fluctuates for the individual. After all "to lead a life soaked in the passionate consciousness of one's gender at every single moment, to will to be a sex with a vengeance—these are impossibilities" (Riley 1988, 6).

However, Riley argues that the fact that identities are not fixed or foundational does not mean that people are cast adrift in a sea of indeterminacy and endless fluidity. In no way does Riley intend her analysis to "vault over the stubborn harshness of lived gender" (3); nor does she necessarily mean it to celebrate "the carnival of diffuse and contingent sexualities" (5). Such directions are an anathema to many feminists, either because of the suggestion that we *can* easily have limitless freedom in our sexual and gender identities—something that is clearly untrue—or because of the suggestion that we *should* have unlimited freedom of the kind that would sanction, say, sex abuse of children. Returning to Butler, we can see that her concept of gender performance does unintentionally lean toward or invite such interpretations, again because of the lack of limiting context.

Riley instead uses the idea of indeterminacy to investigate particular historical variations in the dominant narratives surrounding the term *woman*. She argues that before the seventeenth century, European women were seen to have autonomous souls but women's bodies, which made them physically inferior to men but equal by grace. Gradually, with the process of secularization and the arrival of a new and feminized concept of nature, women's souls and psyches also came to be seen as saturated with their sex, until by the nineteenth century they were virtually seen as a race apart from men. Both the content and strength of female identities changed, over time and in relation to other changing social concepts and institutional developments.

Riley includes the body in her analysis of variations in the intensity and content of gender identity:

Only at times will the body impose itself or be arranged as that of a woman or a man . . . for the impress of history as well as of individual temporality is to establish the body itself as lightly or heavily gendered, or as indifferent, and for that to run in and out of the eye of "the social." It's more of a question of tracing the (always anatomically gendered) body as it is differently established and interpreted as sexed within different periods. (Riley 1988, 103)

This approach to the body allows that it has an extradiscursive reality of basic anatomy, but that the weight and significance attached to this is always discursively and historically constituted.

Looked at historically, it is clear that "women" is an unstable category. Riley considers how feminism should respond to this situation. Rather than assert a mythical, timeless bond of womanhood, or reject the category and risk dissolving the feminist constituency altogether, she argues that feminism is and should be about the metaphorical fighting out of that instability. After all, whether "women" exist or not, the world behaves unambiguously as if they did. Under such circumstances "while it's impossible to be thoroughly a woman, it's also impossible never to be one. On such shifting sands feminism must stand and sway" (114). Riley's approach avoids the pitfall of seeing gender identity as fixed, and yet is sensitive to the history of cultural, material, and institutional restraints on its fluidity. Although her analysis consists of a history of "women," she suggests that a completion of the project would include a similar radical look at the whole category of men, which also would be subject to historical variation (8).

## A Multidimensional Approach to Gender Identity

Perhaps in the enthusiasm to embrace discursive approaches, there has been a recent tendency among poststructuralist feminists to dismiss too hastily all earlier feminist theorizing. Critics of earlier feminist theory should remember that radical feminists have always paid attention to the way in which femininity is produced through the manipulation of women's bodies, even if this aspect of gender has been undertheorized in the past (Bordo 1993a). The construction of gender identity is a multidimensional process, dependant neither solely on embodiment, institutional practices, nor discursive formations. As Robert Connell argues:

The body as used, the body I am, is a social body that has taken on meanings rather than conferred them. . . . The physical sense of maleness is not a simple thing. It involves size and shape, habits of posture and movement, particular physical skills and the lack of others, the image of one's own body, the way it is presented to other people and the ways they respond to it, the way it operates at work and in sexual relations. In no sense is this all a consequence of XY chromosomes, or even of the possession on which discussions of masculinity have so lovingly dwelt, the penis. The physical sense of maleness grows through a personal history of social practice, a life-history-in-society. . . . The social definition of men as holders of power is translated not only into mental body-images and fantasies, but into muscle tensions, posture, feel and texture of the body. . . . We may say then that the practical transformation of the body in the social structure of gender is not only accomplished at the level of symbolism. It has physical effects on the body; the incorporation is a material one. (Connell 1987, 83–87)

Identities are not fixed, neither at birth nor in childhood. Connell uses the concept of "personality as practice" (219–36) to illustrate the possibility of lifelong development and change. In this view, gender is neither a thing nor a property of individual character. It is a property of collectivities, institutions, and historical processes. It is also a linking concept, whereby biological difference is engaged with, and social practices are organized in terms of, or in relation to, reproductive divisions. Gender is more properly used as a verb, so that "engendering" is the process of making such links, which may be many and varied and do not have to conform to any social dichotomy (140). It is this view of engendering as a variable process that opens up the possibility of multiple interpretations of gender and gets away from the monolithic assumptions that have dogged so much of the theory so far. On the other hand, there is a macrodimension to gender that prevents such multiplicity from dissolving into voluntarism.

A multiple, multidimensional approach, in which gender identity is theorized in radically historicized accounts of the construction of sexed bodies and gender identities in different cultural contexts, would acknowledge the integration of gender with other ingredients of identity. It has become increasingly difficult to theorize gender identity in isolation from other identities, and the intersections of gender, class, race, and sexuality have become preoccupations of both feminism and cultural studies. The intervention of lesbian, nonwhite, and non-Western voices into the feminist debate has highlighted the heterosexual and racist bias of much earlier feminist writing and led to debates about double and triple oppressions. The recognition that earlier feminist theory was middle-class, heterosexist, and Eurocentric has forced the issue of differences between women to the center of feminist debates (Harding 1986; Nicholson 1990).[16] Initially, issues of heterosexism, racism, class position, and homophobia were treated as added burdens that some people carry, but it has now become clear that they intersect in the way gender identities are constructed in the first place, so that, for example, gender identities are always already racialized and racial identities are always already gendered (Ware 1992). Whiteness is a racial category as much as blackness is, so that a white, middle-class, heterosexual male is implicated in the mix as much as any other gender identity.

The literature on intersections between gender, race, class, and sexuality and their political significance will be considered in detail in the next chapter. For now it is sufficient to note that one important point to emerge from this literature is that marginalized and oppressed peoples rarely experience their identities as unitary, but rather tend to find them contradictory and confusing. This can be seen as either a disadvantage that needs correction, an opportunity for progressive change, albeit a problematic one, or both. For Seyla Benhabib, fragmented identities are an unwelcome reality. They represent the powerlessness of the marginalized to tell their own stories, to create a personally meaningful life history out of their interactions with the world, rather than having others' perspectives thrust upon them, a situation that would be remedied under the ideal speech conditions of reciprocity and mutual recognition (Benhabib 1992, 198). The problem with this approach is that coherent identities are always constructed on the back of exclusionary practices and therefore can never be available on an equal basis to all, as the pursuers of feminist identity politics have found (Phelan 1989).

For others, the normative embracing of contradictory multiple or mobile identities and weaving them into new kinds of life stories represents an opportunity to bring the marginalized into the center and at the same time move away from fixed-identity politics whose divisions threaten our increasingly complex, contradictory, multicultural societies. Concepts such as hybridization (Hall 1992, 258), and cultural diaspora-ization (ibid.), mestiza consciousness (Mohanty 1991, 36), mobile subjectivities (Ferguson 1993), and nomadic subjects (Braidotti 1994) attempt to capture some of the alternative ways of integrating the self when identification is lived as a multiple process rather than being experienced as a fixed feature of personhood. Given the explosive possibilities of identity politics in the context of the resurgence of ethnic divisions after the collapse of Communism, together with an ever-shrinking globe, such moves would seem generally progressive, although not without their own pitfalls.[17]

While the privileged and powerful may be more likely to experience their identities as unitary, no identity is truly coherent. As was mentioned earlier, we are all bound up in the configurations of race, class, and sexuality, so that, as Chantal Mouffe argues, any one individual is constituted by an ensemble of "subject positions" that is always contingent and precarious. "Not only are there no 'natural' or 'original' identities, since every identity is the result of a constituting process . . . [but] this process itself must be seen as one of permanent hybridisation and nomadization. Identity is in effect, the result of a multitude of interactions that take place inside a space whose outlines are not clearly defined" (Mouffe 1994, 110).

However, as Kathy Ferguson (1993) points out, provisional political identities are still strategically necessary for political action. Although our class, race, gender, and erotic identifications are themselves constitutions rather than discoveries, it is their very constitution, Ferguson argues, that gives them their political potency.[18] First, while they support a degree of fluidity, such identifications are not infinitely elastic and must depend on some shared experiences. Second, to have any political clout, it is necessary to adopt an identity for strategic reasons—to be recognized and to have a political voice, even if this involves a danger that such identities might solidify because it can be hard to give up even a disadvantaged identity if it provides one with a political voice. Ferguson recommends the conscious adoption of "mobile subjectivities," so that one's sense of self has the quality of a journey or an ever-changing story with a series of stronger and weaker identifications along the way; this, she suggests, would mitigate against the twin dangers of exclusion and sedimentation (Ferguson 1993, 160).

THE DEBATE OVER gender identity has been complex and wide-ranging. Rather than plump for any of the competing theories that center on reproductive biology, institutional and psychological processes, or discursive constructions, this chapter has argued for a multiple and multidimensional approach that can draw on all of these theoretical insights but places them in historical and cultural context.

Gender identity is perhaps best seen as something that is constantly ne-gotiated and renegotiated as we simultaneously engage with our own physi-cal embodiment, participate in social practices, and take up or refuse dis-cursive positions that are enmeshed in a network of power relations whose intricacies are peculiar to our own epoch and culture. Within this frame-work, the degree and range of choice of gender identities available to us is constrained by the particular conjunction of our bodily possibilities, our material circumstances, and our social position. Therefore gender identities are neither totally self-created nor completely determined, but are subject to historical development and may vary according to context. Nor can they be separated from other factors of identity formation; notably, class, race, and sexuality. Although biology is relevant to gender identity, it is not the foundation upon which our identities are built. Meanwhile, our experi-ences of gender identity will vary in coherence and intensity, according to circumstances.

In this chapter, I have argued that gender identities are fluid and are al-ways in the process of being produced through the interaction between these three dimensions. In chapter 2, I consider how gender identities relate to gender politics, particularly with regard to men and masculinities.

# CHAPTER TWO

# Masculinities and Masculinism

O NCE gender identities are recognized as constructed by open-ended, multiple, and multidimensional processes rather than being seen as fixed constructs, then the politics of masculinity can be seen as a contested field of power moves and resistances, rather than being construed as a fixed set of power relations. This chapter analyzes the politics of masculinity, using material from both the sociological men's-studies literature and feminist contributions to the discipline of international relations. In particular, I aim to reconcile feminist critiques of "masculinism" with the recognition and analysis of multiple masculinities.

I first want to make some initial points. Although I shall draw on a wide variety of practical and historical examples (using literature relevant to international relations where possible) the intention here is not to verify or argue the case for any particular example of masculinity or interpretation of masculinism, but rather to draw on existing studies in conjunction with theoretical literature to develop and illustrate a theoretical perspective that will be applied in later chapters. Therefore, this chapter should be read as mainly theoretical.

The preceding chapter identified how gender identities are constructed through the three dimensions of embodiment, institutional practices, and language/discourse, using a perspective that combined the Foucauldian concept of productive power operating in a diffuse manner throughout society, with postmodern understandings of the fluidity and multiplicity of identities. However, as I noted, while Foucault's notion of productive power is very useful in understanding how gender identities are produced, it is blind to gendered power inequalities. To now bring gender inequalities and gender politics into the picture, I supplement the Foucauldian emphasis on productive power and micropolitics with a broadly Gramscian approach to cultural hegemony, applied not to class, but to gender.[1]

This chapter also introduces feminist insights into gendered language and dichotomous thinking that originally derive from a different theoretical tradition, that of post-Lacanian French feminist poststructuralism. However, my interpretation of such insights has been cut loose from its Lacanian roots. Such insights are useful in illuminating how language and interpretation play an important part in the politics of masculinity, but my perspective is not one of Lacanian psychoanalytic explanation, with its view that the phallocentric structure of language unproblematically constitutes the social. Nor is it derived from the post-Lacanian, poststructuralist accounts and critiques of binary phallocentrism, which tend to embody the view that the gender order can be understood by examining such linguistic constructions and textuality alone. Language is important in the discursive construction of the gender order, but as I argued earlier, so are the other two dimensions of analysis (embodiment and institutional processes). Although I do not deny that language plays a constitutive role in general, the part that the particular linguistic constructions identified in Lacanian and poststructuralist thought play in constituting gendered social life is highly variable. It needs to be examined in context.

Michèle Barrett makes the useful point that there is a clear distinction between the role of language in the work of poststructuralists who emphasize textuality and the Foucauldian notion of discourse, which is very much related to context (Barrett 1991, 124). This is not to say that a focus on textuality is isolated from questions of political and social practice. Both Foucault and the poststructuralists see social life as being discursively produced through the organizing power of language. However, poststructuralists such as Jacques Derrida and French feminists such as Luce Irigaray, Hélène Cixous, and Monique Wittig tend to generalize from the dualistic structures of language they identify and deconstruct. They assume that such dualisms are overarching, or even totalizing, producing social reality in a uniform fashion. Foucault however, uncovers the individual histories of how and where particular kinds of language have informed particular social practices, and as such is making less sweeping claims about the totalizing power of the structure of language in general.[2]

A note about terminology: I use the term *masculinism* throughout when discussing male privilege and power in the gender order, not *patriarchy* or *androcentrism*. *Patriarchy* has been used extensively by feminists to describe and account for the historical and contemporary oppression of women.[3] In recent years the concept has proved increasingly problematic for some feminists, including those influenced by Foucault's conception of power (Ramazanoglu and Holland 1993, 243). In spite of reformulations that emphasize that patriarchy can come in a variety of forms, both familial and public, and intersects with other hierarchies such as race and class (e.g., Walby 1990), it is by and large associated with universalizing, ahistorical theories and vague generalizations. As a number of feminists have argued, gender relations are insufficiently coherent to warrant the term *patriarchy* in general; these writers prefer to confine the term to its older, sociological sense, where it describes (largely preindustrial) familial "father rule" (Bradley 1989, 55).

One could use the less-loaded substitute term *androcentric* to describe contemporary gender relations. *Androcentric* means man-centered, and an androcentric gender order is one that privileges men over women. Few feminists would dispute that the current gender order does just that. However, the term suggests a direct link between male anatomy and male power, which as the analysis in the following chapters shows, I would not wish to endorse. I make a distinction between men and masculinity and argue that men gain access to power and privilege not by virtue of their anatomy but through their cultural association with masculinity. It is the qualities of masculinity that are closely associated with power, rather than men per se, and the term *masculinism*, which implies a privileging of masculinity, best captures this relationship.

THE BASIC ARGUMENT of this chapter, in sum, is as follows: Feminist interventions into international relations have relied heavily on critiques of masculinism in both the discipline and practices of international affairs.[4] These arguments have their roots in broader feminist debates over the inherent masculinism of science, in general, and the shape of feminist successor sciences (Harding 1986). One of the questions that has arisen from this debate relates to the ways in which women are divided by differences such as race, class, and sexuality, and the epistemological challenges that such differences have generated for feminism.[5] However, in this literature the concepts of men and masculinity are often inadvertently still treated as unproblematic, undifferentiated wholes. While many feminist theorists (particularly poststructuralists) might acknowledge the existence of multiple masculinities, when it comes to discussing multiple gender differences in detail, the main focus remains on women and femininities—with one or two notable exceptions (e.g., Segal 1990, Cornwall and Lindisfarne 1994).[6]

Meanwhile, in "men's studies" literature,[7] where discussing masculinities in the plural has rapidly become a convention (Brod 1987), there has been some discussion of whether an overall theory of masculinity would be useful,[8] but little engagement with either the concept of masculinism or recent developments in feminist theory. This lack of engagement between feminist critiques of masculinism and the emerging literature on masculinities means that the relationship between masculinity and masculinism, on the one hand, and masculinities, on the other, has yet to be fully articulated.

However, feminist critiques of masculinism can be usefully combined with a recognition of multiple masculinities, when such masculinities are seen in terms of hegemonic and subordinate varieties, as advocated by Connell (1987) and discussed below. Such a combination retains the best of both approaches, illuminating the way in which hegemonic masculinity can remain dominant in what appears to be a relatively fluid process of gender constructions and identifications. Feminist insights into the political (rather than psychoanalytic) relationship between masculinism and power remain central, while the diversity of masculinities, the capillary nature of power struggles, and the varying degrees of access to power and the benefits of masculinism between different groups of men are also highlighted.

Although the construction of masculinities and masculine hierarchies is an ongoing, fluid, and diverse process, for analytical purposes it is useful to delineate different archetypes or ideal types of hegemonic masculinity and to attempt to periodize changes in the construction of masculinities. This would provide a history of men as opposed to a history of man, and could be used to try to identify whose interests and which historical developments have been or are being served by the deployment of masculinist strategies, and how. All men do not benefit equally from masculinism; nor do all women suffer equally.

The remainder of the chapter will explain, expand, and illustrate this basic argument.

### The Feminist Critique of Masculinism

The feminist critique of masculinism depends at its core on the uncovering and deconstruction of pervasive gendered dichotomies. It is argued that the opposites of masculine/feminine form a powerful binary symbolism that operates within an epistemology of dualisms at the center of modern Western philosophy and culture.[9] This critique was first elaborated by French psychoanalytic feminists as they reworked Lacan's theory of the developmental and linguistic separation of Self from Other. Hélène Cixous, in particular, focused on hierarchic binary oppositions, arguing that the equation of masculinity with activity and victory and femininity with passivity and defeat is a phallocentric logic that leaves no positive space for women.[10]

In the pair *masculine/feminine*, the terms are constructed as opposites, with the first term, *masculinity*, being valued over the second, *femininity*. Masculinity and femininity are defined in relation to each other, so they are in fact relational terms within a linguistic system. As masculinity is the valued term, it can be argued that femininity is merely a residual category, a foil or Other for masculinity to define itself against. Although the terms are relational, when we use this system as a conceptual apparatus through which we look at the world, they become naturalized and appear as absolute qualities. The dichotomy masculine/feminine is linked to other dichotomous pairs, which operate in a similar fashion. Thus such pairs as hard/soft, rational/irrational, strong/weak, tough/tender, culture/nature, mind/body, dominant/submissive, science/art, active/passive, inside/outside, competitive/caring, objective/subjective, public/private, abstract/concrete, independent/dependent, aggressor/victim, Self/Other, order/anarchy, war/peace, and prudence/impulsiveness are either used to define masculinity and femininity, respectively, or are otherwise associated with them, with the former term always constructed in relation to its opposite, and generally privileged over it. Often what counts as active and therefore masculine is a question of semantics, so that for example while passivity is a devalued feminine trait, restraint is a valued masculine one.

This association of masculinity with positive value and activity is the common thread holding together all the contradictory ingredients that appear in such dichotomized thinking. In post-Lacanian analysis it is closely tied to the centrality of phallic symbolism in culture. Phallocentric discourse is based on a metaphorical link between language and a particular interpretation of male and female anatomy and sexuality. The basic argument runs thus: the penis is positively valued, whereas female genitals are not—they are associated with "lack" (of a penis). Power and activity are associated with the erect penis and the female role in heterosexual intercourse is interpreted as passive. Thus masculinity is culturally constructed as being psychologically associated with value and activity, while femininity is deemed passive. This essentially linguistic construction then permeates all other relations between the sexes and, through gendered dichotomies, social life in general (Moi 1985).

The use of dichotomous thinking, then, is a way of trying to fix the gender order in a way that keeps masculinity both naturalized and privileged. The exposure of this gender symbolism has led to valuable feminist work on the inherent masculinism of both science (Harding 1986; Haraway 1991) and politics (Elshtain 1981), including international relations (Grant and Newland 1991; Tickner 1992; Peterson and Runyan 1993, 1998; Peterson 1994).[11] The association of various qualities such as rationality, autonomy, prudence, strength, power, logic, boundary setting, control, and competitiveness with both masculine values and perceptions and their concurrent centrality in the disciplinary values and practices of science and politics helps to reinforce the links between masculinity and the disciplines themselves.[12] The downgraded or distrusted qualities of intuition, empathy, vulnerability, and cooperation are associated with the feminine, and as a result women are often downgraded or excluded.

In the post-Lacanian framework elaborated by Cixous and other feminist poststructuralists, the masculine/feminine dichotomy is also seen as an organizing principle of economic, social, and political life. Because it informs numerous practices that shape identities, this dichotomy produces the very gendered divisions it purports to describe, such as gendered divisions in labor, codes of dress, emotional styles, behavior, and so on. However, the strict dualism of Lacanian analysis pays insufficient attention to the numerous contradictions between the strategies to fix gender characteristics in binary divisions and the fluidity and complexity of social life that ever threatens to reveal itself, exposing the limits and failures of such strategies and revealing them for what they are. It also underestimates the diversity of uses to which strategies of masculinization and feminization are put and the complex ways in which such strategies interact with divisions other than gender such as class, race, and sexuality. While both phallic symbolism and phallocentric discourse are fairly ubiquitous in modern Western cultures, this does not mean that the phallus is necessarily *the* transcendental signifier, or that *all* gendered language is phallocentric, even in the contemporary West. While the linguistic networks of phallocentric dichotomies undoubtedly play a major role in the constitution of the gender order, they do not determine it completely.[13]

Spike Peterson and Anne Sisson Runyan (1993), in their discussion of gendered dichotomies, appear to drop Lacanian psychoanalytic discourse as an explanation for gendered dichotomies in favor of a more straightforwardly political account.[14] Gendered dichotomies, rather than uniformly constructing gendered social relations through universal psychoanalytic mechanisms, are seen more ambiguously, as playing a dual role. Where gendered dichotomies are used as an organizing principle of social life (such as in the gendered division of labor) they help to construct gender differences and inequalities and thus are constitutive of social reality, but in positing a grid of polar opposites, they also serve to obscure more complex relationships, commonalties, overlaps, and intermediate positions (Peterson and Runyan 1993, 24–25).

Elaborating on this view, it can be argued that gendered dichotomies are in part ideological tools that mystify, masking more complex social realities and reinforcing stereotypes. On one level, they do help to produce real gender differences and inequalities, when they are used as organizing principles that have practical effects commensurate with the extent that they become embedded in institutional practices, and through these, human bodies. They constitute one dimension in the triangular nexus out of which gender identities and the gender order are produced. But at the same time, institutional practices are not always completely or unambiguously informed by such dichotomies, which may then operate to obscure more complex relationships. It is a mistake to see the language of gendered dichotomies as a unified and totalizing discourse that dictates every aspect of social practice to the extent that we are coherently produced as subjects in its dualistic image. As well as the disruptions and discontinuities engendered by the intersections and interjections of other discourses (race, class, sexuality, and so on) there is always room for evasion, reversal, resistance, and dissonance between rhetoric, practice, and embodiment, as well as reproduction of the symbolic order, as identities are negotiated in relation to all three dimensions, in a variety of complex and changing circumstances. On the other hand, the symbolic gender order does inform practice, and our subjectivities are produced in relation to it, so to dismiss it as performing only an ideological or propagandistic role is also too simplistic.

The power of gendered dichotomies and the way in which strategies of masculinization and feminization work to promote inequalities between the sexes can be seen clearly in the gendered division of labor. "Masculine" and "feminine" traits and qualities have been used not only to support the division between paid employment and unpaid domestic work, but also to structure the segregation of employment into predominantly male and female occupations or grades within an occupation. For example, in Britain in 1985, men formed 99.5 percent of the total number employed in construction and mining; 96.4 percent of those in professional science, technology, and engineering; 96.4 percent of those in transport; 83.1 percent of those in farming and fishing; and 77.1 percent of those in professional and related fields supplying management and administration; while women formed 79.2 percent of workers in personal services (such as catering, cleaning, and hairdressing); 77.2 percent of those in clerical work; and 65 percent of professionals in education, welfare, and health (Bradley 1989, 13).

There is an extensive literature on this subject, providing both quantitative evidence on trends and numerous in-depth empirical examples of how jobs become gendered, and I will not rehearse it here. Instead, I cite Harriet Bradley, who, after surveying the literature and elaborating a number of case studies, came to the conclusion that "ideas about feminine and masculine nature and behaviour were highly involved in the gendering of jobs and resulted in the formation of gendered work cultures" (1989, 229). Gendered dichotomies here operate as an organizing principle in the workplace. Moreover, to the extent that men and women self-select "masculine" and "feminine" jobs, respectively, these dichotomies are to some extent constitutive of gender identity. Bradley found that ideas about suitable jobs for women came in part from the ideology of domesticity, but "social meanings of masculinity and femininity were also negotiated within the workplace itself" (Bradley 1989, 229). The outcome of such negotiations is important, not least because "men's jobs" and grades, which are deemed to require masculine characteristics, generally attract higher pay and status. However, there have been numerous struggles over the gendered interpretation and representation of production skills and the qualities needed for particular jobs. The propagandistic element of gender dichotomies is highlighted when one considers that some varieties and grades of employment have switched sides. The same activities can be alternatively masculinized or feminized depending on interpretation. When women have performed similar tasks to men on the production line, what counted as natural aptitude and dexterity for women (nature) has often been reinterpreted as trained skills for men (culture), with pay and conditions of work following accordingly. As Anne Phillips and Barbara Taylor argued, "skill definitions are saturated with gender bias" (1980, 79). Attempts to reverse the poor status of women's employment have also included the introduction of "masculine" management styles, such as the adoption of militarism in civilian nursing (Starns 1997).

To take another example—one perhaps more relevant to international relations: the associations between military service, masculinity, and citizenship have been strong in the modern era. Soldiering is characterized as a manly activity requiring the "masculine" traits of physical strength, action, toughness, capacity for violence, and, for officers, resolve, technical knowhow, and logical or strategic thinking. It has historically been an important practice constitutive of masculinity (Connell 1989; Bourke 1999). But traditionally the "feminine" qualities of total obedience and submission to authority, the attention to dress detail, and the endless repetition of mundane tasks that enlisted men as opposed to officers are expected to perform are downplayed or interpreted as nongendered, at least to the outside world (even while, at the same time, confirming the men's subordinate status to officers within the services themselves). As Laura Marks suggests, "in general military service forces people into extraordinarily passive roles, requiring that they give up individual agency, endure humiliations and unthinkingly obey orders" (Marks 1991, 74). To highlight such aspects of soldiering in the lower ranks would be to some degree to "feminize" this activity, reduce its contribution to the reproduction of masculine identities, and simultaneously signal a reduction in its overall status. It is not the actions themselves but the gendered interpretations placed on them that are crucial in determining which activities count as masculine and valued and which count as feminine and devalued.

## Dichotomous Thinking and Oppositional Strategies

The pervasiveness of dichotomous thinking on gender and the corresponding difficulty in transcending it can be seen when one examines some of the strategies that have been deployed to dismantle masculine power and privilege. As long as masculinity is perceived as a relatively unitary, stable, and coherent phenomenon that corresponds to the experiences of all men, dichotomous thinking remains either obviously or secretly at the core of these solutions, compromising their radical potential. Three such strategies are discussed below:

The simplest proposal for the overthrow of masculinist privilege is the route taken by some radical feminists: they accept all the qualities associated with the feminine as women's natural domain but privilege these qualities over the masculine. This approach has informed some interpretations of the women's peace camp at Greenham Common, in Berkshire, England, and has been significant in radical feminist thought on the nature of war and peace (Jones 1983; Segal 1987). Radical feminist thought has inspired the sharp end of feminist activism and has consequently been successful in bringing a number of issues, especially around women's health and sexuality, to the forefront of mainstream politics.

However, in spite of this practical legacy of effective campaigns, which have, as Joan Cocks (1989) argues, improved many women's lives, radical feminist thought itself does nothing to dismantle dichotomous thinking. Rather than transcend the masculine/feminine dichotomy, the conceptual framework that radical feminists employ would attempt to replace the rule of violent and "masculine" men with the rule of peaceloving "feminine" women. As I argued in chapter 1, such a view is essentialist. Moreover, while power is generally associated with masculinity rather than femininity, such a philosophy is likely to remain marginal. Thus "the oppositional imagination" is a good deal less radical than it might at first appear because, rather than questioning the dominant discourse, it reproduces it by reinstating masculinist dichotomies in reverse (Cocks 1989).

Those who prefer to integrate the masculine and feminine halves of the dichotomies often suggest that the solution to the dominance of masculinism is to increase the participation of women in the public sphere, and particularly their representation in political, economic, scientific, and academic elites. In what is known as the standpoint feminist view, it is argued that because the gendered division of labor has given women different experiences to those of men, women would bring different perspectives and practices to these fields, thus filling in the missing feminine half of the picture (Harding 1986; Hartstock 1987). Their increased participation would improve both theory and practice by engendering wider and more rounded perspectives in policy making and more holistic theoretical approaches to human subjectivity. Masculinist practices and disciplines are seen as handicapped by operating with only half of human experience. Early feminist interventions in international relations have tended to adopt this line.[15]

The problem with this kind of argument is that it, too, like radical feminism, assumes that the qualities associated with masculinity and femininity are clearly attached to men and women, respectively; if they are not, the increasing participation of women may not yield the desired results. For example, large numbers of women might be absorbed into international politics as soldiers, diplomats, and academics with minimal disruption if they were willing to adopt so-called masculine values. Admittedly, to sustain such values in public life, such women would largely have to be from the privileged middle classes. They would have to have "wives" or servants to take care of their domestic responsibilities, if they were to adopt such a "masculine" lifestyle wholeheartedly.[16] An invisible army of support workers would still be needed to underpin the public face of international politics. Class and race are also relevant here (as they are in all gendered situations) so that while white, middle-class women might be increasingly "masculinized" as they participated more fully in the public world of international politics, it would be at the expense of working-class women and women from other ethnic groups who would remain "feminized" and marginalized. The attempt by U.S. President Bill Clinton to appoint Zoe Baird to the position of attorney general, only to come unstuck over her employment of illegal immigrants as domestic staff, showed both the possibilities and limits of women's incorporation into political elites on these terms (*The Economist*, January 30 1993, 4).

It may be necessary for women to adopt so-called masculine attributes to gain acceptance in the political world and be seen as politically powerful.

Peterson and Runyan (1993) argue that a no-win situation applies to women who are politically successful. They are either accused of propping up the status quo by supporting masculine agendas or, if they appear to act "like women" or represent "soft issues," they are accused of reinforcing the traditional feminine stereotype, so that

> as long as female political actors are perceived either as traditional women or "invisible women" (because they are acting like men), gender expectations are not really disrupted. Paradoxically, even when women wield the highest state power, by continuing to behave in gender-stereotypical ways, they reinforce rather than challenge the politics of gender. . . . There is no simple, one-to-one relationship between the presence of women in power and the extent of feminist politics. (Peterson and Runyan 1993, 71)

Only if the proportion of women in international politics became very large, and their visibility very high, might their simple presence seriously disrupt the association of its particular values with masculinity. Otherwise (to return to the dimensions discussed in chapter 1) swapping female for male bodies in traditionally masculine arenas does little to disrupt either the symbolism or practices of the gender order.

Just as an increase in women participating in the public side of international politics on its own would not guarantee a change in the practice of politics, neither would the importation of feminine characteristics automatically redress the gender imbalance, especially if women themselves were still underrepresented in positions of power. The limitations of attempting to reclaim traditionally "feminine" values for men as a radical strategy can be seen in men's-studies literature, where this was a prominent theme in the late 1970s and early 1980s. Men were urged to discover and develop their emotional, intuitive, and nurturing sides through therapy and consciousness raising in men's groups of various kinds.[17] Loosely based on object-relations psychology,[18] the argument was that men en mass were somehow emotionally retarded or emotionally illiterate, locked into lonely isolation and incapable of intimacy, as this quote from an antisexist newsletter suggests:

> As men we are very out of touch with our feelings—we have had the language of feeling beaten out of us, often literally, during childhood. Those

feelings we are left with have acquired connotations which make us shun or misapply them. So—love and warmth imply shame; joy and delight imply immaturity; anger and frustration imply physical violence. We need to reclaim our feelings and shed the connotations—to learn that feeling is good for us. (quoted in Middleton 1992, 119)

Male power is either ignored in these accounts or is seen as not worth the price of such emotional self-denial. Emotional vulnerability is seen as the key to "authenticity," to unraveling male power and violence, and removing inequalities between the sexes.[19] Being impersonal and unemotional is equated with being powerful.

However, not only does it not necessarily follow that emotions undermine power, but the argument that men are less emotional itself derives from the rational/emotional dichotomy of masculinist discourse and in itself reinforces gender stereotypes. At the level of social experience, the picture is much more complicated. A certain amount of aggressive competitiveness is sanctioned and the public expression of male anger and rage is sometimes tolerated (Hodson 1984, 9)—for example, in combat. In private, as David Jackson argues, there exists "a whole range of unsettling emotions that they [men] try to keep buttoned up but that leak out in personal relations, usually at home" (Jackson 1990, 2).[20] The social positions of the persons involved and the power relationships in which they are enmeshed matters, too. For example, the high-ranking U.S. general, Norman Schwartzkopf (known to the British media as Stormin' Norman) was seen to weep in public at a moment of power and victory at the end of the Gulf War. Far from signaling weakness, appropriate public displays of sensitivity such as crying can be a legitimizing sign of the New Man's power (Hondagneau-Sotelo and Messner 1994, 204). It is not that emotional expression per se is prohibited for men, but rather that the circumstances and ways in which it is sanctioned vary. By oversimplifying and overgeneralizing from the rational/emotional dichotomy, this approach tends inadvertently to universalize the experiences of white, middle-class, Anglo-American, heterosexual men and has thus been criticized for being both racist and heterosexist (Mercer and Julien 1988; Dowsett 1993; Rogoff and Van Leer 1993). In Mediterranean and Latino cultures, for example, men are far more open to public emotional expression and sentimentality than this line of argument would suggest, without any undermining of their "machismo."

## Transcending Dichotomous Thinking

It is very difficult to transcend dichotomous thinking altogether since we are limited to some extent by the structures of language we have inherited.[21] Nor should one underestimate the usefulness of the feminist insight that gendered dichotomies construct masculinity and femininity as opposites, treat masculinity as active and femininity as passive, and valorize the masculine. This insight illuminates the close association between masculinity and power in modern Western culture.

However, if the masculine half of gendered dichotomies is always valued more highly but the ingredients of the masculinity are ambiguous or contradictory, then there is room for political and interpretative struggles over what counts as masculine, and consequently who gets power and status. Peterson (1994) argues that a critical analysis of gender dichotomies must include an examination of both their concrete power effects and their conceptual aspects.[22] This can be achieved by the use of historical contextualization, which includes an appreciation of the relational nature of the "masculine" and "feminine" in any particular situation. So critiques of "masculinist" international relations must specify *how* the ingredients of "masculinity" and "femininity" get to be defined in relation to each other in the particular context under examination. Such a contextualization might include spelling out the specifics of how the deployment of gendered dichotomies forms part of power struggles over the *interpretation* of practices and groups of people—groups that are not necessarily made up of women. It would show how apparently stable gender divisions are the temporary result of strategies of masculinization and feminization in which dichotomous thinking is used as a tool of masculinist power struggles.

Such a perspective employs an understanding of power forms and power struggles as relatively diffuse and widespread and is therefore much closer to Foucault than Lacan. However, this kind of analysis, while moving from a fixed picture of binary symbolism to one of process, still retains an underlying male/female division. If only the division between men and women is constantly examined, then even such contextualized analysis as advocated by Peterson can increase the attention paid to and apparent salience of the very gender differences that feminists wish to dismantle.

Criticisms of "masculinism," whether in international relations or elsewhere, need to go well beyond the mere identification of the widespread use of gender dichotomies and the privileging of so-called masculine traits if they are to achieve anything other than a reinforcement of these dichotomies. If neither the increasing presence of women, viewed as honorary men, nor the importation of "feminine qualities" into political life will of themselves necessarily disrupt the prevailing gender order, and radical feminist prescriptions would disrupt, only to reverse it, then a more sophisticated approach is required, an approach that deconstructs gendered dichotomies more thoroughly and pays attention to their contradictions.

## Multiple Masculinities

One way of transcending dichotomous thinking on gender is to move away from an analysis of *masculinity* (singular), albeit relationally defined and historically contextualized, toward an analysis of *masculinities* (plural). In feminist terms this is a risky project because if the postmodern emphasis on difference is already threatening to undermine the feminist project by dissolving the category of women as an oppressed group,[23] then an examination of the differences between men threatens to dissolve, or at least obscure, our view of the oppressor as a group. On the one hand, theorists need to avoid reinforcing gender dichotomies, but on the other, in emphasizing a pluralism of masculinities, they may well ignore or underplay masculinist power relations and the overall privileges of men. Susan Bordo warns that "there are dangers in too wholesale a commitment to either dual or multiple grids" (Bordo 1990, 149).

Walking this tightrope is not easy. For example, in men's studies the earlier tendency to reinforce stereotypes has since the late 1980s progressively been replaced by more sophisticated theoretical approaches that acknowledge the complexities of masculinities and contextualize them historically.[24] However, even in these accounts there is a constant problem of slippage back to merely reproducing taken-for-granted concepts of masculinity or to providing more refined versions of role theory, as their own authors sometimes admit (Hearn and Morgan 1990, 9; Seidler 1990, 223).[25] Alternatively, when masculinities are adequately historicized there is a tendency toward a bland pluralism in which relations with women drop out of the picture altogether, so that men's studies still often loses its grip on power, subordination, and potential radicalism (Brod 1994, 86).[26]

One strand of the literature on masculinities that avoids this problem is derived from the article "Towards a New Sociology of Masculinity" (Carrigan, Connell, and Lee 1985) and a subsequent book by Connell (1987). The article suggested that multiple masculine identities existed in a hierarchy of power relations, and Connell's book both developed this theory and provided a multidimensional account of gender identity with a particular focus on masculinities. In Connell's account, gender differences and hierarchies are seen as being produced through social structures (the sexual division of labor, the relations of power, and the sociopsychological structuring of sexual desire and emotional attachments) that are themselves constituted by repeated practices, including discursive practices. Connell argues that there are many masculinities and, presumably, femininities in existence at the same time, but that there are nonetheless dominant patterns of masculinity, or "hegemonic masculinity," that operate at the level of the whole society and that shore up male power and advantage (Connell 1987, 183–88). Hegemonic masculinity is constructed in opposition to a range of subordinate masculinities, as well as their female corollary, the ever-compliant "emphasized femininity." In Connell's view there can be no equivalent hegemonic femininity, because while there may be prevailing constructions of femininity, and some women may be more privileged than others, all femininities are subordinate to hegemonic masculinity. Of course, Connell's theory does not necessarily mean that women are entirely unable to reconstruct femininity in an empowering way, and indeed overturning this inequality in the power to define gender identities remains a central goal of feminism.[27]

In this gender hierarchy, gender intersects with other factors such as class and sexuality. Connell argues that hegemonic masculinity is above all heterosexual and is defined in opposition to homosexuality. This point is backed up by Jeffrey Weeks (1987), who argues that although erotic activity between men and men and women and women is probably universal, the concept of a distinctly homosexual identity is not. In Europe, male homosexual identities (and their corollary, heterosexual identities) did not emerge until the late nineteenth century, and close relationships between women were not demarcated until even more recently. Previously the emphasis was on prohibited behavior, such as sodomy, but there was no concept of a special type of person who indulged in it, with distinctive desires or aptitudes. As Lynne Segal argues, even now, when male homosexual identities are well established and are seen as founded on homoerotic desires and behavior, not all homoerotic behavior confers such an identity. The phenomenon of male rape in prisons and other all-male institutions rarely confers a homosexual identity on the rapist. Indeed, such rape occurs, various studies conclude, as a way of asserting power and masculinity: "A male who fucks another male is a double male" (Segal 1990, 247).

But while the relationship of sexual identities to particular kinds of behavior remains fairly loose, male homosexual identities have been clearly constructed in opposition to hegemonic masculinity (female homosexual identities have until recently had a more shadowy and ambiguous existence, due to the passive cultural construction of female sexuality).[28] Heterosexual hegemonic masculinity depends for its existence on the presence of a stigmatized subordinate homosexual masculinity. Otherwise it would cease to be clearly heterosexual.

Connell himself does not stress this point, but other commentators have argued that hegemonic masculinity is also racist and is defined against a number of nonwhite subordinate masculinities. A global, racialized hierarchy of masculinities was created as part of the institutionalization of a complex set of race and gender identities sustaining European imperialism — identities that still have a cultural legacy today. Broadly speaking, British and French imperialists imagined "the Orient" as an exotic, sensual, and feminized world, a kind of halfway stage between "Europe's enlightenment" and "African savagery." While oriental men were positioned as effeminate (and oriental women as exotic), black Africans of both sexes were deemed uncivilized and, in a projection of European sexual fantasies, seen as saturated with monstrous lust. In Britain, sex was seen as both natural (uncivilized) and a threat to the moral order. White women, particularly middle-class women, were regarded as lust-free symbols of this moral order who, unless they were protected, were potentially in danger of being raped by black male "savages." The "English gentleman" positioned himself at the top of this hierarchy as a self-disciplined, naturally legitimate ruler and protector of morals. He regarded his sexuality as overlaid and tempered by civilization. He became the embodiment of imperial power, seeming to rule effortlessly, and justifying his colonial mission as a civilizing one. As a type, then, the Victorian English Gentleman was at least as much a product of imperial politics as of domestic understandings of Englishness, aristocracy, and masculinity (Hall 1992a). In the United States, a similar sexualization of race took place under slavery, where the construction of white women as chaste, domesticated, and morally pure was accomplished through the positioning of black slave women as promiscuous, black men as brutes and potential rapists, and white men as protectors (Said 1978; Mercer and Julien 1988; Mohanty 1991). Chinese male immigrants, who occupied the halfway house of indentured labor, were seen as both effeminate—because they often did women's work in laundries and kitchens—and as a sexual threat to white women (Fung 1995).[29]

Connell suggests that because of its generalized and ideological nature, hegemonic masculinity is a very public, simplified, and idealized model of easily symbolized aspects of interaction, rather than a statement of the actual personalities of the majority of men. But he is sufficiently post-Marxist to view ideology as a productive, discursive practice, rather than as a species of false consciousness. Hegemonic masculinity is also constitutive of, and embodied in, numerous institutional practices, such as enforced competitive sport for schoolboys. Individuals are therefore forced to negotiate their identities in relation to practices and relationships informed by hegemonic masculinity and the alternative gender models on offer. The more that individual men publicly identify with hegemonic masculinity, or collaborate with such public images, the more they help to boost their own position. However, compliance—in any degree, and no matter how unconscious or grudging—helps to shore up existing inequalities. The interplay between different masculinities is as much a part of the gender order as the interplay between masculinities and femininities. Posing challenges to hegemonic masculinity at both the individual and the institutional level is therefore at the heart of sexual politics.

The concept of hegemonic and subordinate masculinities is extremely useful in that it acknowledges multiple masculinities while keeping sight of power relations, and it has been successfully applied by feminists and others in recent British literature on gender identity and gender that focuses on men.[30]

There are, however, three drawbacks with Connell's approach. First, he is not entirely successful in his own theoretical attempt to move beyond structuralism: there is, on the one hand, a tension between his focus on practice, dynamic relations, fluidity, and change in the construction of gender identities and, on the other, a more than residual structuralism when discussing the gender order. His separation of the gender order into structural categories of analysis (labor, power, and cathexis) brings with it a static logic, as he argues himself when criticizing other categorical approaches (Connell 1987, 60). Moreover, his categories themselves are inconsistent. As Segal argues, power and desire are really ubiquitous and should be ingredients in all structures; whereas labor is more specifically a structure. The state and language are also specific structures, but the trilogy of labor, state, and language would take him back to the economic, political, and ideological categories of Althusserian structuralism. (Segal 1990, 102).

Second, Connell's reduction of discourse to ideology is crude. While discourse does indeed contain a strong ideological element, discourse does not run counter to the material world; rather, it informs material practices — just as Connell himself argues that practices affect bodies.

And third, Connell's theory of hegemony is somewhat underdeveloped. He references Gramsci and clearly belongs to the tradition that has extracted Gramsci's (1971) theory of cultural hegemony from its Marxist and class-based context. However he does not distinguish this particular interpretation of hegemony from other uses of the term.[31] More importantly, Connell does not really specify whether hegemonic masculinity is consciously promoted by elite groups of men to serve their interests or whether it is wholly sustained by the largely unconscious identification and collaboration of the majority. If it is the former, then he stays closer to Gramsci's original understanding of hegemony, which is achieved largely through an ideological ascendancy over a cultural mix; moral persuasion and consent rather than brute force (although such ascendancy may be backed up by force). If the latter, then he would be adopting a more Foucauldian approach to hegemony. In this case, while elites and knowledge producers are heavily implicated in the production of hegemonic masculinity, masculinism is not a conspiracy of elites. Rather, it is endemic at all levels of society as different groups and interests jockey for position in micronetworks of power relations. Heterogeneous, vital, and unstable power relations operating at the "molecular" level produce weighty and relatively rigid "hegemonic effects" (Foucault 1980, 93), as opposed to the alternative vision of an oppressive power radiating out from a central point. As Raymond Williams argued, elites are implicated in the dissemination of cultural hegemony through their participation in a lived system of meaningful practices that reproduce and confirm their own identities, rather than through a conscious or deliberate strategy of domination (Williams 1977a, 110). Arguably, this latter approach is more satisfactory since it avoids dubious conspiracy theories.

## Masculinity, Masculinities, and Masculinism

An analysis that pays attention to how masculinism creates hierarchies of masculinities as well as inequalities between men and women goes some way toward undermining a simple dualism of masculinity/femininity, without losing its grip on power relations. This is where a contextualized understanding of the feminist concept of masculinism, such as Peterson's, can mesh with the literature on multiple masculinities that draws on Connell's theory of hegemonic and subordinate masculinities (shorn of its problematic structuralism).

Ann Tickner moves in this direction in her feminist analysis of IR theory. She emphasizes the "masculinist underpinnings" (Tickner 1992, xi) of the discipline, but at the same warns against the essentializing tendency of separating women from men as undifferentiated categories. This tendency "ignores the ways in which women's varying identities and development interests as farmers, factory workers, merchants, and householders bear on gender relations in different contexts" (Tickner 1992, 95). At various points in her book, she explicitly examines different models of "man" and "masculinity" (see my introductory chapter), and offers a variety of feminist critiques. She also mentions alternative conceptions of masculinity not featured in IR theory, and in her final chapter discusses the possibilities of a nongendered model of human action.

However, in spite of these nuances in the detail, her book's overall structure and main thrust, in counterposing "international relations" against "feminism," tends to oppose a monolithic and one might say essentialized masculinity—identified as "hegemonic masculinity" (e.g., 131, 136) or "idealized manhood" (e.g., 132)—in IR theory against an equally monolithic opponent known as either "feminist theories" (57, 132), "feminist approaches" (132), or "feminist perspectives" (133–34). The overall effect is one of theoretical confusion and an undifferentiated eclecticism in deploying incompatible feminist approaches.

Tickner also slides all too easily between different terms and models that are not all defined by the same characteristics. For example, it is not clear whether Connell's concept of hegemonic masculinity, introduced in the first chapter and then used throughout the book, refers to one or all of the various models of masculinity discussed in different chapters. Meanwhile, the main thrust of her argument, which is to make a case for the reformulation of IR theory to redress the masculinist balance by including women and so-called feminine qualities, tends to divert attention from, and hence play down, the significance of the different masculinities she identifies. Moreover, the goal of integrating explicitly feminine values into IR is presented as a step toward the development of a nongendered approach to IR. However, these two aims may prove contradictory. The assumption that they are inherently compatible is another example of the lack of differentiation in Tickner's otherwise groundbreaking book.

In order to integrate the critique of masculinism with a recognition of multiple masculinities fully, it is necessary to shift the focus away from an exclusive interest in the exclusion and devaluation of women and femininity and toward an analysis of the politics of "masculinity" itself. One needs to specify the relations between the terms *masculinity, masculinities,* and *masculinism,* and explore the role of masculinism in relationships between different masculinities. Tickner goes halfway to doing the former. Implicit in her analysis is the assumption that active and positively valued traits and qualities associated with masculinity in general are more closely representative of hegemonic masculinity than of subordinate varieties. This seems a reasonable assumption, so that, in the masculinist practices outlined above, the qualities identified as masculine in gendered dichotomies can be seen to relate most closely to hegemonic masculinity. Thus, gendered dichotomies promote and reinforce not just any masculinity but the hegemonic masculinity of white, heterosexual, middle-class men. That this is so can be instantly seen when one considers the rational/irrational or rational/emotional, mind/body, and culture/nature dichotomies. The superior male mind that lies behind these masculinist dichotomies is a white, imperial one—since, as discussed above, black men are associated with the body, as are women and homosexuals.

Hegemonic masculinity itself is tied to phallocentrism through the scientific imagination that posits masculine reason and culture as active and acting on the relatively passive body of nature within which woman is apparently mired—*active* (signifying the phallus) and *passive* (signifying lack) here being the operative terms. Similarly, both the image of penis as weapon and the conventional construction of heterosexual relations revolve around phallocentric discourse. Hegemonic masculinity, then, can be seen to be largely, but not exclusively, phallocentric in modern Western culture. To argue this is not necessarily to endorse a Lacanian psychoanalytic perspective. Arthur Brittan (1989) argues for a broadly Foucauldian analysis of phallocentrism: the phallic myth is propagandized by priests, psychiatrists, and doctors, and enters the practice of sexuality through the embodiment processes of social practices and their associated emotional power. However, it is not safe to assume that hegemonic masculinity has always been or always will be dominated by phallocentric imagery (as Lacanian analysis would imply).[32] As noted in chapter 1, the equation of women with passive nature and men with active culture itself constituted a reconceptualization of gender as part of broader philosophical changes during the Enlightenment period. Phallocentric imagery, although prevalent in contemporary culture, is only one of several ways of characterizing hegemonic masculinity.

Joan Cocks argues that the transition to modernity has been accompanied by a gradual change in the form of male dominance, from a power primarily based on patriarchal rights to one won through phallic superiority (Cocks 1989, 210–14). This change is linked not only to Enlightenment philosophical developments but also to the whittling away of the spatial base of patriarchal relations through changing economic and cultural factors related to the industrial revolution and the rise of capitalism and bureaucratic power. For example, patriarchal rights were undermined by the collapse in the family/household system of production, large-scale urbanization, and increasing state regulation of social life. The shift toward phallocentric legitimation was a way for male power to save itself, but it was also facilitated by the new liberal championing of individual freedom, the scientific disenchantment of desire, and the rise of utilitarian beliefs that paved the way for a commodification of sexual gratification, so that "one could thus argue that the triumph of phallic right was as much the consequence of as the antidote to patriarchal right's decline" (Cocks 1989, 214).

Moreover, Cocks argues that the eclipse of patriarchal power is not complete and even now antagonistic masculinist interests representing these two forms of power still compete,[33] suggesting that there are struggles between men over the constitution of hegemonic masculinity. Such long term changes in the legitimating grounds of male dominance suggest that hegemonic masculinity itself can be seen both as a plastic phenomenon, and as a vehicle for keeping the associations between masculinity and power alive under changing circumstances. Hegemonic masculinity gets transformed, through constant challenges and struggles, to resemble whatever traits happen to be most strategically useful for the getting and keeping of power.

Such a perspective has its critics. Victor Seidler argues against any social constructionist approach that would view masculinity as power: "If we adopt a conception of masculinity which simply defines it as a relationship of power, or as the top place within a hierarchy of powers, then we are tempted into thinking that it is possible to "abandon our masculinity" (Seidler 1990, 219). He argues that such a temptation is itself a typically masculinist, rationalistic stance that follows Kant in believing that one can change one's inclinations by will. Seidler sees contemporary Western masculinity as principally defined by the Enlightenment legacy of rationalism and detachment, combined with the Protestant ethic of self-denial. Although Seidler's desire to undermine a particular variety of elitist bourgeois Protestant masculinity is laudable, his methodology is problematic. If gender identity is seen in the terms in which it was described in the preceding chapter, then, even if hegemonic masculinity is, in the end, a relationship of power, it cannot easily be "abandoned," because that power is produced through practices and inscribed in men's bodies and their psychologies as much as in language or the rational mind. Seidler's critique grossly underestimates the material consequences of productive power, which cannot be negated at will.

On the other hand, if the term *masculinity* is treated as an empty referent, having no stable content at all beyond its association with power, there is the danger of dissolving the meaning of masculinity altogether.[34] Even if masculinity is subject to endless revision and reinterpretation, it still has to be recognizable as masculinity, otherwise, the gendered divisions its construction supports are erased.[35] This question of gendered meaning operates on at least two levels. First, all masculinities have to appear to have enough in common to qualify as masculinities; and second, if each individual variety of masculinity is itself unstable, it must have sufficient continuity to be recognizable as a distinct variety. While subordinate varieties of masculinity may and do become indistinct at times, hegemonic masculinity, in particular, has to be recognizable as "real" masculinity to keep its powerful position in the gender order.

A useful way of looking at both masculinity as a generic term and the existence of plural masculinities is proposed by Harry Brod, who applies Wittgenstein's philosophical concept of "family resemblances" to masculinities: "Just as members of a family may be said to resemble each other without necessarily all having any single feature in common, so masculinities may form common patterns without sharing any single universal characteristic" (Brod 1987, 275–76). If this model is adopted, it can be seen that there is considerable room for fluidity in the construction of masculinity or masculinities. As long as there are enough common characteristics with some other masculinities, to make each variety recognizable as such (in terms of the particular historical and cultural context in which it is produced), new elements can be introduced to accommodate change. Hegemonic masculinity can then be seen not as a fixed set of dominant traits but as a constantly negotiated construct that draws on a pool of available characteristics, which, although they may be mutually contradictory can be put together in different combinations depending on circumstances. Different pools of characteristics may be available at different times and in different cultures (some are delineated below in a genealogy of hegemonic masculinities). No two images or manifestations of masculinity need be exactly alike. Thus, the mix-and-match nature of hegemonic masculinity accounts for its many contradictions, while the overlap in constructions and the incorporation of individual characteristics into gendered dichotomies provide continuity and naturalize "masculinity" as a powerful, timeless, and stable phenomenon.

The pool of available characteristics is also subject to gradual change over time, and characteristics of subordinate masculinities can be plundered to reinvigorate hegemonic masculinity, while previously hegemonic characteristics can be dropped or devalued. For example, the homoeroticism of ancient Greek martial masculinity was largely dropped in later Western martial masculinities. On the other hand, the contemporary positioning of heterosexual men as consumers in the West is involving a reincorporation of sensual and eroticized images of men into mainstream Anglo-Saxon culture not seen, in Britain at least, since the eighteenth century.[36]

The perspective outlined here tries to avoid dissolving *masculinity* altogether, on the one hand, and reinforcing gender dichotomies, on the other. Critics might argue that if men routinely exhibit so-called feminine characteristics, and if the similar activities and qualities can be labeled masculine or feminine depending on interpretation and a change of emphasis, and if the term *masculinity* has no stable ingredients, then why take the claims of feminists seriously at all? It took years for feminists to establish that gender oppression is significant in its own right—that it is neither an ideological distraction from the real divisions of class nor the result of an easily rectified faulty application of liberal values. This achievement is important and should not be undermined.

However, the perspective outlined here still allows for such gender divisions to be taken seriously, not least because of the practical consequences of the widespread interpretation of people, activities, and qualities as masculine and feminine. Such practical consequences include the largely gendered division of labor, as discussed above. Further, however contradictory the term *masculinity* appears on close examination, it remains meaningful to large numbers of people and is associated with power. Therefore men, even men at the bottom, have generally been more successful in claiming power (through its association with masculinity) than have women. In a complex intertwining of the hierarchies of race, gender, sexuality, and class, men as a whole have always had an edge over women, even though particular groups of men may have been less privileged than particular groups of women.

The trend toward discussing masculinities rather than masculinity does not completely escape the problems of inadvertently reinforcing the very social constructions that are ostensibly under attack. The use of concepts such as hegemonic and subordinate masculinities, rather than the adoption of a completely deconstructionist stance, is a compromise, as the very identification of power relations itself is part of their reproduction, and as such may reinforce them.[37] Rogoff and Van Leer question the usefulness of the concept of masculinity (even as masculinities) by arguing that this merely renews the academic currency of an oppressive concept: "if we do not in our readings relentlessly dismantle culture's boundaries, we may find that our studies leave us stranded in hegemony, not "speaking to" the topic, but speaking for it" (Rogoff and Van Leer 1993, 760). This is a risk that cannot be avoided if theory is to be constructed rather than deconstructed. Unless one is convinced that the deconstruction of theory will of itself entirely dissolve such power relations, it is a risk that has to be taken. It can be minimized, however, by starting from the premise that there is a good deal of

*gender
constructor*

contradiction, complexity, and fluidity in gender constructions, and by deploying the concepts of hegemonic and subordinate masculinities as useful analytical constructions rather than as concrete phenomena to be observed.

## A Genealogy of Hegemonic Masculinity

The hegemonic model is fleshed out in the following sections. I do this by drawing on a wide variety of historically and geographically disparate accounts of masculinities (although all focusing on Anglo-American constructions in one form or another). My aim is to reflect upon some of the numerous points of overlapping and cross-cutting of the available narratives, to build theory from the bottom up. In particular, I want to extract some understanding of the periodization and ingredients of hegemonic masculinity in order to identify some archetypes, to highlight the flux and change in hegemonic masculinity, and to examine the pattern of relationships between hegemonic and subordinate varieties and the role of masculinist practices in these relationships.

The focal point lies not in the history of masculinities itself, but rather in how patterns identified in historical and contemporary accounts can illuminate the question of the relationship between different masculinities, power, and the masculinist practices discussed above. It is, therefore, a minor kind of genealogical inquiry.[38] The accounts drawn on were, of course, originally provided in the context of a variety of different agendas: they are embedded in different perspectives and thus contain different emphases. Some emphasize the role of the economy, some race, others sexuality. Between them, they offer a wealth of useful material for identifying patterns in masculinities and illustrating the deployment of strategies of masculinization and feminization in the construction of masculinities and the policing of male behavior.

*history of hegemonic ideas*

An examination of the literature that attempts to trace the history of hegemonic masculinity in the West reveals at least four ideal types, or social categories, of dominant masculinities. These are inherited from different periods of European cultural history. The ideal types consist of the Greek citizen-warrior model; the patriarchal Judeo-Christian model; the honor/patronage model; and a Protestant, bourgeois-rationalist model. These types have been identified from a variety of sources. The Greek citizen-warrior model and its legacy is discussed by Stearns (1979), Elshtain (1981), and

Tickner (1992), among others; the patriarchal Judeo-Christian model by Stearns (1979), Elshtain (1981), and Cocks (1989); the honor/patronage model by Morgan (1992) and Connell (1993); and the bourgeois-rationalist model by Seidler (1987, 1988, 1989, 1990, 1991), Morgan (1992), Tickner (1992), and Connell (1993).

These types are heuristic devices and are not completely distinct. The honor/patronage model is heavily indebted to the Judeo-Christian legacy, and as Stearns and Elshtain suggest the bourgeois rationalist model is to some extent the result of a fusion of the Greek citizen-warrior with Judeo-Christian ideals. The Greek model combined militarism with rationalism (Stearns 1979) and equated manliness with citizenship in a masculine arena of free speech and politics (Elshtain 1981). In contrast, the Judeo-Christian ideal of manliness emphasized a more domesticated ideal of responsibility, ownership, and the authority of the father of fathers. The honor/patronage model was an aristocratic ideal in which personal bonds between men, military heroism, and taking risks were highly valued, with the duel as the ultimate test of masculinity (Connell 1993). The bourgeois-rationalist model idealized competitive individualism, reason, and self-control or self-denial (Seidler 1988), combining respectability as breadwinner and head of household with calculative rationality in public life.[39]

The influence of the various archetypes of hegemonic masculinity has waxed and waned historically. For example, martial masculinities, prominent in Greece and Rome, lost status in the Middle Ages. Under the papal "domestication" of Europe (in which there was a series of overlapping jurisdictions, national sovereignty being muted), power was in the hands of clerics, and mainstream masculinities tended to be agricultural or monastic in the Judeo-Christian mold. Meanwhile the military life was by and large relegated to a soldier caste. The revival of military service as an important feature of masculinity and citizenship, central to the identity of men, was associated with the rise of city-states and then nation-states (Stearns 1979; Elshtain 1981). As argued above, modernity has also brought a slow decline of the patriarchal Judeo-Christian model and its replacement by bourgeois-rationalism.

At any one time, the core ingredients of hegemonic masculinities can be made up of elements drawn from various of these ideal types, whose previous layers, reformulations, combinations, and manifestations lend an air of continuity and timelessness to today's construction. The mutual incompatibility of these basic types has not prevented some creative combinations of their elements in constructing apparently unified and singular masculinities. Realist masculinity in international relations is a case in point, having borrowed from all of these traditions. In fact, the credibility and durability of the realist approach may partly lie with the fact that it does appear to combine and embody traits that have been associated with male power and dominant masculinity under different historical conditions (see chapter 3).

## Flux, Change, and Crisis in Hegemonic Masculinity

A brief reading of the recent literature on the history of masculinities suggests that, even within the modern period, dominant styles of masculinity can change quite rapidly, almost from one decade to the next. There was a change from the "men of letters" in Britain in the mid nineteenth century to the "hypermasculinity" and flight from domesticity of the new colonialism in the 1890s (Roper and Tosh 1991; Mangan and Walvin 1987). There was a crisis of masculinity in the United States associated with the symbolic closing of the frontier in the 1890s (Kimmel 1987a), and an attempt to regain the strenuous masculine life culminating in World War I (Filene 1987). Alternatively, World War I was the beginning of a twentieth-century crisis in masculinity and a terminal blow to martial masculinities (apart from a brief fascist interlude that attempted to turn the clock back) (Tolson 1977; Stearns 1979; Brittan 1989; Connell 1993). Then came the twentieth-century splitting of Victorian hegemonic masculinity into varieties based on expertise, domination, and the emergence of working-class hegemonic masculinity (Connell 1993); another period of hypermasculinity in the cold war of the 1950s, also associated with the flight from the domestic in both Britain and the United States (Segal 1987) or, alternatively, with rigid domestication in the breadwinner role (Ehrenreich 1983). This period, too, has been identified as one when masculinity was again "in crisis" (Brod 1987).

Finally, there are the proliferating diagnoses of change in recent times, culminating in what Connell describes as a "contemporary multilateral struggle for hegemony in gender relations" (Connell 1993, 613). This variously seems to point to progressive change and the unraveling of hegemonic masculinities (e.g., Abbott 1987; Connell 1990; Kroker and Kroker 1991; Simpson 1994); less progressive change and the reconfiguration of hegemonic masculinities (e.g., Moore 1988; Stacey 1993; Messner 1993; Forrest

1994); resistance (e.g., Faludi 1991; Le Doeuff 1993); a crisis of masculinity (e.g., Kimmel 1987a; Brod 1987; Buchbinder 1994; Faludi 1999); a lesser legitimation crisis (e.g., Brittan 1989); or an ambiguous mixture of all of these (e.g., Segal 1987, Pfeil 1995).

One reason for the different and apparently contradictory histories outlined here is that different authors may be focusing on different sections of society or different constructions or archetypes of masculinity, and possibly generalizing too much. It is very likely that crises of masculinity occur for different groups of men and different strands within hegemonic masculinities at different times. As for contemporary changes, they are still unfolding. The different interpretations to some extent reflect ongoing struggles where the overall direction of change is still ambiguous.

Such a plethora of crises and changes identified in the literature lends weight to the argument that masculinities are fluid constructions and that dominant masculinities are constantly being challenged, reconstituted, and reinvented in different sections of society, in adaptation to changing economic, political, and social circumstances. Indeed, one might be led to expect crises or subcrises of hegemonic masculinity in particular locations or sections of society to be an almost permanent social feature. But such crises should not necessarily be seen as a sign of the imminent demise of male power for they are part-and-parcel of the adjustment process, so that, as Brittan argues, "while styles of masculinity may alter in relatively short time spans, the substance of male power does not." (Brittan 1989, 2). The pessimistic view (from the perspective of feminism) is that unraveling masculinities is "a utopian aspiration because new hegemonic masculinities are always being refigured and reconstituted, perhaps more quickly than the older ones unravel" (Stacey 1993, 711).

Some contributors see current challenges to hegemonic masculinity as particularly significant, however. Stearns, Segal, Weeks, and Connell all agree that by the end of the nineteenth century a clear and distinct, definitively heterosexual, Anglo-American model of manhood had crystalized, emerging through industrialization, bureaucratization, medical classification, British "public schools" (which actually are top private schools) and their U.S. counterparts, and imperialism, and that this model has survived, with modifications,[40] as the manly ideal throughout most of the twentieth century. It is perhaps this ideal of hegemonic masculinity that is now breaking down, or at least being seriously challenged by the strain of globalization, economic restructuring, the positioning of men as consumers, changes in family structure, and feminist, gay, and postcolonial political challenges, to mention only a few of the elements that make up "the condition of post-modernity" (Harvey 1989).

The idea that changes in dominant forms and constructions of masculinity can be provoked by wider economic and social changes is supported by some readings of gender history. Kimmel argues that major crises in hegemonic masculinity and consequent redefinitions have occurred at particular historical junctures, during times of rapid social change and disorder, when structural changes transformed the institutions of marriage and the family, often bringing new opportunities for women. Masculinities have then changed in reaction to new constructions of femininity, as "since men benefit from inherited definitions of masculinity and femininity, they would be unlikely to initiate change" (1987a, 123–24).

Kimmel's two cases were Restoration England (1688–1714) and the late-nineteenth-century United States. In the former, large numbers of men suffered contradictory loss of occupational autonomy and at the same time were led to expect increased individual independence when family craft workshops were threatened by the rise of liberalism, mercantilism, and migration to cities. On top of this, women were becoming wageworkers rather than partners in the old family workshops and they were consequently asserting sexual agency—equality of desire and equal rights in marriage. Many men abandoned their traditional role within the family, moved to the city, remained unmarried and/or (according to female pamphleteers) became feminized through their concern with dress, hairstyles, and cross-dressing—with becoming a beau or a fop. This feminization was linked to city life, to exotic foreign "French" influences, and was associated with sexual and political treason (Britain was at war with France at the time). Meanwhile, in a conservative backlash against such developments, traditional masculinity was promoted by association with patriotism and virility (successful resolution of the war with France).

In the case of the United States, the city was also linked with the threat of feminization, in the economic context of rapid industrialization, the deskilling of male workers, the closing of the frontier, mass immigration, the economic crash, and industrial unrest. By the late nineteenth century, expansive U.S. "frontier masculinity," for which the West signaled freedom and a virile optimism, was no longer tenable. Instead, the industrialized, bureaucratized, closed in world of the city beckoned. In contrast to the frontier, Frank Lloyd Wright described the city of New York as a "mantrap of monstrous dimensions" (quoted in Kimmel 1987a, 142). The city was seen to threaten masculinity through vice, cultural threats from immigrants and Jews, the increased public presence of women, and the loss of authority of traditional institutions such as the church. The crisis of masculinity formed part of the general social unrest that brought U.S. society to the brink of collapse, as all the familiar routes to manhood became blocked at the same time as women were demanding suffrage. Male responses to the crisis included accusing women of being "mannish" lesbians and an abhorrence of the idea that boys should be brought up almost exclusively by women in nuclear families—part of a dangerous feminization of U.S. culture. Masculinity was revived through appeals to religious fundamentalism, the "country life" movement, and health and sport fanaticism.[41] From these two cases Kimmel concludes that "masculinity was a relational construct and was to be reconstructed, reasserted or redefined in relation to changing social and economic conditions and the changing position of women in society" (1987a, 153).

Hearn (1992) criticizes Kimmel's historical approach to change in hegemonic masculinity as economically determinist. There is danger in seeing changes in dominant masculinities as purely reactive processes, determined by wider forces and structural changes. This undermines the claim that gender divisions are powerful in their own right (Donaldson 1993). Kimmell's analysis is overdependent on examining economic and structural changes to the neglect of the interplay between gender and other axes of hierarchical differentiation. In the second period that Kimmel examines, the late 1890s, Anglo-American hegemonic masculinities were not only being challenged by economic restructuring, they were also being defined in relation to the newly emerging category of "homosexual," and in terms of super-Darwinistic theories of racial superiority (discussed above). Kimmel's observations are instructive, but the picture is more complex than his rather economically determined analysis allows.

The relationships between hegemonic and subordinate masculinities play a key role in the gender order, at least as much in the policing of male behavior as in the subordination of women. As Donaldson remarks,

through hegemonic masculinity most men benefit from having control of women; for a very few men, it delivers control of other men. To put it another way, the crucial difference between hegemonic masculinity and other masculinities is not the control of women, but the control of men and the representation of this as a "universal social advancement," to paraphrase Gramsci. (Donaldson 1993, 655)

### Feminization, Conformity, and Subordination

The threat of feminization is a tool with which male conformity to hegemonic ideals is policed. This threat works when subordinate masculinities are successfully feminized and then demonized. The creation and labeling of the homosexual as a distinct deviant type served this purpose (Weeks 1989). As Barbara Ehrenreich argues, the threat of effeminacy, or latent homosexuality, was used to coerce men in the United States in the 1950s into forming a reliable workforce that would voluntarily support wives and children. Masculinity was equated with adulthood, marriage, and the breadwinning role, and homosexuality was demonized as the ultimate escapism (Ehrenreich 1983, 24). This ideology was backed up by theories from a host of psychological, medical, and sociological experts. Any man who failed fully to live up to the breadwinning role by walking out on wife or job—or worse, failing to get a wife or job in the first place—might be diagnosed as suffering from "latent" or "pseudo" homosexuality. Every heterosexual man was on his guard against such possibilities. It was the equation of latent homosexuality with femininity as well as with sexual deviance that guaranteed its effectiveness as a threat.

Ironically, it was not until the 1970s, when (largely through their own efforts to turn around their subordinate position) the increased visibility of gay men as a distinctive cultural and political group allowed more freedom for heterosexual men to indulge in formerly suspect behavior without losing their heterosexual citizenship privileges:

> Where the notion of latency had established a secret continuum between the heterosexual and the homosexual, there was now a sharp divide, like a national boundary: Gays on one side, "straights" (as they now became by default) on the other. . . . Homosexuality might still be feared and stigmatized, but it could no longer be used as the null point in a hypothetical scale of masculinity. With the old equations between homosexuality and effeminacy broken, "straight" men were free to "soften" themselves indefinitely without losing their status as heterosexuals. (Ehrenreich 1983, 130)

*subordinated mass*

Clearly, feminization as masculinist strategy operates not only to circumscribe and downgrade female activities, but is also a powerful tool in the construction and maintenance of hierarchies of masculinities. It has been used not only to police the boundaries of hegemonic masculinity and ensure a large measure of conformity, but also to differentiate between and create hierarchies of subordinate masculinities—although not without contradictions. An illustration of this can be seen in the context of British imperial rule over India. While all "orientals" were deemed effeminate, some were more effeminate than others, so that a hierarchy of racialized masculinities emerged, based on degrees of manliness and effeminacy. Mrinalini Sinha (1987) demonstrates how Bengali men were successfully subordinated by nineteenth-century British rulers by being given a political status below that of the "martial races" of northern India and the Punjab, as part of an imperial divide-and-rule strategy. Bengali men were seen as both effeminate and morally corrupt because of their sexual practices and their diminutive size, which in the British imagination were linked. The Bengali practice of consummating marriages at puberty was interpreted by the British as a sign of an effeminate lack of self-control, the cause of moral corruption, debilitating masturbation, and stunted physical growth (through early pregnancy). The British introduced a "consent" act, which prevented the early consummation of marriage and made Bengali men the only men subject to accusations of rape within marriage. That the British had removed Bengali men's sexual power over Bengali women was interpreted by Bengali men as a slight to their manhood, which emasculated them still further in their own eyes. It is ironic that a group of men labeled as effeminate should be stigmatized by charges of rape, that most masculine of offenses. Nonetheless, the successful feminization of Bengali men put them below the Punjabis in political clout and status. Punjabi men, the recruiting ground of the Indian Army, consummated their marriages later (late teens), and were, needless to say, taller than Bengalis.

Strategies of feminization used to downgrade groups of men may be more contradictory and precarious than strategies that straightforwardly masculinize men and feminize women, but their relative success in the above examples indicates that masculinism can privilege elite males at the expense of feminized Others, regardless of sex or gender. Such masculinist strategies at least partially separate the concept of masculinity from its association with the male sex because they deny that some men are masculine. Once masculinity is thus separated from men, feminist analyses of patriarchy—whether seen as a single ahistorical system of male domination, as operating in a dual system with capitalism, or even as a unified system of capitalist patriarchy—are no longer tenable, for this is not the rule of all men over all women on the basis of their sex alone; it rather involves multilayered hierarchies, in which gender, race, sexuality, class, and other factors mix in a relatively fluid process.

## Subordinate Masculinities

In the proliferating literature on the representation of subordinate masculinities, the twin themes of effeminacy and pathological deviance crop up again and again. The psychological legacy of imposed racist gender identities is complex.[42] However, broadly speaking, the racist legacy of empire still positions indigenous men and those with ethnic roots east of Turkey (including Jews in the Diaspora) as effeminate (Brod 1994; Fung 1995),[43] while blacks and men with roots in South Europe are seen as pathologically "hypermasculine" (Mercer and Julien 1988; Segal 1990).[44] Mexicans, who have links both with Southern European and with indigenous cultures, are labeled as both effeminate and, perversely, "macho."[45]

Class and sexuality cut across this racial hierarchy, giving many permutations and nuances, in highly attenuated grades of masculinity.[46] Homosexuality is deemed effeminate, while working-class masculinities get the "hypermasculine" tag in comparison with the middle-class "new man." Thus a working-class black man might be doubly hypermasculine, while a middle-class, Asian gay man would be doubly, or even triply, effeminate. Other composite positions are more contradictory, such as the gay, black, middle-class man.[47] In practice, most men find themselves in composite, contradictory, and shifting positions with regard to the finer nuances of differentiated masculinities, aligned with hegemonic masculinities in some respects, subordinated in others.

Much of the literature on subordinate masculinities is couched in terms of oppression and resistance. There are divergent and contradictory assessments of both working-class and black machismo. Afro-Caribbean and Afro-American machismo (as represented in the 1990s by gangster rap), plays on colonial fantasies and fears about black-male sexuality, "brute" strength, and danger, while perpetuating homophobia and misogyny (Mercer and Julien 1988, 113). It can be seen as a kind of negative and ultimately self-destructive form of resistance to emasculation by white culture; on the other hand, it can be seen as an ironic, unsettling, and empowering way of manipulating the stereotypes thrust upon black men by the dominant culture, or even as a positive display of fraternity and cultural pride (Zinn 1989).

Asian youths in Britain have tried to circumvent being feminized through the adoption of black American street styles in an attempt to shake off the image of oriental effeminacy that they think makes them more vulnerable to racist attack, with contradictory results (Mac an Ghaill 1994). The 1980s "butch shift" among gay men can similarly be interpreted as either a positive form of resistance to their feminization (Segal 1990), a regressive capitulation to hegemonic codes of masculinity (Kimmel 1990; Edwards 1994) or as a contradictory phenomenon that has successfully dislodged the association between macho masculinity and heterosexual men in Britain, while also reinforcing gender stereotypes (Forrest 1994).

Meanwhile working-class masculinities are characterized either as outdated, regressive, and misogynist (Kersten 1993) or are seen to have provided the solidarity and aggression needed for real collective power in the labor force, at least in the past (Tolson 1977). Some racist, white, male youths in South London have even taken to mixing black cultural forms in with their racism, as a kind of "cultural dowry" that endows toughness and machismo (Back 1994, 182).

These differing interpretations suggest that nonhegemonic groups of men are more often than not caught up in a contradictory and complex process of simultaneously participating in and resisting their oppression and the constructions of masculinity that are thrust upon them, so that subordinate and oppositional styles of masculinity are neither wholly regressive nor wholly progressive. Indeed discussing styles of masculinity in isolation from other practices can obscure rather than illuminate both structural inequalities and progressive changes.

For example, on the basis of style alone, New Man sensitivity might be seen as more progressive than Chicano machismo, but in terms of domestic practices it may well be the other way around. Hondagneau-Sotelo and Messner (1994) argue that in the United States hegemonic masculinity is being reconstituted in the New Man image: among other things, middle-class men can now enjoy the emotional fruits of parenting without losing their class and gender privileges, and simultaneously deflect feminist criticism. New Men cultivate a public gender display of emotional sensitivity and participation in parenthood that may be at odds with the reality of their day to day lives.

The public face of subordinate masculinities, with their collectively constructed displays of masculinity and machismo, might also be at odds with men's experiences. Hondagneau-Sotelo and Messner point to three arenas where male Mexican immigrants to the United States have lost their patriarchal privileges: in spatial mobility, familial authority, and household labor. Mexican immigrant family life, with its high rate of female employment and shared domestic chores, may well be more egalitarian in practice than the family life of New Men, who often pay only lip service to domestic responsibilities.[48] But the ideological image of the New Man needs a counterimage to stand against, and hence "those aspects of traditional hegemonic masculinity that the New Man has rejected—overt physical and verbal displays of domination, stoicism, and emotional inexpressivity, overt misogyny in the workplace and at home—are now increasingly projected onto less privileged groups of men: working class men, gay bodybuilders, black athletes, Latinos and immigrant men" (Hondagneau-Sotelo and Messner 1994, 207). Similarly, Barbara Ehrenreich reports that blue-collar males have been seen as "the lowest level of consciousness, the dumping ground for all the vestigial masculine traits discarded by the middle class" (Ehrenreich 1983, 136).

This projection of currently unwanted characteristics onto subordinate groups, branded as pathological or aberrant varieties of masculinity, appears to be ascendant over the earlier projection of effeminacy, as hegemonic masculinities increasingly soften.[49] If subordinate masculinities are being increasingly pathologized through accusations of hypermasculinity, then this will have consequences for the effectiveness of the feminization strategies discussed above. There may be an opportunity for educated women and other previously "feminized" groups such as middle-class Asian men to alter their position in the gender hierarchy, as the qualities associated with them in gender ideology more closely match the requirements of a softer hegemonic masculinity. As hegemonic masculinities change, so might the whole pecking order shift and reform in a slightly different configuration.

Struggles over the representation of subordinate masculinities form part of the political process of their construction and disruption, but it is important to recognize that such representations are no more a mirror of the actual social experiences of men in subordinate groups than the masculine/feminine dichotomy is a mirror of male and female experience. None-theless, as Rosa Linda Fregoso argues, while white Euro-Americans have access to a heterogeneous body of masculinities from which hegemonic masculinities are fashioned and refashioned, subordinate groups of men have far less choice: "Contrary to the historically variable and shifting range of hegemonic masculinities, the representation of the identity of racially subordinated groups stands out for its monologic and homogeneous economy, resting virtually on the negative side of the masculine equation" (Fregoso 1993, 661). It is perhaps this difference in the range of choices that, more than any other factor, distinguishes the construction of restricted and restricting subordinate masculinities from enabling and powerful hegemonic ones.

To SUMMARIZE THE theoretical perspective endorsed in this chapter: there is no single narrative of masculinity. The concept of masculinity is revealed as a plural and fluid construction as soon as it is historically contextualized. The proliferation of differing interpretations of the history of masculinities merely highlight this fluidity and draw attention to the importance of interpretation itself in the construction of masculinities. For analytical purposes, it is useful to draw out different models or ideal types of masculinity, even though such types are very generalized and do not conform to the lived experience of particular men.

Feminist critiques of masculinism offer insights into the association of masculinity with power, but tend to view masculinity as a monolithic entity. The reconciliation of such critiques with the identification of plural masculinities can be achieved by using the concepts of hegemonic and subordinate masculinities. These heuristic devices indicate plurality while also highlighting power relations, both those between men and women and those between different groups of men. In a masculinist culture, anything that is associated with hegemonic masculinity carries a higher status and better access to power than anything associated with the feminine. However, as masculinities have no necessarily fixed ingredients, what qualities, organizations, practices, or peoples get to be associated with masculinity is a political question and is the subject of a series of heterogeneous power struggles going on at all levels of society. Masculinist practices work both to maintain the status of hegemonic masculinity and to ensure that it evolves to meet the requirements of retaining power and privilege for elite (usually white, middle- or upper-class, heterosexual) men under changing circumstances. Masculinist strategies do have their limits: since they depend on an arbitrary list of qualities being anchored by a metaphorical association with male anatomy, they are obviously less effective when masculinities become denaturalized and may be especially vulnerable to failure in times of rapid change.

Hegemonic masculinity is constantly being challenged and reconstituted in struggles that involve the strategies of masculinization and feminization of peoples, groups, values, occupations, and practices. Feminization, masculinization, and the identification of pathological varieties of masculinity are all tools in the war of interpretation that position different masculinities and groups of men in relation to each other, as well in relation to women, under changing circumstances. Changes in the gender order, including changes in the construction of masculinities, are often triggered by structural changes in society and form part of the political struggles over the direction of change. Competing visions of masculinity then are mobilized simultaneously in the pursuit of different ends. The power of hegemonic masculinity appears to lie in part in its flexibility in comparison with the restricted and monological representation of subordinate masculinities.

In the arguments put forth in the first part of this book, it can be seen that the overall approach to gender endorsed is one that emphasizes identifications rather than fixed identities, and power-laden political processes rather than static structures. In part 2, this approach will be used to help reveal and clarify the unfolding politics of masculinity that saturate the discipline and practices of international relations.

PART TWO  *Masculinities, IR, and Gender Politics*

# CHAPTER THREE

# Masculinities in International Relations

S o far the discussion has revolved around the construction of gender identities and the politics of masculinities. What, one might ask, has any of this to do with international relations? In reply, I would challenge the disciplinary assumption that international relations and the politics of identities (including gender identities) are discrete areas of research that have no important interconnections. Rather I would ask: How might the perspective on the politics of masculinities and masculinism that is discussed above illuminate our understanding of international affairs, and be brought to bear on the discipline of IR? To attempt to answer such a question is to refuse the boundary between IR and political theory or political science, and to make the boundary itself (which hides these connections) an object of enquiry. In doing this, I will follow critical and postpositivist approaches that examine the construction of IR as a discipline, rather than operating from within it.

The chapter sets out to indicate some of the complex and circular links between international relations, the discipline of IR, the politics of identity, and the production of masculinities. After briefly discussing how the study of multiple masculinities relates to the research agenda at an applied level, I will concentrate on the relationship between some aspects of hegemonic masculinities and IR at the symbolic level. The focus here is not on the practices of international relations per se, but on the symbolic role they play in linking the politics of culture and gender identity with the discipline of IR. The chapter therefore considers some of the connections between masculinist practices, multiple masculinities, and theoretical controversies within the discipline itself.

### International Relations and the Production of Masculinities

There is an interesting anomaly between the significant role that international affairs play in the production of identities, including gender identities, and the relative absence of discussions of identity in mainstream approaches to the discipline of IR. Masculinities are not just domestic cultural variables: both political events and masculine identities are the products of men's participation in international relations. As noted earlier, the Victorian English Gentleman was defined and constructed in relation to a complex, global set of racialized gender identities. As a type, therefore, he was at least as much a product of imperial politics as of domestic understandings of Englishness, aristocracy, and masculinity. In terms of the three dimensions of gender identity discussed in chapter 1, a number of two-way links can be made between international relations and the production of specifically masculine identities, as depicted in figure 3.1.

It is a commonplace observation that international relations reflects a world of men in that they influence international affairs through their physical capacities, through (masculinist) practices at the institutional level, and through the symbolic links between masculinity and power. But there is also a relationship flowing the other way (as Ehrenreich, among others has argued—see below). International relations also make men through the same channels in reverse. These two-way influences are illustrated by the arrows in figure 3.1, which demonstrate how the relationship between men and international relations is mediated.[1] The separation of elements in the diagram is illustrative only. Of course, there are complex relationships between the dimensions of embodiment, institutional practices, and symbolic meanings—which are often all present in the same "event." Nevertheless, for explanatory purposes the connections shall be briefly separated here. To illustrate this diagram and explain these connections, a fairly arbitrary selection of examples have been chosen. Some illustrate the links through all

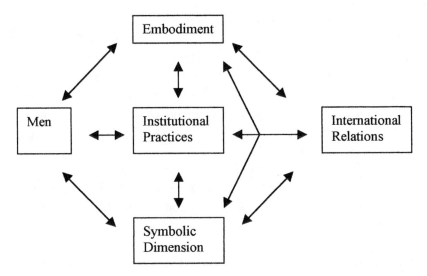

FIGURE 3.1. The relationship between men and international relations.

three dimensions, while others operate most clearly through one or two dimensions. All have been chosen to highlight the influence of international relations on masculinities rather than vice versa, as this is the more novel claim.

Military combat in the pursuit of war is a clear example of how international relations helps to shape men. War has been deemed central to the discipline itself and has historically played a large part in defining what it means to be a man in the modern era, symbolically, institutionally, and through the shaping of men's bodies. First, the symbolic dimension: the argument that men take life while women give it, is a cornerstone of one powerful ideology of gender differences (Segal 1987). This ideology has been central to modern warfare and underpins the masculinity of soldiering and the historic exclusion of women from combat (Elshtain 1987). In symbolic terms, engaging in war is often deemed to be the clearest expression of men's enduring natural "aggression," as well as their manly urge to serve their country and "protect" their female kin, with the one implying the other (Tickner 1996).[2] The popular myth is that military service is the fullest expression of masculinity, and in 1976 there were about twenty million men under arms in about 130 standing armies worldwide, compared with only two million women (Connell 1989).

However, as Ehrenreich (1987, xvi) argues, "it is not only men that make wars, it is wars that make men"—literally and physically. Military service has served as a rite of passage for boys to be made men throughout much of the modern era, while at the level of embodiment, military training explicitly involves the physical and social shaping of the male body. Indeed it can be argued that "war and the military represent one of the major sites where direct links between hegemonic masculinities and men's bodies are forged (Morgan 1994, 168).

Joanna Bourke (1996) has examined the relationship between masculinities and embodiment in Britain in World War I, when soldiering became intimately bound up with notions of masculinity. Soldiering disciplined the male body, helping to shape its style of masculinity as well as its physical contours. This shaping was inflected by class. As one middle-class soldier, Ralph Scott, graphically noted in his diary: "I looked at my great murderous maulers and wondered idly how they had evolved from the sensitive manicured fingers that used to pen theses on 'Colloidal Fuel' and 'The Theory of Heat Distribution in Cylinder Walls.' And I found the comparison good" (quoted in Bourke 1996, 15–16).

If middle-class men found themselves transformed from bourgeois rationalists to warrior-citizens, then for the working classes the emphasis was much more on basic fitness. At the beginning of World War I, British authorities had been horrified at the quality of their raw material, as British manhood was by and large malnourished, disease-ridden, of stunted growth, and poorly educated.[3] Such men had to be "converted" into soldiers, both physically and mentally. The increased surveillance and regulation of male bodies that this entailed was sustained through the interwar years, when regular exercise through military-type drills was widely adopted in schools and other institutions. Military drill therefore constituted an institutional practice that had been established through war and that had a widespread effect on men's bodies. Drill was also deemed to make men economically efficient, to promote emotional self-control, and even to enhance brain development (Bourke 1996, 178–80).

Men who did not fight were looked down on, while the "real" men, those who fought, carried a high risk of death or physical disablement. The return of thousands of youthful war-mutilated servicemen, who were hailed as masculine heroes, changed the medical and technological approach to disablement for good, and even modified public attitudes for a while. Initially, although the most disfigured men were kept out of sight, the lightly maimed soldier was regarded as "not less but more of a man" (quoted in Bourke 1996, 58). These were "active" rather than "passive" sufferers, who deserved respect, not pity, and who were even deemed especially attractive to women as marriage prospects (Bourke 1996, 56). To be physically maimed was far more manly than to be a "malingerer," although many "malingerers" were in fact men psychologically damaged by "shell shock." The dead were also heroes. So for a while, Bourke argues, manliness was equated with physical dismemberment. In the long term however, sympathy changed to disgust at the carnage involved, and disabled former servicemen who could not fulfil a role as breadwinners became increasingly marginalized and feminized.

Although Bourke finds evidence to suggest that the majority of soldiers in World War I retained a longing for a quiet domestic life, at the extreme the relationship between masculinity, male bodies, and war can be brutal and misogynistic. Klaus Theweleit (1987) investigated the literary fantasies of the Freikorps. This was a volunteer army, derived in part from World War I "shock troops," who helped to put down the attempted socialist revolution in Germany following the war and who later became the core of Hitler's SA. These troops lived for battle and had a reputation for enjoying violence. Apparently, they both hated and dreaded women's bodies and viewed their sexuality with a kind of fascinated horror. In their novels and memoirs, the male body was depicted as dry, clean, hard, erect, and intact, but always threatened by contamination from feminine dirt, slime, and mire (Theweleit 1987, 385–402). Women's bodies were seen as messy, open, wild, and promiscuous—as engulfing swamps in which men could be annihilated. Women, communists, and the rebellious working class represented a "flood" or "tide" threatening to break down both masculine integrity and established social barriers (Theweleit 1987, 405–38). This enemy had to be repeatedly smashed to a bloody pulp to make the world safe for men and masculinity again (an activity that provided the added "thrill" of coming close to the horror of dissolution). Thus physical violence was integral to the construction of the masculine self—without it the Freikorps could not sustain their bodily integrity in the face of desire, pain, and internal viscera—the feminine Other forever lurking within (Theweleit 1989).

Continuing with the military example, militarization as an institutional process has followed different paths under different international circum-

stances. Cynthia Enloe (1993) has discussed the varied relationships between women, degrees and types of militarization, constructions of masculinity, and international practices in different locations and at different
times. That the links between masculinity and militarism are contingent
and are produced through institutional practices is highlighted in her account. For example, under British colonial rule, the construction of imperial armies was no mean feat, as colonized groups of men often took some
persuading that soldiering was in any way a manly pursuit. Complex bar-
gains over conditions of service had to be struck, depending on differing local requirements of manly respectability (Enloe 1993, 79). Recruitment
policies have also helped to define hegemonic and subordinate masculinities. In many countries, ethnically or religiously subordinate groups of men,
along with homosexuals, have historically been barred from active military
service or have been given restricted roles (Enloe 1980). Such restrictions,
justified by nationalist security ideologies, have helped to construct the subordinate status of these groups more generally, through the implicit and explicit links between military service and citizenship. Full citizenship rights
are often denied to men who do not participate in defending the state, in
much the same way as they have been for women.[4]

Within the military itself, institutional practices also help to shape different masculinities and masculine identities. Connell (1989) argues that the
basis of military organization was historically a relationship between two
masculinities—one based on physical violence but subordinate to orders,
and another dominating and organizationally competent (in Britain this relationship between "officers" and "ranks" has reflected and helped consolidate the class system). In the last century, a third masculinity—that of the
technical specialist—has become increasingly important, necessitating a
"general staff" of planners, strategists, and, latterly, technicians, separate
from the command of combat units (Connell 1989).

Moving on from the military example to colonialism, the institutional
practices of European colonialism have also helped to consolidate hegemonic and subordinate masculinities on a global scale (as mentioned in
chapter 2). Backed up with pseudoscientific theories such as craniology,
which linked skull size with intelligence and personality, the ranking of
masculinities according to race was organized around the dimension of embodiment. In 1849 the craniometrist Samuel George Morton used skull
measurements to rank Caucasians at the top of the scale, blacks at the bot-

tom, and Amerindians and Asians in the middle (women ranked with blacks, but this—see below—was in terms of "intelligence"). The Caucasian group was further subdivided, with Anglo-Saxons and Germans at the top, Jews and Arabs intermediate, and Hindus lowest (Halpin 1989). As well as skull dimensions (which were later proved to be linked to nutrition, rather than intelligence), other body parts were deemed important, with black Africans in particular being seen as super-muscle-machines suited to heavy labor (Mercer and Julien 1988). In local differentiations, paler races tended to be ranked above darker ones, and taller above shorter ones—as in the case of tall Punjabis versus short Bengalis, mentioned in chapter 2 (Sinha 1987).

This ranking was not only organized around embodiment, but was also institutionalized in colonial administration. To cite a British Empire example, in India middle-ranking locals were heavily involved in the administration itself (albeit in the lower ranks), while Parsees of Persian stock were promoted to relatively high positions and became more thoroughly immersed in British culture (with some even being educated at British public schools and universities). This contrasted with Africa, where the lower-ranking of African males meant that even junior officials were imported from Britain.

In the twentieth century, the legacy of this "scientific racism" was reflected in the ranking of mandated territories by the League of Nations in the aftermath of World War I, through which European imperial ambitions were also realized. Mandated territories were ranked into A, B, and C categories according to their degree of "civilization" and readiness for self-rule. The A category covered Iraq, Palestine, and Syria—Arabs and Jews, who were deemed nearly ready for independence. The B category covered tribal African countries such as Rwanda, Togo, and Tanganyika, which would require decades of stewardship. The C category covered "stone age" Pacific Islanders and the Hottentots of Southwest Africa, who were deemed to need centuries of external rule (Louis 1984).

Contemporary links between institutional practices in international relations and the construction and ranking of masculinities are often more subtle. Nonetheless, the legacy of colonialism, combined with the dominance of the United States, is such that the education and socialization of senior politicians, diplomats, generals, international civil servants, and other players on the international stage is still heavily influenced by European, if not Anglo-Saxon, values of hegemonic masculinity, regardless of the cultural origins of the predominantly male players themselves. The role of elite educational establishments in the West in producing hegemonic masculinities over the last hundred years is well documented and theorized (e.g., Connell 1987; Mangan and Walvin 1987) and such institutions still tend to churn out a high proportion of international elites. Even those postcolonial political leaders most vociferously against the hegemony of Western values in international society have rarely escaped the influence of those values.[5]

The production of masculinities and disciplining of male bodies through competitive team games is another legacy of the Victorian colonial era with strong contemporary relevance in terms of embodiment and institutional practices as well as symbolism (Mangan and Walvin 1987; Jackson 1990). It affects not only sporting relations between states and the lives of international sportsmen, but also the everyday lives of boys and men in schools, clubs, and leisure time, throughout the world. The training techniques and the languages of sport and war overlap considerably, with each being used as a metaphor for the other, strengthening the connections between them (Shapiro 1989b). At the symbolic level, international sporting competitions, particularly in gender segregated team games such as football, rugby, and cricket, also mobilize and fuse national feeling, masculine identification, and male bonding among players and spectators alike (Simpson 1994).

Specific foreign policies also lead to the institutionalization of particular kinds of masculinity. Take, for example, the cold war, which according to Enloe was "best understood as involving not simply a contest between two superpowers, each trying to absorb as many countries as possible into its own orbit, but also a series of contests within each of those societies over the definitions of masculinity and femininity that would sustain or dilute that rivalry" (Enloe 1993, 18–19).

David Campbell (1992) argues that in the case of the United States, an explicit goal of foreign policy was the construction and maintenance of a U.S. identity. A "society of security" (Campbell 1992, 166) was created in which a vigorous loyalty/security program sought to define Americans in terms of excluding the Communist Other, both externally and internally. Campbell notes the gendered nature of such exclusionary practices, so that, for example, Communists and other "undesirables" were linked through feminization, as indicated by the abusive term *pinko*.[6] Although he does not emphasize the point, this U.S. identity that was constructed through Communist witchhunts and the associated tests of "loyalty" was essentially a masculine identity. Indeed, it was the very same form of masculinity that was also shaped by fear of "latent homosexuality" as discussed by Ehrenreich (see chapter 2). Integrating Campbell's and Ehrenreich's (1983) work, it becomes clear that vigilance against the possibility that unsuspecting liberals might unwittingly help the Communist cause, paralleled and intersected with the vigilance needed to ward off the threat of "latent homosexuality." While the institutional practices that supported this identity were eventually reduced in reach and scope, Ehrenreich suggests that the symbolic legacy lasted longer, so that "communism kept masculine toughness in style long after it became obsolete in the corporate world and the consumer marketplace" (Ehrenreich 1983, 103). Eventually, it was not only the increasing visibility of gay men, but also the Vietnam War and its aftermath that engendered a crisis in this hegemonic masculinity of anti-Communist machismo. Not only did the enemy turn out to be women, old men, youths, and children, but U.S. masculinity was shown nightly on television, in a pathological, brutal light (Ehrenreich 1983, 105). The "emasculation" of American men following the defeat in Vietnam, and the desire to reverse this, helped to provide support for both the politics of the Reagan era and the Gulf War (Jeffords 1989; Niva 1998).

Finally, the popular media operate largely through the symbolic dimension of the links between men and international relations (see fig. 3.1). Between them, television, radio, films, books, newspapers, and magazines disseminate a wealth of popular iconography that links Western masculinities to the wider world beyond the borders of the state. There is a long-standing and continuing association in the popular media of foreign adventure with virile masculinity, ranging from boys' stories of the nineteenth century (Kanitkar 1994), through the legend of Lawrence of Arabia (Dawson 1991) and the myth of the French Foreign Legion, to contemporary potboilers and adventure films. Diplomacy, spying, and the reported activities of presidents and statesmen have helped to define hegemonic masculinities in the popular imagination. As James Der Derian has suggested, the relationship between the real and fictional worlds of espionage has been close, with influences in both directions (Der Derian 1989). The symbolic link between espionage and hegemonic masculinity is demonstrated by James Bond films, which promoted a "gentlemanly" and "aristocratic" ideal of manhood: a man of leisure leading a glamorous lifestyle—updated for cold war politics.[7]

Meanwhile, in the nonfictional world, media attention is focused on personalities, "international players" who are icons of glamorous wealth and power. In current affairs, statesmen and presidents are presented as the ultimate hero figures (or sometimes as villains)—popularized larger-than-life images of exemplary masculinity, judged constantly in terms of their manliness or lack of it. John Fiske considers "hard" news and current-affairs programs, which place such "heroes" in the context of distinctively masculine styles of production, narrative structure, and presentation, as the masculine cultural equivalent of feminine soap operas (Fiske 1987, 281). Even everyday language reveals the gendering of the world beyond state borders: not just explicitly sexual phrases such as "conquest of virgin territory," but also more mundane phrases and slogans such as "a man of the world," "travel makes a man of you," and "join the army, see the world"—these all invite men to flee the domestic hearth in the search of manhood, and the farther the better.

Much of the appeal of these glamorized connections between international adventure and masculinity is that the worlds depicted are worlds where women have traditionally been entirely absent, or were presented as threats to masculinity (Fiske 1987; Roper and Tosh 1991; Kanitkar 1994). The very word *international* implies privileged access to a higher plane above and beyond the borders of the state behind which most of us are confined. Although this may no longer be literally the case, it still carries symbolic meaning. These cultural connections, between notions of masculinity and the "international" and media representations of glamorized masculinities in an international context, whether fictional or in the guise of news and current affairs, are no less important in constructing masculinities than practices on the ground. They provide a continuing source of imaginative inspiration that informs the meaning of such practices and also help to reflect and produce the highly gendered cultural framework within which such practices are shaped and interpreted. Although they are not all directly relevant to international politics, they form a network of cultural meanings within which international relations are embedded, and without which its practices cannot be fully understood.

As well as operating at a general level, these cultural connections must also inform the nexus of personal, intellectual, and professional interests that practitioners and academics bring to their work. Academics and practitioners do not work in a cultural vacuum. It would be interesting to investigate how much men in the field use their own participation in international relations to achieve or bolster masculinity for themselves, as a core of their identities, whether self-consciously or otherwise. Challenging the gendered nature of IR will be an uphill task if it not only proves threatening to mainstream practitioners at an academic or even a professional level, but also at the level of personal identity and psychology.

## Academic IR and the Politics of Identity

There may be numerous ways in which international relations are implicated in the construction of masculinities and masculine identities: through the direct disciplining of male bodies, through numerous political and institutional practices, and through broader cultural and ideological links. In contrast to this possible wealth of examples, IR as a discipline has generally shown little interest in, and has been ill-equipped to deal with, issues related to the politics of identity construction.

Before the intervention of feminists, the closest mainstream IR got to acknowledging the relevance of gender identities was in the assumptions about (masculine) human nature that underpinned theory in the classical tradition—assumptions that tended to mirror the prevailing naturalized discourses of gender. For example, Keohane quotes Morgenthau as describing the "limitless character of the lust for power," which "reveals a general quality of the human mind" and that accounted for war (Keohane 1986, 11–12). After World War II, much of IR theory was revolutionized by behavioralism, which sought to turn it into a science of quantifiable and measurable exactness. Such assumptions about human nature were questioned and criticized as being vague and unprovable, but rather than the criticisms opening up a series of interesting political questions about the absence of foundational identities in politics, attempts were made to contain questions of identity in bureaucratic or psychological models of human behavior (Allison 1971; Jervis 1985), to mechanize them in the ubiquitous rational-actor model (Keohane 1984), or to do away with them (along with many other relevant topics) by resorting to purely systemic explanations (Waltz 1979),[8] all in the name of science.[9] Given these moves either to codify or, in Waltz's case, remove "human nature" from the discipline, it is hardly surprising that the politics of identity construction has been neglected.

The structuring of IR theory to exclude questions of the politics of identity has some interesting effects that serve to uphold the existing gender order and indirectly confirms the importance of international politics as one of the primary sites for the production and naturalization of masculinities in the modern era. Consider the way in which the discipline of IR itself has historically been conceptualized in mainstream theory and analysis. International politics has been divided from politics within states in disciplinary terms because of apparently distinct features that make international politics qualitatively different from other kinds of politics. In the 1950s and 1960s, the dominant view was that, while politics and "the good life" (Wight 1966, 30) could be pursued within the secure borders of states, survival, fragile laws, and uneasy alliances and balances were all that could be expected in an international arena that is above all characterized by anarchy. With anarchy (between states) and sovereignty (within states) as its principal guiding forces, IR theory found it easy to "black box" the state, deeming all that goes on in it as irrelevant except where it is expressed as "national interests" (Hollis and Smith 1990).

As the discipline of IR has developed since then, the division between domestic politics and international relations has not been strictly adhered to. It has often been breached, for example in foreign-policy analysis, when both the domestic determinants of foreign policy and the international determinants of domestic politics have been examined (Gourevitch 1978). Such breaches have led to debates over the "levels of analysis" problem, which asks whether international relations should be explained by reference to properties of the system of states, to the behavior of individual states, to pressures arising from domestic politics, or to the activities of individual people such as particular statesmen (see Hollis and Smith 1990). Moreover, characterizations of international "anarchy" have also become much more varied and sophisticated.[10]

It would be unfair and inaccurate to say that mainstream IR now "black boxes" the state, except in one or two influential examples.[11] However, anarchy of one kind or another is still the defining feature of international relations for mainstream analysis, and the domestic politics/international relations divide retains a crucial symbolic importance, as it remains the principal justification for the existence of a separate discipline of IR in the first place.

### Private/Public/International Boundaries

Breaching the domestic politics/international relations division, however, will not in itself lead to a clearer understanding of the involvement of international relations in the politics of identity construction or the production of masculinities. This is because of a second boundary (or rather series of overlapping boundaries) that is rarely referred to in mainstream IR literature but that is also highly relevant to its conceptual space. This is the boundary between the public sphere of politics (and economics) and the private sphere of families, domestic labor, and reproduction, which has been challenged by feminists (Peterson 1994). In political philosophy, the private (familial) and public (political) spheres have been deemed to have different moral requirements (Grant 1991).[12] The domestic/nondomestic or familial/nonfamilial boundary has been accompanied or overlaid by other public/private divides; notably, the political/social or state/civil society division of liberalism and the more recent, and romantic, social/personal division, in which both the state and civil society fall into the public realm (Kymlicka 1990).[13] Domestic and family life has tended to fall outside both the state and civil society in liberal schemes, and the position of women and children in families was neglected in classic liberal discussions of justice and freedom. As for the newer distinction between the public realm and personal life, the right to privacy has merely tended to reinforce the idea that family relations should be exempt from questions of public and social justice (Kymlicka 1990). In spite of some contradictions between these different definitions of the public and private, together they add up to a formidable barrier to women's equality, in general, and inclusion in civil and public life, in particular.

Gender divisions and inequalities depend to a great extent on the segregation of social life into separate spheres for men and women, so that gender differences can be constructed and the lines of difference made visible.[14] The cultural and social production of gender differences and gendered character traits segregates the sexes in various ways, in order to construct and make visible the lines of difference between them. Generating gendered constructions is an integral part of any such segregational practice. The construction of conceptual boundaries between the private and the public has been challenged as just such a gender segregation. By arguing that the personal is political, feminists have successfully bridged these private/public divisions and have to some extent politicized the private spheres of family life, domestic labor, and intimate relations. Whilst few feminists would wish to abolish the notion of privacy altogether, they have successfully put such formerly private issues as domestic violence and sexual harassment on the public political agenda and have helped to promote tax equality and benefits—entitlement equality between husbands and wives.

Putting these private/public and domestic/international boundaries together, modern life is conceptually divided into a number of highly gendered separate spheres. These can be categorized in a number of ways, but include the domestic/private (which can be divided into familial and personal); the nondomestic/public (in which public can be further divided into state and civil society); and the international. IR symbolically becomes a wholly masculine sphere of war and diplomacy, at the furthest extreme from the domestic sphere of families, women, and reproduction in the private/public/international divides of modernity. Thus personal life, domestic and family life, and even much of civil society has been evacuated from IR.

Where IR dips into the "black box" of the state, it is usually to deal with public, political, or economic issues and affairs of the state. Women and their traditional supporting roles—for example, as army and diplomatic wives, as nurses and prostitutes servicing armies, or even as production workers in defence industries—are outside the traditional remit of international relations, their activities by and large occupying lowly positions in the public sphere or being wholly confined to the private or domestic realms (Enloe 1990). As the private/public/international divisions define international relations as a virtually all-male sphere, then it follows that the activities and qualities associated with this gender-segregated space cannot help but inform the definition and production of masculinities. The emphasis on power politics in both theory and practice then reinforces the associations between such masculinities and power itself, associations that are crucial to masculinism.[15]

The private/public/international divisions inscribe an all-male sphere that serves as an arena for the production of masculinities. However, this productive power is hidden, as these very same divisions help obscure the processes of identity production. The production of masculinities is rendered invisible because an examination of the interconnections between the international and the private world of personhood is discouraged—ruled out of court as outside the remit of the discipline. Questions of gender identity are generally assumed to be private aspects of adult personality (invoking the right to privacy from public scrutiny) and are rooted in the domestic realm of childhood and family life (invoking the familial/nonfamilial or domestic/nondomestic divide), if not determined at birth—far from the reach of IR's focus of analysis.

The private/public/international divisions that have informed the construction of IR as a discipline have rendered it utterly blind to gender politics. This traditional framework is not a natural reflection of external events, and it has rightly been challenged from within the discipline. For example, as Richard Ashley argues, the domestic politics/international relations division is a mutually defining one. In realism and neorealism, sovereignty reigns within the state, while the international realm is one of danger and uncertainty, which intrepid statesman attempt to tame.[16] However, it is the very inscription of danger and uncertainty in the international realm that allows the space within states to be defined as a well-bounded domestic social identity within which progress and the good life can take place (Ashley 1989, 305).[17] Ashley's work seeks to problematize the paradigm of state sovereignty with its division between inside and outside, domestic politics and international relations. He advocates a theoretical stance that lies at the "borderline" or "margins" of domestic and international politics (Ashley 1989, 309).

But Ashley ignores the public/private division. It took a feminist, Cynthia Enloe, to bridge the private/ public/international divide explicitly. Enloe uses the phrase "the personal is international" (1990, 195). Of course, feminist contributions by their very nature refuse the boundaries of IR as narrowly conceived. Any interest in gendered constructions is already outside the remit of mainstream IR, not to mention bringing into view gendered divisions of power, labor, violence, and resources—thus incorporating not only the marginalized spaces of women's economic activities and politicized resistance movements (Peterson and Runyan 1993; Sylvester 1994), but also the "private" worlds of diplomatic wives and migrant domestic workers (Enloe 1990; Sylvester 1994) and the international relations of sex (Enloe 1990; Pettman 1996).

Rob Walker (1992, 1993) acknowledges that the private/public boundary obscures gendered analysis as much as the domestic/international one. He recommends that critical approaches should rename the discipline to indicate a wider remit that transcends these boundaries. However renaming the discipline is not so easy. Walker's (1992) preferred title is "World Politics," a phrase that has a respectable history.[18] However, feminists and other critical contributors have not necessarily endorsed this particular change. Peterson and Runyan (1993), for example, prefer to use "Global Gender Issues"; Connolly (1989) uses "Global Politics."

There are clearly problems of definitions in the usage's of the words *international, global, world,* and *politics.* The problem with *international* is that in IR it tends to denote relations between discrete states. Replacing *international* with *world* is an attempt to move beyond this to include the supranational, subnational, and transnational. If IR has also been associated with a technical, problem-solving approach, as argued above, then to substitute the term *politics* for *relations* is clearly not only an attempt to bring back the political but also serves to emphasize the scope of political theory beyond state borders. *World politics* thus suggests a discipline that is not bounded by any particular "level of analysis" and that acknowledges the relevance of political theory. On the other hand, many activities that Walker and other critics of mainstream IR wish to cover might not fall within the definition of "politics"—even fairly widely cast. Peterson and Runyan's use of the word *issues,* instead, indicates the wider nature of the topics they cover. The word *global* instead of *world* also signals the fact that they acknowledge the new global gender division of labor associated with globalization (see chapter 5 for full discussion). This is in keeping with the trend in which the subdiscipline of international political economy (IPE) is increasingly being referred to as global political economy.[19] Perhaps while *world* signifies a flexible approach to the place/space of relevant activities, *global,* through its association with the term *globalization,* implies that the world has itself become a more tightly integrated space. On the other hand, Pettman (1996) prefers the combination of *Worlding Women* and *international politics*— even while discussing the global division of labor. Meanwhile, Sylvester (1994), Tickner (1996), and Stearns (1998) stick to *International Relations.*[20] If nothing else, this confusing state of flux shows that the process of inscription is never complete and indicates the degree to which traditional boundaries of the discipline are now being challenged.

The implication of the above critique is to take seriously the cultural production and interpretation of masculine identities as a political process in its own right, a process that both informs and is informed by other, more conventionally defined, political and military struggles identified in IR literature. That this cannot be done within conventional approaches should be clear. If one cannot simply take mainstream IR and "add women" or "add femininity" to get a properly gendered analysis (Peterson 1992b), neither can one take mainstream IR and merely "add men," or "add masculinity," or even "add masculinities." This is where Adam Jones (1996), who wrote an article on the subject of introducing masculinities into IR analysis, is misguided. Critical of feminists who seek to overturn mainstream analysis altogether, he takes the view that a realist/neorealist perspective should be reworked to include different masculinities as gender "variables," with a particular focus on subordinate groups of men. However, this approach would take masculinities as already given variables and would largely ignore the way in which international relations is implicated in their production. The epistemological limitations of such analysis would obscure the politics of masculinities—that is to say, the relational and power-laden processes of their construction.

## Multiple Masculinities in IR Theory

Having established that IR as a discipline is implicated in the production of masculinities, and in particular hegemonic masculinities, one can then tease out a number of different and competing masculinities at play in the field and consider the relationships between them. In order to do this, it is convenient to follow the common practice of dividing the discipline into several competing perspectives. Over the years there have been a number of different ways in which this has been accomplished. Steve Smith (1995) identifies ten different categorizations of the discipline, arguing that as tools of the power/knowledge nexus, such categorizations are constitutive and that they obscure as much as they illuminate.[21] They are constructed to reflect normative concerns and to silence alternative interpretations, and they suffer from lumping together sometimes disparate arguments. In the case of this text, the normative concern is to uncover and challenge gendered constructions, to identify disciplinary divisions with contemporary relevance and the models of masculinity that underpin them.

To this end it is useful to follow a modified version of the interparadigm debate characterized as between the three perspectives of realism/neorealism, liberalism/pluralism, and neo-Marxism (Smith et al 1981). This division has been widely used since the beginning of the 1980s; it is the basis of many IR textbooks and "has become the accepted wisdom of most international theorists" (Smith 1995, 18).[22] It also shares a good deal in common with Wight's earlier (more ideologically based) three Rs categorization of realism, rationalism, and revolutionism (Wight 1991), providing some historical disciplinary continuity. This kind of threefold division has the benefit of being widely used and easily recognized both in IR and IPE, and has previously been adopted by feminists. For example, Tickner, in her "three models of man" (1992), sees models of masculinity as dividing broadly along realist, liberal, and Marxist lines.

However, as Smith (1995) argues, there is no even division between the three perspectives in terms of academic output. Since World War II, IR has been dominated by the realist/neorealist camp, with the liberal/pluralist (now neoliberal institutionalist) perspective coming a respectable second. There has been a real debate between these two perspectives (probably reflecting U.S. foreign-policy concerns), but the neo-Marxist camp has been largely marginalized, especially since the collapse of Soviet Communism. Meanwhile, other "revolutionary" theories have emerged. Andrew Linklater has usefully remodeled the three Rs for the 1990s with critical theory replacing neo-Marxism in the third (the revolutionary, or emancipatory) category (Linklater 1990). One might add that the new poststructural and postmodern perspectives in IR share in this revolutionary zeal, and all three come under the category of postpositivists (as do feminists). In this spirit, I here divide the discipline into three broad categories. The first two, realism/neorealism and liberalism/neoliberalism, form the most prominent prongs of modern IR theory. They can be seen to draw on well-established models of hegemonic masculinity. The third category is of (admittedly diverse) theorists. They fall into a postpositivist perspective, which, although it currently occupies a marginal position, promises to remodel (in the case of critical theorists), overthrow (in the case of poststructuralists), or otherwise transcend modernity and modern theories—including, by implication, the entrenched forms of hegemonic masculinity that such modern theories represent. While this categorization is immensely crude, it captures the main fault lines in contemporary debate and divides the upholders of the status quo from those who might be expected to be more gender aware and more sympathetic to feminist concerns.[23]

Symbolically, realism can be seen to embody hegemonic masculinity, in that it is the perspective of elite white men, in which the ideal of the glorified male warrior has been projected onto the behavior of states (Tickner 1992). However, even within realism a number of different and contradictory archetypes and formulations of hegemonic masculinity are in play.

Machiavelli, for example revised the Greek archetype of the warrior-citizen for modern times, while Hobbes combined elements from the patriarchal model uneasily with an individualism associated with the emerging bourgeois-rationalist model (Elshtain 1981). In spite of their incompatibility, both are considered founding fathers of contemporary realism.[24] The postwar importation of scientific methods and economistic assumptions has now overlaid the warrior-citizen and patriarchal elements with bourgeois rationalism. The historical eclipse of realism by neorealism is usually presented as one where vague generalizations about human nature were superseded by the promise of positivist scientific rigor, but it can also be seen as a reversal of the relationship between man and nature as conceptualized in IR theory. In the Hobbesian view, man in the international arena is in a state of nature, not standing over nature. Indeed, rather than man having control over nature, nature is in control of man. It is this apparently unmediated natural anarchy that provides the excuse for "stag fighting" over territory and helps to legitimate hegemonic masculinity by naturalizing it. This is a very different use of the concept of nature than the one projected by the scientism of neorealist discourse, with its emphasis on control.[25]

Such contradictions do not appear to have undermined the appearance of continuity in the realist/neorealist tradition. Indeed, the credibility and durability of the realist approach may partly lie with the fact that it does appear to combine and embody traits that have been associated with male power and dominant masculinity under different historical conditions, providing a manly trait for every occasion. For example, a combination of warrior and patriarchal masculinities lay behind what Connolly (1989) describes as the twin strategies of European imperialism: conquest and conversion. Conquest involved the supremacy of adventurous men in the warrior mold, while conversion to Christianity involved a patriarchal approach. In the twentieth century this was overlaid by the mantra of modernization—a bourgeois-rational practice that has replaced religious conversion as the key Westernizing tool. In embodying all three of these models of hegemonic masculinity, realism can implicitly lay claim to this history of imperial masculinity as its own, now thoroughly sedimented and naturalized, source of authority.

In contrast, rival liberal and pluralist perspectives have depended more singularly on the bourgeois-rationalist model. Given that realism and neorealism (which by this account appear to draw on a number of varied masculine archetypes) have dominated international relations for decades in spite of regular announcements of their demise, it is worth recalling the argument above, that masculinities that are hegemonic have a broader range of traits to draw from than others.

These different archetypes of masculinity imply different relationships to women and feminism. The heroic warrior-citizen model tends toward overt misogyny since "it involves a notion of manliness which is tied to the conquest of women. In Machiavelli's own words, 'Fortune is a woman, and it is necessary if you wish to master her, to conquer her by force'" (Tickner 1992, 39). Meanwhile the patriarchal model ignores women. Where were the women in Hobbes's state of nature? As Rebecca Grant argues, "men dominate the conceptual scheme, leaving no room for the question of how gender relations affect the transition out of the brutish state of nature and into society. Women are invisible in the 'state of nature'" (Grant 1991, 10). Presumably, the "invisible" women were in a state of *nurture* (producing the next generation); otherwise, life would have been nonexistent rather than merely "nasty, brutish and short" (Tickner 1991, 31). Women fared little better in the alternative, romantic, republican tradition, as in Rousseau's state of nature, reason and understanding could be attained only by men (Grant 1991, 11).

The bourgeois-rationalist model of masculinity is less aggressive, more egalitarian and democratic. As outlined in chapter 2, it idealizes competitive individualism, reason, and self-control or self-denial, combining respectability as breadwinner and head of household with calculative rationality in public life. In this model, superior intellect and personal integrity is valued over physical strength or bravery. The relationship between this model of masculinity, women, and feminism is more subtle and complicated than in the case of the warrior-citizen or patriarch. Its philosophers have championed women's rights, and feminism itself has its roots in bourgeois-rationalist thought (Pateman 1988; Coole 1993). It is above all a modern form of masculinity, the first New Man—linked to the Enlightenment, the modern state, and the development of capitalism. In its purist and most abstracted form, as the rational-actor model, it is also the most ubiquitous characterization of human action in contemporary IR, not just in liberal approaches but rather directly or indirectly informing much mainstream neorealist and neoinstitutionalist scholarship, ranging from IPE, through public-choice approaches to politics, to strategic studies.[26]

Victor Seidler (1987; 1988; 1989) traces the history of this model of masculinity, viewing it as the dominant contemporary form, not only in terms of theoretical categories but also in terms of gendered identities. He explores the rational/emotional, mind/body, and reason/madness dichotomies of Western thought and their association with developing notions of masculinity and femininity in the post-Enlightenment period. Seidler argues that the rationalist tradition sees emotions and desires as threatening. Both Kantian thought and Protestant culture posit an inner freedom from emotionally driven inclinations as the ideal. Feelings and emotions are seen as both imperiling masculine superiority and questioning the sources of masculine identity. The body, its desires and frailties, similarly poses a threat to masculinity and pure reason. Acting only from reason and duty serves to strengthen the autonomy of men. Otherwise they are in a position of servitude, when reason becomes a slave to the passions. Therefore self-control over one's emotions and body have come to be hallmarks of masculinity. Emotional and dependency needs as well as sexual desires are transformed into issues of performance and control or displaced onto "feminine" Others such as women, gays, Jews, and blacks (Seidler 1987, 86–90). Including himself in this tradition, Seidler argues that "the connections we might otherwise have developed to our somatic experience and emotional selves have become so attenuated that we can no longer experience them as a basis for grounding our experience" (Seidler 1989, 18). As a result, bourgeois-rational men have been locked into externalizing and intellectualizing their experiences and have a bias toward self-denial and self-rejection.[27] With their identity defined in opposition to "feminine" dependency, emotionality, and bodily enslavement, they are, by and large, instrumentalist in thought and goal-oriented in action (Seidler 1989, 12).

The rational-actor model, as used by IR theorists (although it is not exclusive to IR, by any means) fits this psychological profile well. It posits that actors have exogenously given preferences or aims that they can rank in order of importance; that they will then seek to optimize these aims, and that they will weigh up the expected costs and benefits (and, in more sophisticated versions, risks) of alternative courses of action in seeking to achieve their goals. Physically disembodied and socially disembedded, it assumes personal autonomy, instrumental rationality, and goal orientation. Various modifications to the model have been introduced to take into account of the constraints on pure rational action that actors may encounter in practice

(Keohane 1984). Although its adherents claim it as an objective, politically and culturally neutral model of behavior into which any values can be inserted, it contains implicit normative and prescriptive aspects.[28] The model's power to socialize is evidenced by the abstract "rational" discourse of defence intellectuals, where dry euphemisms reign and for whom any display of emotion or recognition of human frailty is the ultimate "feminine" taboo.[29] Carol Cohn reports a conversation with a white male physicist who had been working with a group of defence colleagues on the modeling of "counterforce attacks": "All of a sudden," he said, "I *heard* what we were saying. And I blurted out, 'Wait, I've just heard how we're talking— Only thirty million! Only thirty million human beings killed instantly?' Silence fell upon the room. Nobody said a word. They didn't even look at me. It was awful. I felt like a woman" (Cohn 1993, 227).

In spite of its pretence at being a universally applicable model of human behavior, the rational-actor model is clearly grounded in highly individualistic and instrumental values. It both derives from and promotes a particular variety of hegemonic masculinity emanating from post-Enlightenment North Europe: the bourgeois-rational individual of liberalism. This variety (which is more Lockean than Rousseauian or Machiavellian) requires certain social and political conditions in order to flourish, such as a strong private realm in which relatively autonomous individuals capable of critical self-reflection can develop (Benhabib 1992).

Although some feminists have criticized the paradigm of autonomous rational man for universalizing masculinity through its generic pretensions (Harding 1986; Tickner 1992), defenders of the rational-actor model might argue that women need not be excluded—that the assumption that women, too, are capable of autonomy and reason is an egalitarian one, to be counterposed to centuries of contrary propaganda. They might follow the early feminist Mary Wollestonecraft (1929) in arguing that to view all forms of reason and rationality as masculine is to essentialize gender difference and buy into the very gender dichotomies that feminists are trying to escape. This line of reasoning is very seductive and has led some contemporary liberal feminists, such as the economist Nancy Folbre (1994), to embrace a modified version of the rational-actor model. In her account of gendered global economic development, incorporating the political economy of family policy and the hitherto invisible economics of reproduction and family welfare into her analysis of economic-development strategies, Folbre tries to subsume the rational-actor model within a feminist diagnosis of the structure of patriarchy. In her scheme, patriarchy and capitalism are structures that constrain the actor's options in different ways. In the case of patriarchy, it is according to gender.

The problem with this type of argument is that it ignores the basis on which liberalism (and liberal feminism) developed. As Carole Pateman argues, the social contract of liberal theory contains within it an implicit and hidden sexual contract. The social contract between freedom-loving individuals takes place only in the public sphere, a sphere that (as was argued above) not only excludes familial relations, domestic labor, and the unequal position of women in marriage, but also depends on them for its existence. The private sphere is a necessary foundation for public life, and as such is part of civil society but is kept separate from politics and "civil" life. While men could pass back and forth between the two spheres, women were not just excluded from the original social contract: they were the subject of it. Women represented everything that the individual was not. Thus the social contract was a fraternal pact and "far from being opposed to patriarchy, contract is the means through which modern patriarchy is constituted" (Pateman 1988, 2).[30]

On the other hand, there is an affinity between liberalism and all feminism. After all, it was the bourgeois-liberal tradition, with its rationalist approach and universalizing concepts, that provided the intellectual climate for feminism to develop in the first place, in the name of universal equality (Banks 1981; Coole 1993). This is where the tangled and contradictory roots of feminism and bourgeois-liberal thought begin to show themselves. Liberal feminism thus remains hampered by its contradictory aspiration to (masculine) rationality (Pateman 1988). The demand for female equality has grown out of liberalism, but cannot be realized within it (Eisenstein 1981).[31] Returning to Folbre's scheme, we can see that as the rational-actor model of free individuals relating to each other in civil society itself underpins capitalism and implicitly relies on modern forms of "patriarchy," then neither can be seen as structures that lie outside the model.

The affinities and connections between early feminism and bourgeois rationalism might explain some of the similarities between feminist and liberal critiques of realism, which have encouraged neoliberal institutionalists such as Robert Keohane to take an interest in feminist perspectives (Keohane 1991). Keohane is a great supporter of the rational-actor model and has done much to popularize game theory in the subdiscipline of IPE.[32] His initial interest in feminism stemmed from what he saw as some mutual common ground. For example, while the concept of cooperation, often highlighted in standpoint-feminist approaches, may be a dangerous sign of feminine weakness for realists, bourgeois-rationalist men such as Keohane can accommodate it when it is deemed to be in one's rational self-interest to do so (Keohane 1984). In striking contrast to liberal political theorists, liberal institutionalists in IR and IPE often adopt communitarian values, although these are derived from liberal individualistic premises.[33] Thus, as Keohane notes (1984 and 1991), he and standpoint feminists alike tend to emphasize cooperation, interdependence, empathy, community, reciprocity, networks, mutual enablement, and confidence-building measures as ways out of the security dilemma and other international problems (Keohane 1991). Whether such qualities count as feminine or not rather depends on one's model of masculinity.

However, in spite of considerable overlap between liberal and standpoint-feminist critiques of realism, bourgeois rationalism remains problematic for all but liberal feminists for a number of reasons, not least its paternalism. Perhaps unsurprisingly, then, Keohane has been accused of merely incorporating those aspects of feminism that suit him, those aspects that are least threatening to the status quo and his own concerns. As Cynthia Weber argues (1994), rather than engaging with feminist claims seriously, Keohane has dismissed the more challenging and radical strands of feminism in pejorative terms. This twin strategy of incorporation and demonization thereby dilutes feminist threats to the orthodoxies of IR theory.

The rational-actor model cannot easily be divorced from the historically specific and highly gendered framework of meanings within which it was developed. Although less prominent in IR, the Marxist model of Man also suffers from the problem of universalizing a particular model of masculinity. Cast in the image of the worker-hero derived from an industrialized, blue-collar masculinity, he, too, inhabits the nondomestic world and leans heavily on masculine reason and fraternal relations. This strategy has helped some previously subordinate men—namely, peasants and manual workers—to get more political power, at least for a while, in many parts of the world. But the Marxist understanding of class and labor excludes and naturalizes women's domestic labor (Tickner 1992). So as Soviet women found, they could enjoy "the dignity of labor" and join "the brotherhood of man" as long as they shouldered a double burden, and molded themselves in the image of the masculine industrial laborer—while continuing their "invisible" work as women in the family as well.

## Interparadigm Debates and Multiple Masculinities

Below I will consider postpositivist constructions of gender, but first I would like to suggest that gendered rivalries between different models of masculinity may have had a hidden and unacknowledged influence on the interparadigm debate. In chapter 2 I argued that masculinities are relatively fluid, combining different traits to suit the occasion. Then strategies of masculinization and feminization are often deployed to upgrade or downgrade rival masculinities in a pecking order, or hierarchy of masculinities, with gendered power and status as the potential reward for the hegemonic position. As each perspective in IR is associated with particular constructions of masculinity, there is scope for such strategies in the often-acrid rivalry between them.

Realism, largely developed in a cold war climate, had an affinity with the type of cold war masculinity discussed above—the masculinity of tough-talking presidents and of John Wayne and James Bond. Its ascendancy over prewar liberalism was in part achieved through a successful "emasculation" of liberalism and of liberals as "failed men" (Ashworth and Swatuk 1998, 82) who had sought to domesticate international politics with Enlightenment reason but had ended up appeasing Hitler. However, by the early 1970s and the era of détente, the dominance of realism was coming under attack from new perspectives, particularly liberal transnationalism. One of realism's critics, Robert Rothstein, argued that realism was outdated and dangerous:

> What it has done has been to foster a set of attitudes that predisposed its followers to think about international politics in a particularly narrow and ethno-centric fashion. . . . And once decisions have been made, it has provided the necessary psychological and intellectual support to resist criticism, to persevere in the face of doubt, and to use any means to outwit or dupe domestic dissenters. The appeal of realism is deceptive and dangerous, for it rests on assumptions about state behaviour which have become increasingly irrelevant. (Rothstein 1991, 416)

In Rothstein's view, realism was an oversimplified perspective in which "the only guide to the future is the past" (ibid., 415). He considered that it remained popular only because it suited statesmen, allowing them the dominant role as general operators in all manner of international affairs. However, generalist statesmen were themselves no longer up to the challenges posed by international relations, which would be better handled by suitably qualified experts.

The point of outlining Rothstein's argument is not to establish its veracity (or otherwise) but to show how it makes use of a gendered subtext. Rothstein's loyalties were clearly to bourgeois-rational experts rather than citizen-warriors. Statesmen, who followed the Machiavellian antidemocratic requirement of secrecy in diplomatic affairs, embodied a citizen-warrior masculinity, bolstered by patriarchal privilege. Such citizen-warriors and patriarchs were no longer what was required to run international affairs — but rather bourgeois-rational experts would usher in a new age of international cooperation. Rothstein was in effect deploying a New Man strategy here. Just as New Men in chapter 2 boosted their own position by pathologizing blue-collar workers as being unsophisticatedly macho and crudely violent, so Rothstein bolstered bourgeois rationalism and its associated liberal theories by implying that realism embodied a pathological variety of masculinity, with dangerous outdated traits.[34]

For a while, liberal transnationalism was in the ascendancy. However, in the late 1970s Kenneth Waltz led a counterattack and defence of realism, now reconfigured as neorealism, a perspective that in terms of intellectual rigor would "meet philosophy of science standards" (Waltz 1986, 27). In this "scientific" turn, Waltz was clearly grafting bourgeois-rational masculinity onto the base of citizen-warrior masculinity bolstered by patriarchy, which Rothstein had earlier criticized. In order to fend off the threat of bourgeois rationalism, Waltz was trying to incorporate it into a realist perspective, to regain realism's historic postwar ascendancy. He was particularly keen to emphasize the importance of parsimony and theoretical "elegance." He warned against "the accumulation of more and more data and the examination of more and more cases" (Waltz 1986, 30), arguing that this leads to being "overwhelmed with useless detail." He criticized "today's students of politics" (Waltz 1986, 31) — that is, the pluralists and liberals of the 1960s and 1970s — for doing just that.[35] He also, in his "systemic" theory, was intent on cutting out all factors that he saw as irrelevant to the "laws" governing the system of states, including the "low politics" that liberals and pluralists concentrated on at the time. He dubbed their theories with the pejorative term *reductionist* because they "explain international outcomes through elements located at national or subnational levels" (Waltz 1986, 47). When analysis erroneously considered factors that by rights should have been confined to domestic politics, the consequence was that "so-called variables proliferate wildly," leading to "endless arguments that are doomed to being inconclusive" (Waltz 1986, 52).

The gendered subtext here is that pluralist and liberal perspectives were being feminized by Waltz in order to put them down. Theoretical overcomplication that creates confusion is akin to so-called feminine woolly mindedness, in signifying lack of masculine reason and purposefulness. Lack of parsimony and the wild proliferation of variables is akin to a feminine propensity for uncontrolled verbosity and indulgence, and signifies a lack of masculine self-control. Such failings contrast neatly with Waltz's own punchy, curt, and slightly aggressive prose.[36]

Liberals and pluralists were also contaminating the discipline through its domestication. Although this charge of domestication was made on the basis of bringing "domestic politics" into international relations, its force could only have been strengthened by the fact that the bourgeois form of masculinity that liberal and pluralist perspectives embodied was itself more domesticated in the other sense: the sense of home and hearth. Both domesticity and lack of mental clarity have feminine connotations, and one could argue that through such arguments Waltz and others strove to reinforce their rehabilitation of realism by subtly feminizing the Other of pluralism. While Waltz himself yokes bourgeois-rational method onto a fundamentally citizen-warrior tradition, he wields a compact and pushy style to give it "muscle." Yoked to the idea of "parsimony," this style gives the manly impression of being the academic equivalent of those popular male heroes of few words but many deeds.[37]

In the 1980s, neorealism and neoliberal institutionalism converged around a core methodology of rational actors, game-theoretic models, and an increased interest in international political economy. Their principal disagreement was over the degree of cooperation or conflict inherent in the international system, as modeled by game theory, rather than the bigger issues that had divided earlier realists and liberals (see, for example, Keohane 1984). This convergence coincided with, and may have been prompted by, the deregulation of international finance and global economic restructuring. But at the same time, there was a transformation of masculinities associated with international banking and finance (Thrift 1994). Just as academic neorealists were starting to take political economy more seriously (e.g., Gilpin 1987), so new financial forces in the global economy were being clothed in the cold war imagery of masculinity, images redolent of the diplomat and spy, complete with high-tech gadgetry. Both these developments might reflect the interplay between a reorientation of hegemonic masculinities and the processes of globalization.

This will be discussed in later chapters. For now, it is sufficient to note that the concerns of neoliberal institutionalism and neorealism have increasingly converged. Their rivalry is more muted. Instead, the latest big debate in IR theory is one between the combined forces of positivist neoliberal and neorealist institutionalists, on the one hand, and postpositivists, on the other (Lapid 1989). This debate, too, is informed by gendered rivalries. In particular, it is worth considering the relationship between changing constructions of hegemonic masculinity (which as will be argued later are connected to globalization) and the influence of postpositivist approaches.

## Hegemonic Masculinity and the Postpositivists

Rather than initially looking for the types of masculinity embodied in postpositivist approaches to IR, this section will first focus on the gender awareness of selected postpositivist approaches and their relationship with feminism. This is because the best safeguard against inadvertently embodying forms of hegemonic masculinity and continuing the masculinist rivalries that have hitherto inhabited the discipline would be through explicit gender awareness, critical self-reflection, and the incorporation of feminist insights into theory and analysis. Critical self-reflection in theory (through deconstruction) has been held up by a number of postpositivists as their guarantee against replicating the power/knowledge constructions of modernity (Ashley 1988; Der Derian and Shapiro 1989; Walker 1993; Smith, Booth and Zalewski 1996), and therefore one might expect them to extend such self-reflection to issues of gender.

However, some feminists have expressed concern over the continued absence of sustained gender analysis in some other postpositivist approaches to international relations, despite the obvious compatibilities and epistemological affinities (such as deconstructing dualisms and identities; abolishing the international/political divide; exploring exclusionary strategies, and transforming the agenda) between these and feminist approaches to international relations (Whitworth 1989; Peterson 1992b). Christine Sylvester discusses the claim of some postpositivist dissidents to write from the margins and to bring into view that which has been excluded from modern perspectives. While such contributors acknowledge that both woman as the Other of man and femininity as the Other of masculinity fall into the category of exclusion, and even discuss the gendering of core concepts such as sovereignty, anarchy, autonomy, and dependence, they have so far failed to follow this observation up by drawing on feminist scholarship in their own work, or including feminist contributions in their edited collections.[38] In this respect, they have ended up implicitly reproducing the masculinism they might otherwise undermine (Sylvester 1994, 149–50).

Even the most apparently sympathetic renderings of poststructuralist critique may miss important gender implications. Take Richard Ashley, a prominent IR poststructuralist, for example. He has exposed and deconstructed the paradigm of "sovereign man" (Ashley 1989) that lies behind the concepts of sovereignty, anarchy, and states as rational actors. In a widely used analogy, the state is treated like an individual, who as an autonomous rational actor is implicitly a male individual (discussed above). The state's territorial integrity is seen as analogous to an individual's bodily integrity, and its sovereignty is analogous to an individual's autonomy.[39]

Ashley argues that the practice of combining atomistic conceptions of man and state sovereignty with systemic arguments about the logic of anarchy is inherently contradictory. For example, in Waltz's *Man, the State, and War*, although Waltz himself emphasizes the need to combine explanations based on human nature, the state, and the international system, Ashley argues that such methodological contradictions make this difficult. In Ashley's deconstructive reading, even though men and states are characterized as rational actors—decision-making autonomous individuals who maximize self-interest—the logic of anarchy at the systemic level of international relations leads to the conclusion not that "man" makes war, but rather that war makes "man."[40] "Man" is thus revealed as an unstable concept, being conceived of at one and the same time as both an original or foundational identity and as a subject whose behavior is determined by the international system. To expose these contradictions is to uncover one of the "transversal struggles" (Ashley 1989, 296) through which knowledgeable practices of power inscribe meaning, to reveal that a paradigm of sovereign man, far from being a pure and autonomous source of history's meaning, is never more than an effect of indeterminate practical struggles in history. It is to see the figure of man as an effect that is always resisted, always an effect that might not happen, and therefore, always an effect in the process of being imposed, resisted, and reimposed, often in transformed form. (Ashley 1989, 297)

Ashley argues that modern statecraft projects the paradigmatic voice of sovereign man as a textual strategy that externalizes dangers and that "shall be disposed to recognize as intrinsically problematic or troubled—and at a minimum to exclude from serious discourse—other persons not similarly disposed to recognise these dangers, externalise them and try to bring them under control" (Ashley 1989, 303). In the context of his discussion of IR theory, the "other persons" can be taken to mean the "feminized" discourses of alternative approaches to the discipline. The paradigm of sovereign man is explicitly linked in Ashley's analysis to bourgeois-liberal conceptions of the autonomous self—that this is a particular form of hegemonic masculinity should be clear from the discussion above. However, because of his focus on the totalizing discourses of modernity, Ashley sadly has less to say about the citizen-warrior model of masculinity that also informs such "heroic" constructions (so that *sovereign man* equates with *sovereign statesman*—see discussion above).

Ashley clearly uses the word *man* knowingly—he is aware that it is both a generic and a gendered term, which is opposed to the feminine Other of anarchy. He even quotes Julia Kristeva, a feminist poststructuralist, in his consideration of texts (Ashley 1989, 281). Yet he does not explore even the more obvious gendered dimensions of his discourse: the exclusion of women in this paradigm. While Ashley chooses to treat his material purely as a discussion of rhetorical strategies in the production of academic knowledge, his material is also relevant to the identities of men and the ongoing construction of hegemonic masculine identities. He concludes that "modern statecraft is modern mancraft. It is an art of domesticating the meaning of man by constructing his problems, his dangers, his fears" (Ashley 1989, 303). Such a conclusion should apply not only to the production of modern theories of IR, and to the creation of "man" as a subject in the text, but also to the production of hegemonic masculine subjectivities on the ground through its association with practical participation in modern forms of politics. Ashley's analysis is too abstract and disembodied to acknowledge or explore this dimension. In spite of his critique, he remains in the rarefied mental world of metanarrative and the philosophy of "Man." The real Other(s) of such a paradigm include not only "woman" but also subordinate masculinities and marginalized groups of men.[41]

Ashley is heavily influenced by both Foucault and Derrida, neither of whom address the question of male power directly, in spite of their preoccupations with the power/knowledge nexus (Nicholson 1990; Ramazonoglu 1993). The failure to take on board the insights of feminist scholarship (in Ashley's case, even while quoting feminist scholars) is not confined to poststructuralists in international relations. Moreover, as Jane Flax argues, male poststructuralists still largely operate within the mentalist tradition of Western philosophy, however much they argue they are displacing it. In privileging abstract thought over lived experience in their consideration of the production of knowledge, they reinforce phallogocentrism—the fantasy of control and omnipotence associated with "the Word"—even as they criticize it (Flax 1990).[42] As Susan Bordo, discussing Flax's argument, concludes: "The Great White Father (who also has a class identity . . .) just keeps on returning, even amid the seeming ruptures of post-modern culture" (Bordo 1993, 281). Continuing to recuperate the Other in conceptual terms alone will not necessarily mean progress as far as women and subordinate men are concerned. To quote Bordo again, "we deceive ourselves if we believe that post-modern theory is attending to the 'problem of difference' so long as so many concrete others are excluded from the conversation" (Bordo 1990, 140).

These criticisms also apply to some extent to the work of critical theorists. Although critical theorists (like feminists), straddle the modern/postmodern boundary, they are regarded as postpositivists in Smith's (1995) categorization of the postpositivist debate in IR. As Benhabib argues, critical theory and Habermasian discourse ethics remain in the rationalist tradition of Western philosophy, with its emphasis on abstract principles and procedures—paying all too little attention to concepts such as "the concrete other" and the "ethic of care" traditionally associated with feminine morality in their rendering of ethics and politics (Benhabib 1992). As such they embody and promote bourgeois-rational masculinity. However, it must be said that recent efforts have been made to incorporate Benhabib's and other feminists concerns on this issue (see, for example, Linklater 1996), and critical theorists such as David Campbell and Rob Walker (both discussed above) have to date offered the most satisfactorily gendered analyses outside of explicitly feminist circles.[43]

A cynical argument is that, these exceptions notwithstanding, for the majority of academic postpositivists, challenging Enlightenment dualisms allows the "pimps of post-modernism" to get "a bit of the Other" by indulging in academic cross-dressing. Like 1970s and 1980s New Men, they enjoy playing with the previously forbidden fruits of femininity (and other exotic cultures) without engaging with feminism seriously or surrendering their gender privileges (Moore 1988). In spite of such accusations, there is no doubt that in challenging the assumptions of modern theory, academic postpositivists have opened up a conceptual space for change, with possible gender implications. Peterson has noted that "to the extent that masculinism is privileged, forms of knowledge—including postpositivism—associated with the 'subjective' and the 'feminine' are devalued and resisted as inferior to 'hard science' with its claims to objectivity, certainty and control" (Peterson 1992b, 196). Postpositivist approaches remain marginal to the bulk of IR scholarship.[44] Under these circumstances, incorporating feminist scholarship might expose such perspectives and the male academics who pursue them to further marginalization.[45] However, failing to do so will undoubtedly play into the hands of masculinist interests

Indeed, some dissident discussions may even unwittingly mark out new agendas for emerging hegemonic masculinities to colonize, particularly those by contributors such as James Der Derian (1989, 1990, 1995) and Michael Shapiro (1990), who are influenced by Baudrillard's postmodernism of "hyperreality" and "simulacra" (Baudrillard 1983).[46] And here I would like to discuss Der Derian's work in more detail than I have hitherto given to other contributors to IR. This is not to demonstrate that he has ignored gender issues (which he has), but rather to identify more clearly what new form of masculinity his work might embody. The significance of this will become apparent in later chapters.

Der Derian's more recent work takes fragments of texts from different genres and interweaves them into a "magic world, a pastiche of science fiction, cartoons, Disneyland, CIA reports, spy novels, IR theory, movies and so on" (Huysmans 1997, 337).[47] This is an interpretive method designed to pull together popular culture and political and academic sources and to de-differentiate between genres, refusing conventional disciplinary boundaries.[48] As such, it has some common ground with the aims of this book and could in theory be sympathetic to feminist concerns. However, Der Derian displays a particular fascination with speed and the virtual world of new technology, and the language that goes with it. He has in fact been accused of being excessively "techno-celebratory" (Der Derian 1995, 1).

At first sight, Der Derian's approach to technology, and particularly the technology of war, is critical. In a 1990 article, he argues that poststructural analysis "can help us understand something that cannot fully be understood: the impact of an array of new technological practices that have proven to be resistant if not invisible to traditional methods of analysis" (1990, 297). He then discusses the antidiplomatic discursive power associated with such "technostrategic" practices (which make use of technology for the purpose of war) as simulation, surveillance, and speed, drawing on the ideas of Baudrillard, Foucault, and Virilio, respectively. Simulations of various kinds, he argues, are proliferating and displacing reality—so that simulated electronic targeting overrides reality in deciding who gets shot, and the novels of Tom Clancy keep realism in favor in state affairs. Surveillance is being comprehensively extended into international relations through satellite technology and other electronic means. Speed has meanwhile displaced geography as the primary basis of military logistics, giving tactical vision increased strategic importance. The impact of these factors taken together means that "the war of perception and representation demands more of our attention and resources than the seemingly endless collection and correlation of data on war that goes on in the field of international relations" (308).

While Der Derian is clearly against the normalizing power of such practices, which induce both "simulation syndrome" (303) and paranoid, overdetermined decision making, his playful use of language, combining science-fiction terms and a sophisticated, ironic tone with academic analysis, all work against his disapproval and could serve to glamorize or lend legitimacy to his subject matter. For example, his prose is littered with terms such as *chronopolitics, cyberspace, hyperreality,* and *simulation sickness* (303), all mimicking or derived from science-fiction sources. Admittedly, he has not appropriated these phrases for academic use himself: *chronopolitics* comes from Virilio, *hyperreality* from Baudrillard, and so on. However, they are obviously used with relish and in the context of a playful approach to language. When discussing "the panoptic surveillance machine" (308), he even adds a touch of chilling, science-fiction mystery and suspense, describing the machine as a "power" that is "here and now, in the shadows and in the 'deep black.' It has no trouble seeing us, but we have great difficulties seeing it" (304). Through their association with the cutting edge between science and science fiction, such terms do add glamour to the subject matter. Der Derian is aware of the power of the language he uses. He is happy to heavily promote the term *simulation* in spite of, or perhaps because of, the fact that "'simulation' also has the obvious advantage of sounding more serious than 'gaming' and of carrying more of a high-tech, scientific connotation than 'modelling'" (301).

While Der Derian's language can undermine his apparently critical approach to new technologies, other clues suggest that his own relationship with technology is rather more ambiguous. In a piece about Der Derian's visit to the U.S. forces training facility at Hohenfels, Germany—where, in a thinly veiled "Bosnia," simulated battle-training for "operations other than war" was taking place (1995, 8)—Der Derian comments that the briefing officer, one Major Demike, "clearly had a take-no-prisoners attitude toward the English language" (8). However, all the major's high-tech jargon is then served up by Der Derian in a commentary on his briefing, including descriptions of operations training in which, for example, "simulated artillery attacks are launched via Silicon Graphics workstations, and hits are assessed according to probability software which calculates trajectories, terrain and the grid locations of vehicles and troops which are constantly updated by Global Positioning Systems" (9). After this we visit the "Warlord Simulation Centre," with its computer and satellite equipment and the "MILES" (Multiple Integrated Laser Engagement System) laser stores, the trip culminating in a lurid description of battles simulated with lasers in the "cyber-Box."

On one level, this account could be seen as simply an ironic replaying of the techno-enthusiasm of the military—another game Der Derian is playing with the language of new technology. After all, he is attempting to convey the atmosphere at Hohenfels itself, where the technology is clearly revered, and his commentary is wry. He picks up the major on his assumption that soldiers are always male and so a female voice announcing casualties would stand out against the background noise: "My query about what happens when women eventually join combat simulations was met with a blank stare by the major" (9–10). Der Derian's juxtapositions also show the absurdity of statements such as when, after showing video footage of simulated battle in "the Box," a Colonel Wallace said, "None of this stuff is staged, it's all live from live footage taken by the Viper video teams in the Box" (11). Der Derian sums this up as a "knack for paradox" (11). Earlier, Colonel Wallace is reported as having said that "virtually everything we do is real. There's nothing simulated in the Box" (9).[49] The lightly mocking tone of Der Derian's account could be interpreted as a way of displacing the importance or credibility of this heroic techno-babble, and he indulges in frequent, sophisticated wordplay, such as when describing a four-hundred-page "White Paper" outlining the purpose of all this training: "In po-mo terms, this "White Paper" was this year's model for the hi-tech, post–Cold War simulations and training exercises that would prepare U.S. armed forces for pre-peace keeping non-interventions into those post-imperial spaces where once- and wannabe-states were engaged in post-war warring" (13). Unfortunately, any serious criticisms hidden in this light-hearted banter are undermined by Der Derian's own complicity in the underlying technophilia. First, there is always the suspicion that playful enjoyment of the language reflects playful enjoyment of the technology itself. But the relationship between Der Derian and the military technology he describes involves more than ironic language games. Technology is given a central place in Der Derian's account of his tour of Hohenfels and is presented as if self-evidently important.[50] His account of the simulated battle in the "cyber-Box" is not confined to the plot but also comes complete with hardware weaponry specifications. His enthusiasm for technology is signaled not only by the amount of space he devotes to descriptions of military hardware, but also by such statements as "ever since *Kraftwerk* droned their ode to the 'Bahn, Bahn, Autobahn,' I've felt a strong urge to travel at hyperspeed encased in German steel" (6). Here Der Derian not only betrays his love of technology and speed but also invokes a classic image of rebellious youthful masculinity in this fleeting homage to rock-and-roll and fast cars. Of course, any good postmodernist would deny innocence, but Der Derian's fascination with the world of virtual technology comes through very strongly in his work. Later in the piece, he interviews Paul Virilio, a critical theorist of the new technologies and a source Der Derian much admires and draws on repeatedly (Huysmans 1997). In the course of the interview, Virilio reveals his own ambiguous relationship to the new technologies:

I think that the power of technique will lead to its religion, a technocult, a kind of cybercult. Just as there is an Islamic, a Christian, a Jewish integrism, there is a technical integrism in power, which is made possible with the technologies of information. Fundamentalism, in the field of technology, is just as dangerous as the religious one. Modern man killed the god of transcendence, the god of Judeo-Christianity, and he invented a machine god, a deus ex machina. One should be an atheist of technique. I try to be an atheist of technique. I am in love with technique. My image is that of the fight between Jacob and the Angel. He meets god's angel but in order to remain a man he must fight. This is the great image. (quoted in Der Derian 1995, 23)

Virilio's ambiguous relationship with the new technologies, which he both loves and is critical of, is seen as a manly battle, with Virilio cast in the role of tragic hero, a warrior doomed to fight the thing he loves. Grappling with new technology is clearly portrayed as a masculine thing.[51]

Arguably, the struggle against the seductive angel of information technologies and their strategic applications is a struggle that both Virilio and Der Derian are losing. Their fascination with "virtual" technology resembles the earlier "toys for the boys" fascination with missile technology exhibited by more conventional contributors to strategic studies. Both groups, earlier strategists and postmodern contributors, display a degree of nihilism. In the case of earlier strategists, this was through the pathological emotional distance and absurdly abstract air of unreality surrounding such dangerous concepts as mutually assured destruction, or MAD, as it was known (Cohn 1987), and in the case of postmodernists, it is through their invocation of Nietzsche (e.g., Der Derian 1990). Both indulge in playful language games with masculine associations, the earlier strategists using a highly sexualized language of explicit phallic symbolism (Cohn 1987) and the postmodernists through forays into the world of fiction such as *Top Gun* and *Miami Vice* (Shapiro 1990) and through aping the rhetoric of *Boys' Own* science fiction. The main difference is that in the postmodern version, the playful language makes it into the academic journals and books, rather than being translated into the formal language of "objective" science.[52]

However, transgressing the boundaries of acceptable rhetoric and mixing fiction with "hard facts," self-consciously irreverent as it may be, is not enough to ensure the radical credentials of postmodern writers. The U.S. forces clearly do not see Der Derian as a threat; if they had, they would not have given him privileged access to U.S. armed forces state-of-the-art training facilities in the first place. More likely, and in spite of the apparent stupidity of some of the commanding officers, they see him as a tool in a propaganda war in which potential enemies will hopefully be cowed and bamboozled by the appearance of high-tech wizardry. What the armed forces may be less conscious of, however, is how hegemonic masculinity may be being remodeled in the process (a remodeling to be discussed in more detail in the following chapters). Since feminist interventions form a substantial contribution to the postpositivist debate in IR, postmodern academics have less excuse to participate so enthusiastically in such a process.

I HAVE ARGUED here that an awareness of multiple masculinities raises new questions about the relationships between different masculinities and international practices. This chapter also raises questions about the boundaries of the discipline, as one effect of traditional conceptualizations is to inscribe IR as a primary site for the production of masculinities, while at the same time obscuring this process, by eliminating personal life and questions of identity from its scope of analysis. In addition, the relationship between masculinities and IR needs to be seen as part of a broader set of historic and contemporary cultural connections between masculinity and "the international" that are themselves politicized; the relationship needs to be analyzed in the wider context of "world politics," or a similarly broadly conceived successor discipline. Such a perspective would be no respecter of levels of analysis or existing disciplinary boundaries. This is not to suggest that anything and everything should come under the remit of IR, but rather that it should not be viewed in isolation and that its gendering practices cannot be "seen" from within.

Meanwhile, the discipline itself both reflects and (re)produces the dynamics of competing masculinities in the struggle for hegemony. In this context, the struggle between institutionalist and postpositivist approaches can easily become one between competing masculine futures (or may even result in some new hybrid hegemonic masculinity). In crude terms, if realists and neorealists can be characterized as warriors and patriarchs, and institutionalists and liberals as embodying varieties of bourgeois New Men, then some postpositivists (not critical theorists) can be seen as the "rebels without a cause" of IR theory—rebels whose rock-and-roll sci-fi masculinity may become the future orthodoxy.

Intellectual rigor notwithstanding, the academic discipline of IR is not exempt from the general observation that the more men align themselves with hegemonic masculinities, the more they boost their own credibility and perpetuate that hegemony (Connell 1987). This is true in epistemological as well as sociological terms. The further away from hegemonic masculinities their perspectives roam, the more easily such perspectives are marginalized. Most female academics are already on the professional margins (Caplan 1994), and as such have less to lose by endorsing feminist approaches. Postpositivists open up an intellectual space that can either be used for undermining the gender order or for the reconstitution of hegemonic masculinities. Take on board feminist scholarship in a sustained fashion and they risk further marginalization; keep quiet, and they will find their work recuperated for masculinist purposes. Under such circumstances, challenging the gender order is clearly in the interests of all marginalized perspectives in IR, and not just avowed feminists. Without a clear commitment to dismantling the gender order, some postpositivists may merely facilitate the further transformation of hegemonic masculinities to serve a new era of globalization.

# CHAPTER FOUR

# *The Economist's* Masculine Credentials

Tнis chapter and the one following form a case study of *The Economist* newspaper, which uses the theoretical perspective outlined in part 1 to explore changing masculinities in the paper during the period 1989–96. The relevance of this case study to international relations should become clear in due course.

## The Argument in Brief

*The Economist* forms part of the immediate cultural context in which the predominantly Anglo-American discipline of IR operates. Aimed at an international readership largely composed of elite men, it is a weekly newspaper saturated with images of masculinity, and consequently the state of play between different versions of would-be hegemonic masculinity can be read off from its pages.[1] It is a site where models of masculinity are not only reflected but also produced, modified, contradicted, reinforced, and negotiated through the nexus of ideas that circulate within its pages and between its readers. This nexus of ideas is both influenced by, and in turn must itself influence, not only the practices of international relations and political economy, but also the academic disciplines of IR and IPE, which do not and cannot exist in a cultural vacuum.

The following discussion of the images of hegemonic masculinities in *The Economist* (1989 to 1996) will focus on the tensions and overlaps between well-established models that resonate with cold war political realism and economic corporatism, and alternative constructions that resonate more closely with recent developments toward an accelerated globalization of the world economy. In the 1990s "globalization" was a hot topic in IR and IPE circles, as well as in the pages of *The Economist*. The period under discussion covers a time of rapid political, social, technological, and economic change after the relative stability of the cold war, a period in which the term *globalization* has come to the fore. In *The Economist*, images of newer styles of elite masculinity have tended to be associated in particular with the reorganization and expansion of global finance following 1980s deregulation, new managerial strategies, and corporate restructuring, all of which are aspects of economic globalization and all of which have received extensive coverage in the paper. Indeed, *The Economist*, with its radical, liberal, free-market editorial line, has been a self-confessed high-profile "booster" of the ideology of economic globalization and, while it has long had an international circulation and reputation, has itself become one of the key publications of the global financial press (Thrift 1994, 350).

The images of hegemonic masculinity that appear in *The Economist* closely mirror those in the discipline of IR discussed in the preceding chapter—a phenomenon that demonstrates a high degree of overlap and cross-fertilization between academic models and popular-culture. This overlap is a powerful tool in the construction and reinforcement of particular gendered identities. Of special interest is the way in which constructions of masculinity associated with globalization in the paper resonate with some postpositivist approaches to IR. These connections shed further light on the gender politics involved in such approaches.

However, before moving on to the main argument, this chapter first justifies the choice of *The Economist* newspaper as an important site for the cross-fertilization of ideas between the academic world of IR and the wider cultural milieu. I also briefly explain what type of analysis will be made and the conceptual tools that I deploy. The remainder of the chapter demonstrates *The Economist*'s elite masculine credentials. I show how the newspaper is saturated with the imagery of well-established constructions of hegemonic masculinity, which form a generally mutually reinforcing masculinist framework—a lens through which readers are invited to view both the world and themselves. For this, further use will be made of the ideal types of hegemonic masculinity introduced in earlier chapters.

## Why The Economist?

*The Economist*, founded in 1843 as an arm of the City of London financial press, is a weekly, international, news and business journal/newspaper published in London. In the early 1990s it had a rapidly rising circulation of more than five hundred thousand, 81 percent of which lay outside of the United Kingdom, spreading through the United States, Europe, and Asia.[2] I chose *The Economist* because of its position as a mediator of ideas between the worlds of business, international politics, and academics and practitioners in IR and IPE. This position is indicated by and reflected in the following ways in the organization and layout of the paper:

The core sections of *The Economist*'s editorial coverage appeal to and provide useful information for all the groups just mentioned, comprehensively covering politics and current affairs from around the world, economics and international business, as well as financial matters. Considerable attention is paid to states' foreign policies and development policies; international problems and tensions; the activities of supranational institutions such as the United Nations, the G7 group, the European Union, the International Monetary Fund and the World Bank; the activities of multinational corporations; banking and financial institutions; the politics and economics of new technology; and new managerial strategies.[3] Although *The Economist* is not an academic publication itself, articles in the paper often make direct reference to academic papers and books from the fields of economics, IR, business studies, and science.[4] Thus ideas in circulation in the academy are promulgated and popularized for a wider audience. In addition, guest articles have been authored by prominent academics and politicians.[5] In return, *The Economist* provides a useful secondary source of material for academics and is used as a reliable source of factual information and contemporary comment in academic literature.[6]

This mix of topics is both reflected and promoted by the type of employment and education advertisements that the paper carries. Advertising in the paper includes a section entitled "Executive Focus" that concentrates on high-ranking jobs with corporations, international consultants, and development agencies; an "Appointments" section with academic vacancies in IR, IPE, economics, business studies, and development studies, together with lower-ranking jobs in international institutions and agencies; a large "Courses" section that advertises mostly postgraduate degrees in business, IR, and development, along with language tuition, short management courses, and international summer schools; and sections that cover government tenders and business opportunities. The worldview of *The Economist* fits well with the perspectives of the dominant paradigms in IR—neorealism and neoliberal institutionalism. *The Economist* portrays itself as a paper of the "extreme centre" (September 4, 1993, 27) and is thoroughly and consistently liberal in its values, both economic and social. It upholds individual responsibility and free markets; it makes extensive use of liberal economic theory; it promotes business, democracy, and the rule of law;[7] it supports liberal individualism and liberal feminism.[8] It is sympathetic to the goals of liberal international institutions and by and large supports European economic integration.[9] On the other hand, this liberalism and internationalism is tempered by and in tension with a heavy dose of political realism. Coverage of politics is mostly state centric, the analysis of national interests and regional power-balancing looms large, and nationalism is a force to be reckoned with.[10] Political order is generally given priority over liberty (*The Economist* September 4, 1993, 27). Liberal international regimes are seen to depend on the backing of powerful liberal states, while the power and influence of multinational corporations waxes and wanes according to political circumstances.[11] States are seen as rational actors, often characterized as maximizing their own position in a competitive, Darwinistic world, where global economic competition is as much between states as between companies.[12] The basic assumptions about the nature of international affairs and the implicit values of mainstream neorealism and liberal institutionalism are all shared by *The Economist*. Moreover, epistemological concerns are also shared, as *The Economist* itself uses and from time to time discusses, the same positivist tools of analysis as are ubiquitous in mainstream IR research in journals such as *International Studies Quarterly*.[13] The world it depicts and the language it uses are comfortingly familiar to mainstream IR academics, who may quibble over particular arguments but will find their basic stance confirmed in its pages.[14]

Although it is not clear from the 1990 survey of subscribers exactly what proportion of readers were professionally engaged in international relations and related fields as opposed to business, 49 percent of readers had a higher degree and 35 percent were professionals and government employees.[15] The breakdown of the business readership shows "top management" 42 percent, "middle management" 18 percent, and "executive clerical" 5 percent. Of the professionals and government employees, one would expect a proportion to have been IR academics and practitioners (other academic readers would include economists and business-studies faculty). However, readership rates among such groups would probably have been underrepresented because of institutional purchase as opposed to personal subscription. In spite of the lack of concrete readership numbers, the range and regularity of IR jobs and courses being advertised during the period under investigation is ample evidence of a healthy IR readership, and not just in the United Kingdom. Taking 1995 as an example, academic jobs in the field ranged from junior lecturers in international relations, through various postdoctoral fellowships, to senior positions as chairs or directors of international relations programs in universities and research institutes in the United States, Britain, Europe, and Japan.[16] A wide variety of relevant courses for both academics and practitioners were likewise advertised.[17] *The Economist* is also an important recruiting ground for practitioners. In 1995 barely a week went by without the United Nations headquarters or some of its agencies advertising for staff;[18] other supranational and government institutions also recruited regularly in the paper's columns,[19] and various lobbying groups and nongovernmental organizations (NGOs) occasionally looked for international affairs researchers and policy advisers.[20]

In addition to the editorial content and appointments sections linking academics and practitioners in IR, IPE, and business, *The Economist*, like any other newspaper or current-affairs magazine, (re)produces all the iconography and symbolism of the wider culture in which it is produced, both in terms of its own narrative structure and rhetorical strategies and in the more general advertising that it carries. In the pages of *The Economist*, popular culture meets the academic world of IR very clearly and explicitly. Moreover, it is a particular section of popular culture, the cultural iconography of elite males, that is most clearly represented. This makes it a good site to explore the models of hegemonic masculinity in general cultural circulation and their connections to IR.

In order to do this, it is necessary to draw on the methods of analysis used in cultural studies.

### The Analytical Approach: A Textual Analysis

My approach to *The Economist* is by way of a textual reading. The term *text* here is used (following the cultural-studies practice)[21] to refer not just to the written words but also to the graphs, layout, photos, drawings, and so forth and the narrative conventions embedded in these — indeed, all the elements that go toward making up the totality of the paper, including the advertising material. In the case of *The Economist*, this totality is itself enhanced by the practices of having an easily identifiable house style and of eschewing by-lines. These practices make this paper in particular appear as a seamless whole. A textual approach also means that the analysis is not predicated on any assumptions as to the sex, gender, or ethnicity profile of its contributors, nor assumptions as to their individual or even collective views or attitudes to gender politics. The concern here is with the gendered meanings that are encoded in the newspaper, regardless of the intentions of its publishers and authors. Indeed, it is worth stressing that these gendered meanings may often be very different from the conscious intentions of the authors. This is because authors' intentions constitute only one of three key ingredients in the production of meaning from texts, the other two being intertextuality and reading strategies.

The notion of intertextuality is an important tool in cultural studies.[22] It refers to the process by which meanings are circulated between texts through the use of various visual and literary codes and conventions (Fiske 1987). For example, through the endless repetition of certain symbols, images, and ideas, a complex visual language of advertising has developed over the last few decades, a sophisticated shorthand whereby whole strings of associations and carefully nuanced "stories" can be "read" from a single printed image or a few seconds of action on a TV screen, by an audience already tutored in the language of advertising through exposure to past advertisements. When white British television viewers see an image of a tropical palm-fringed beach (used regularly in a number of advertisements such as for Bounty chocolate and Martini vermouth), the associations automatically conjured up are of a paradise, glamorous wealth, escape from the crowds, and endless leisure. Such connotations are achieved through the constant repetition of such images and their relationship to a culture in which leisure travel to the tropics has been the preserve of the wealthy and leisured classes; in which there is a long history of varied but overlapping stories about desert islands and buried treasure that mingle with real adventures that plundered the wealth of tropical islands; and in which, in a more recent colonial past, white Britons were waited on in the tropics by local or imported subjects (the presence of a *white* body experiencing leisure on such a beach brings the colonial associations even more into focus).[23] All these meanings and associations are condensed into an image viewed on the television screen for only a few seconds. Meanings cannot be gleaned by examining a text in isolation. They can be understood only in the context of both the immediate intertextuality of media images and symbolic meanings and the wider cultural context or intertext.

As with television images, so with the advertising material and other pictorial images in the pages of *The Economist.* They, too, operate within a wider cultural context, whose shared meanings they draw on, reproduce, and to some extent modify or redraw. Moreover, the relevance of intertextuality and symbolic meaning is not confined to the advertising material and visual images in the paper. Gendered meanings can often be found in even the driest and most factual passages of editorial, embedded in metaphor and other rhetorical strategies that are used. Such meanings and metaphorical associations are at least as important in gendering the paper as the intended or more obvious subject matter being presented. The written language often operates on two levels at once, the more obvious level of communicative logic, and the less readily noticed level of symbolic, metaphorical message. So when one reads *The Economist,* one gets two kinds of stories at once, on different levels: (1) a logical, abstract, and informative, if opinionated, discussion about current affairs, and (2) a symbolic narrative about who *you* are as an *Economist* reader.[24] This second story is the one that attempts to position you as a man who identifies with hegemonic masculinity.[25] One can, of course, resist the "message" in either or both of the stories. One may disagree with the opinions expressed in the first, intentional level, or find its choice and framing of topics politically incompatible with one's view. One may take in the symbolic messages of the second level unconsciously, or resist them, whether consciously or unconsciously. If, as an *Economist* reader, you strongly disagree with the opinions expressed at the first level, or if you are a female or nonhegemonic male reader, you are more likely to resist routinely and unconsciously at the second level.

This brings me to the third ingredient in the construction of meanings: reading strategies. In analyzing the effects of *The Economist*, I am assuming a readership of people who are themselves inserted into or at least heavily exposed to this wider cultural milieu.[26] Social and cultural outsiders, without prior exposure to the full range of codes and conventions used in a text, which often circulate in specific cultural and social circles, are more likely to fail to grasp nuances, to make wild interpretations, to find novel associations with the imagery of the text (novel, that is, in terms of the dominant culture that is being represented), or even to experience baffled incomprehension at times.[27] However, the following chapters will not be discussing the more tangential readings of *The Economist* that may be made by those who are relatively unfamiliar with Western cultural codes or the nuances of the English language. The consideration of such reading strategies is not directly relevant to the analysis of hegemonic masculinities, save to mention that without the necessary "cultural capital" (to borrow a phrase from Bourdieu) to make sense of all the nuances of meaning in the text, subordinate and non-Western-educated groups of men are at a disadvantage in keeping up with what, in cultural terms, currently counts in elite circles.[28] Thus a hegemonic reading is one that fully grasps the relevant intertextuality of the text because the reader is fluent in the symbolic language (whether written or visual) of the hegemonic culture itself. In this respect alone, *The Economist* already helps to perpetuate the hegemony of white, educated, English-speaking Western males (who are already most thoroughly immersed in the relevant social and cultural circles), whatever its intentions.[29]

On a personal note, as a white, middle-class Englishwoman I am fully conversant with the hegemonic Anglo-American cultural milieu that *The Economist* inhabits. For this research I have deliberately ruled out any contact with journalists and publishers connected to *The Economist*, because to ascertain their views and intentions would inevitably change my own perspective and influence my reading strategy and interpretation of the paper. I thus come to the gendered meanings generated by the paper in much the same way as the majority of elite readers, except for my sex. Reading the pa-

per as a woman probably alerts me more readily to its gendered constructions than might otherwise have been the case.

To summarize, *The Economist* does not carry a fixed set of symbolic
meanings and connotations that can be "read" only in one way. Rather, the
gendered meanings that the paper carries are negotiated between the text,
the intertext, and the reader. However, the textual analysis that follows will
concentrate on showing how *The Economist* has interpellated its readers,
inviting them to identify with various models of hegemonic masculinity. It
will discuss the models themselves in the context of the changing political
and economic environment associated with globalization and will tease out
some specific intertextual connections with IR and IPE, rather than specu-
lating about reading strategies in themselves, or making more general intertextual observations. Hence the discussion is based primarily on my own
textual reading of *The Economist*, which while I hope will illuminate some
of the contemporary ferment in the construction of hegemonic masculinity
and is in no way intended as the definitive interpretation of the paper's gendered effects or meanings.

## The Economist's *Masculine Credentials: Promotions*

Although in theory *The Economist* is presented as a gender-neutral journal
for international business and professional elites, in practice it has been
aimed at elite or would-be elite men.[30] This is illustrated by a U.K. billboard
advertisement (autumn 1994), part of a long-running campaign of witti-
cisms, that used the slogan "Top Cats Prefer *The Economist*." The slogan
was humorous, making reference to another long-running advertising campaign for a brand of petfood that announced: "Ninety percent of all cats prefer Whiskas." It also carried associations with the well-known Boss Cat cartoon series and its "Top Cat" theme song (sung over the opening and
closing credits). Obviously the advertisement drew heavily on the imagery
and reputation of cats as the elite of animal predators. The business world is
often likened to a hostile and competitive jungle in which only the strongest
survive. There was also an association with the term *fat cats* used to refer to
extremely wealthy and successful businessmen. Top cats are unmistakably
masculine—the ruler of the jungle (the "king") is always pictured as a male
lion with a large mane (even though in practice lionesses do most of the

hunting). Top cats are not only wealthy and powerful, they are also sexually successful, as in "cool cats." The idea of elite men as kings of the corporate jungle is so clichéd, however, as to be risible to contemporary educated British males, so the humor was necessary to retrieve this crude symbolism of elite masculinity. The self-conscious irony added to the sophistication of the advertisement—and interpellated the reader as a sophisticated, educated, modern man who was beyond such crass characterizations of masculine identity, but without diluting the message. For all the mocking, the crude symbolism of elite masculine power still got an airing, was still being (re)produced. Not only that, of course, but the billboard campaign, by positioning The Economist reader as a "top cat," drew on a certain kind of "aspirational" masculinity (to use the jargon of advertisers). Subscribe to The Economist and you will join the club of elite males. Being an Economist reader becomes part of (or even proof of) one's identity as an elite man.

According to The Economist's 1990 readership survey cited above (source: The Economist), 89 percent of subscribers at that time were, indeed, male. The Economist's "World Profile" brochure promoted the survey with a narrative that set out to convince would-be advertisers of the elite credentials of the paper's subscribers.[31] Subscribers were described as being "senior decision-makers" who were "concentrated around the dynamic middle years," with an average personal income of $107,600, household income of $155,800 and net worth of $1,152,600 (all figures were expressed in U.S. dollars and were for 1990). They were nearly all graduates (90 percent) and one-half had postgraduate qualifications (49 percent). They were described as holding "some of the most influential positions" (with 37 percent holding board directorships), as being "international opinion leaders" (45 percent had given a speech or addressed a public meeting and 23 percent had been interviewed by the media in the preceding year), and discriminating "style leaders," who frequently traveled by air, stayed in first-class hotels, hired luxury cars, and bought luxury goods. Figures were given for such investments as second homes (27 percent), antiques (24 percent), and vintage-wine cellars (21 percent); and for an array of purchases in the preceding year, including $400-plus suits (38 percent), perfume (30 percent), and $120-plus ladies handbags (28 percent).[32] The "World Profile" concluded by stating that The Economist provided "a prestigious international environment" that delivered an "active" and affluent "global elite" to advertisers.[33]

Accompanying this narrative was a series of photographic still-life pictures laden with images of status symbols that conjured up a picture of elite masculinity: The pictures were of a series of executive desktops, all viewed from directly above, as if the reader himself were sitting at the desks in the pictures. The first picture, "World Personal Profile," was of the desk owner's old school tie; a gold cup for sporting achievement (tennis); a framed photograph of a young woman; a government bond, a corporate report, and a copy of *The Economist* on a desktop. *The Economist* cover featured a picture of Nelson Mandela with the caption "Freedom Man." The reader was positioned as having had an elite education, perhaps in a British public school, as being heterosexual, as valuing his "freedom," and as taking an interest in cosmopolitan, global current affairs.[34] The second picture, "World Business Profile," featured a gold fountain pen; a check for one hundred thousand dollars; a computer, and a telephone on a textured, cream desktop—positioning him as important in the corporate world. The third, "World Lifestyle Profile," had credit cards in a black-leather wallet; a gold man's wristwatch; a cut-glass champagne flute; an American Express card; two theater tickets; a string of pearls; and a horse-shaped paperweight on a walnut desktop. The fourth, "World Travel Profile," showed a briefcase; a glass of whisky; international currency; a handwritten airmail letter to a girl; an outline of a jet; and a copy of *The Economist* on a grey-leather background. The fifth and last picture, "World Quality of Reading," included a whisky flask; a gold-rimmed cup of coffee; a silver clock, another gold pen; a leather-bound diary; and another copy of *The Economist*, this one on a black-leather desktop.

Clearly, the photographs were intended to convey a sense of luxury (gold watch, gold pen, gold-rimmed china, champagne flutes, whisky), wealth (gold again, credit cards), and power (old school tie connoting class power, fat checks, luxury desktops associated with executive jobs, and telephone and computer with which to issue commands). Although not all the objects necessarily connote masculinity, enough of them do to fix the overall meaning in favor of masculine corporate power: the man's old school tie and photograph of a young woman in the first picture help to fix the images as masculine, as does the man's watch in the third picture. The only item that could be described as feminine was the string of pearls, which appeared next to a pair of theater tickets and a champagne flute, probably suggesting a date with a woman for whom the pearls were a present, rather than that the desk owner was female.[35]

To complete the message of elite masculinity, neutral tones—browns and greys—dominate the color schemes of the pictures, which are in sharp focus and have crisp, jagged outlines and angular lines that dominate the layouts of the objects. In photographic and artistic convention, sharp focus, neutral tones, hard surfaces, and sharp lines all connote masculinity, as opposed to the soft focus, pastels, soft materials, and curved lines that connote femininity (Betterton 1987). The sepia tones and slightly quaint paraphernalia (the only ultramodern items on show were the telephone and computer, but these were carefully bathed in an old-world sepia tint) gave an old-fashioned feel to the pictures, suggesting old money and tradition, the slight stuffiness of aristocracy and long-held authority in the corridors of power. The feeling of power was enhanced by the fact that there are no people in the pictures: the ones with power were either the readers or were so important as to be veiled from the public gaze.

*The Economist* was subtly playing with the specifics of a particularly Anglo version of elite masculinity here, drawing on associations with the English Gentleman of years gone by—both in terms of the content and style of the pictures (for example, tennis is a gentlemanly sport; the image of a well-groomed horse is also associated with gentlemanly pursuits; and the old school tie is a very British status symbol, although not exclusively so). As a British publication, *The Economist* itself was milking the status it could gain by association with an aristocratic past. It also promoted itself as a "truly global" publication with a "unique" perspective that distinguishes *The Economist* from other international or pan-Continental titles that are either American-owned or regional in outlook. *The Economist*'s independence, and therefore its authority, is assured because the editor is appointed by a board of trustees. The editorial is written anonymously, ensuring editorial continuity and a consistency of view, independent of political, commercial, or proprietorial control (*The Economist* "World Profile").

The "unique perspective" was promoted here as embodying the ideals of impartiality and fair play, ideals that an English Gentleman would have subscribed to, and that was routinely used to justify the "authority" of British imperialism, which was also a "global" phenomenon. The strategy of juxtaposing the cultural signs of the English Gentleman with such rhetoric must surely have carried imperial overtones, even if unintentionally. These intertextual associations both lent imperial authority to the publication itself and at the same time interpellated readers as would-be English Gentlemen with all the status and power that that implies. This double strategy neatly positioned both the publication and its subscribers as numbering amongst the masculine elite, but also sent a more problematic double message. There remained a degree of ambiguity over to what extent subscribers, who are for the most part *not* British, were invited to partake in this imperial masculinity, and to what extent they were merely subjected to it.

In the case of elite WASP (white, Anglo-Saxon Protestant) U.S. subscribers, whose own "gentlemanly" heritage shares many of the same cultural signs and symbols as the English Gentleman, there would probably have been a large degree of identification. The overlap between British and U.S. models of elite masculinities, which both fall into a broadly Anglo-Saxon tradition, has been, and remains, extremely useful to *The Economist*. It has helped the paper maintain a strong international profile throughout the decline of the British Empire and the rise of the United States as a global power. *The Economist's* global influence must increasingly depend on having a solid base of elite U.S. subscribers; hence, the large section devoted to domestic U.S. politics. The appeal to certain groups of elite U.S. readers must be all the greater where the cultural trappings of the English Gentleman naturally coincide, for historical reasons, with WASP sensibilities.

## Content

Turning to the weekly issues of the newspaper itself, between 1989 and 1996 the elite masculine credentials exhibited in the promotional brochure were confirmed in a number of ways. In terms of content, the staple fare of *The Economist* is made up of topics that are all designated masculine interests: the public world of politics; foreign policy; international affairs; economics; business; science and technology. Although these are clearly not exclusively "masculine" by any manner of means, they are arenas that are dominated by men. That *The Economist* largely reports the doings of men, one might argue, cannot be helped, given its subject matter. However, *The Economist* also displays a rather more enthusiastic and comprehensive interest in science and technology than is strictly necessary for a paper dedicated to serving the current-affairs needs of businessmen and politicians. While keeping up with scientific developments may provide entrepreneurs with new business ideas, the quantity and detail of scientific reporting is more likely to reflect general interest rather than the professional information needs of its readers. Every week new scientific research in a wide variety of fields is faithfully reported and summarized. For example, the issue for February 25, 1995, reported on biological diversity, linguistics, and genetic screening; the March 18, 1995, issue covered new developments in astronomy, photocopier technology, and quantum mechanics. *The Economist* also holds an annual competition for scientific journalism and regularly produces upbeat special surveys on new technology.[36] Although the arts did get some coverage during the period studied, when content as a whole is taken into consideration, there was an overall bias toward science.[37]

This marked interest in science and technology reflects an editorial faith in scientific progress and in scientific discovery as the engine of capitalism, but also resonates with the entrenched practice of making scientific and technical knowledge a source of specifically masculine pleasure in its own right. Such pleasures are constituted as masculine from the nursery onward. For example, research has shown that schoolchildren perceive science as "masculine" (Kelly 1985). Moreover, by the time they get to adolescence, British teenage boys and girls use relationships to science and technology to help define their gender identities. Masculinity is confirmed by an interest in science and/or a degree of technical competence, while femininity is often confirmed through a (sometimes wilful) technical incompetence and a privileging of social knowledge over control of the "natural" world (Kelly 1985).

The reporting of scientific developments in *The Economist* not only assumes that readers have received a basic education in scientific matters, but offers them the chance to confirm their own (bourgeois-rational) masculinity. Scientific knowledge carries the highest status as "truth" and is regulated through complex rules and conventions, such as detachment, logic, internal consistency, replicability of tests, and the ability to predict and control outcomes, all of which guarantee its "objectivity." It is constituted as "masculine" through the gendered dichotomies of modernity, occupying the privileged side of mind (objectivity, order, and masculinity) in the pairings of mind/body, objective/subjective, order/chaos, and masculine/feminine (Harding 1986). Scientific research has also been portrayed as an exciting "frontier" activity, implying that it is far away from the domestic world of women. An article headlined "The Earth's Hidden Life," referring to life in apparently inhospitable conditions, proclaimed: "It is nonsense to say that the Last Frontier has been crossed. Apart from the almost limitless expanses of space, where the physical cosmos may or may not blend into a nonphysical one, there are plenty of places down here on humdrum old earth yet to be opened to human knowledge" (*The Economist* December 21, 1996, 133).

In addition, as high-status scientific knowledge is presented in exactly the same way as political comment and economic analysis, this juxtaposition allows the latter fields to gain masculine authority and credibility as "objective truth" more akin to scientific "fact" than woolly conjecture. This counters the reputation of economics as "the dismal science" and bolsters the credibility of positivist social sciences, which however hard they try, are unable to conform to the strict requirements of science, bedeviled as they are by the inability to replicate controlled experimental conditions, isolate and quantify causal variables, make reliable predictions, or discover consistent laws.[38] The scientific frame of mind is also confirmed by the way in which every opportunity is taken to lace articles in general with empirical and statistical facts and illustrate them with plentiful graphs and charts — again drawing on the "masculine" conventions of rationality and science. Information in graph and statistical form also resonates with the popularly held belief that men have better math and "spatial" abilities than women, and show a preference for knowledge coded in spatial and numerical forms.[39]

## House Style

*The Economist* is designed to be read in short bursts and to provide a comprehensive but condensed picture of the contemporary public world (implying that the readers are all too busy making important decisions to dally with a less concise journal).[40] In terms of its method of delivery, it follows the standard conventions by which politics, economics, and current affairs are predominantly coded as "masculine" interests in Western culture. Virtually all media reporting of news and current affairs uses the discursive conventions of representational realism, and *The Economist* is no exception.[41] There is an extensive cultural-studies literature on the genre of realism, but a useful general summary has been provided by John Fiske (1987).[42] Realism can be defined in a number of ways, but broadly speaking in realism the text is presented as if it is a natural reflection of experienced reality, a transparent window on the world, reflecting the pure truth. The world is taken to be made up of individual people, actions, and events that can be directly sensed by observers and objectively reported in the text. In the genre of news and current affairs, realism ensures that the processes of constructing stories—the selection, the presentation, the built-in assumptions, the relative importance given to different factors, and the fact that news itself is a cultural artifact—are masked (Fiske 1987, 21–22; Hartley 1982). The narrative is structured to produce a more or less unilinear story in sequence, with a beginning, a middle, and an end. This is not to say that it is without sophistication. The narrative itself will most likely contain a range of contradictory discourses and perspectives on a given "event," but as MacCabe (1981) has argued, these are arranged in a hierarchy, with the reporter's perspective having priority over those being reported and the reader occupying a privileged position of "all-knowingness" (Fiske 1987, 25), from which to "understand and evaluate the various discourses" on offer (Fiske 1987, 288). Within the narrative, while less-valued voices are associated with particular individuals, or "nominated," often the most authoritative voice in the hierarchy of discourses (and the one the reader is invited to agree with as the most objective) is not associated with any particular individual, and so is "exnominated" (Barthes 1973; Fiske 1987, 288–90).

The effect of these devices, along with the compartmentalizing of subject matter and the use of clichéd and conventionalized metaphors to make "common sense" of stories, is to achieve narrative closure. Realism imposes a certain kind of coherence on a multifaceted reality, a coherence that cannot help being ideologically inflected, not least in gender terms. As Fiske argues, "objectivity is the 'unauthored' voice of the bourgeoisie" (Fiske 1987, 289). But this is also the voice of hegemonic masculinity—which rather than drawing attention to itself appears as the voice of bourgeois-rational reason. It is no coincidence that the codes of realism (codes of objectivity, transparency, coherence, and narrative closure) closely resemble philosophical realism and the ontological and epistemological assumptions of "masculinist" science, for they developed alongside each other, along with individualism, humanism, and bourgeois capitalism. The way we understand a realist text is thus through the same general ideological framework as the way we make sense of our experiences in the modern world (Watt 1957; Fiske 1987, 21–24).

Realism is, in contemporary gender terms, thoroughly masculine.[43] As a cultural form, it is used to structure "masculine" fiction and TV action serials as well as factual material, where it can be contrasted with the multiple story lines, endless deferment of narrative closure, and serial forms of "feminine" soap operas. When the conventions of realism are used to report politics (the public doings of, mostly, men) and economics (the "dismal science"), the style bolsters the masculine credentials of the content. Realism is also masculinist, in that it promotes order, coherence, and unity over devalued and feminized anarchy, incoherence, and multiplicity. However, in news and current affairs, "masculine" narrative closure and control over the "feminine" formlessness of reality can never be fully achieved, and "the feminine" always threatens to break through (Fiske 1987, 308).[44]

Although *The Economist* makes use of the masculine narrative codes and conventions of realism, it does not reproduce them faithfully. Indeed, *The Economist's* house style is made up of conventions that exaggerate and in some ways parody realism, thereby also exaggerating the masculine coding that realism embodies. Exnomination in *The Economist* is taken to an extreme. The lack of bylines and complete anonymity of the editorial, as well as bearing the imperial associations mentioned above, create a tone of authoritative hyperobjectivity. The convention of referring to the paper as *The Economist*, as opposed to the *Economist* (which for a newspaper would be more usual) adds to this authority. The emphasis that both italics and capitalization place on the initial *The* suggests that the paper shares the status of "the Word" or "the Truth." This phallocentric practice lends added weight to the paper's already exnominated contents.

*The Economist* is also written in a distinct style, or "tone of voice," as its editor would have it. According to an article discussing this style/tone (*The Economist* December 22, 1990, 34), it was largely developed by Geoffrey Crowther, editor from 1938 to 1956, and has been described by its critics as "high droll" of a rather "acerbic" and "patronising" nature. It is written in a terse, urgent style with short, punchy sentences. Purple prose is avoided at all costs and the watchword is to "simplify, then exaggerate." Short words are preferred to long ones, and empiricism is preferred to "avoidable abstractions." In Economese, as it is called, "the aim is to squeeze out un-necessary metaphors, adjectives and other argument-obscuring figures of speech so that the . . . point is got across clearly and economically" (December 22 1990, 34). The prose is thrusting and up-front, there being no hint of timidity or equivocation over its opinions, particularly in the editorial section. Opinions are generally stated as though they were bald facts or commanding imperatives. Typical examples include: "In the present debate [on Europe's unemployment] there are three main camps. . . . All three are dangerously in error. For a start, Europe's unemployment is plainly neither cyclical nor structural, but a mixture of both" (June 26, 1993, 19); and "all communitarians claim that their ideas improve on Western liberalism, which they caricature outrageously, calling it a doctrine of economic atomism that pays no heed to man's social nature. This charge is simply false" (March 18, 1995, 20).

The Economist is rarely tentative,[45] and it is never rambling—it rarely strays far from the main point or argument in an article. The phallic symbolism of such a thrusting style of prose can hardly be missed. Indeed, one disgruntled former reader went so far as to describe it as "cocksure" (December 22, 1990, 34). This excessive style is defended in the paper by the argument that "the world is a complex place, and most readers prefer strongly held opinions to waffle and doubt. Part of the paper's extraordinary success globally lies in its ability to express itself forcefully and consistently" (September 4, 1993, 26).

"Feminine"-coded complexity, contradiction, and confusion are always strictly contained, and "feminine" stylistic embellishments are banished by what amounts to an exaggerated code of coherence. In The Economist, consistent rational analysis is paramount and "sentiment is the enemy" (September 4, 1993, 25). As its founder James Wilson wrote, "reason is given us to sit in judgement over the dictates of our feelings, and it is not her part to play the advocate in support of every impulse which laudable affections may arouse in us" (September 4, 1993, 25).

With the conventions of narrative realism being associated with a bourgeois-rational version of hegemonic masculinity with imperial overtones, the exaggeration of these conventions into a particularly bold, clipped, and aggressive "tone of voice" gives Economese a hard-boiled, tough-talking style. The text is consistently punctuated with short, punchy statements: "It should not have happened"; "It should not happen again"; "They would get nowhere"; "Best to be bold" (all in October 5, 1996, 15); "Consider the fudging"(October 5, 1996, 16); "It is time for a rethink" (October 5, 1996, 17); "You have been warned" (October 5, 1996, 19). This style is generally resonant with the tone of heroic, masculine self-confidence that American detective fiction (in the Chandler/Hammett tradition), Western films, and political thrillers embody.[46] The heroes of such literary and cinematic genres are men of few words and the words they do use tend to be in the form of terse, often ironic, statements.[47] They are isolated individuals who are "up against the world" and are able to deal with seemingly complex and confusing situations incisively. In detective fiction and political thrillers the heroes are generally very intelligent, and while they are usually men of honour, they are often required to be callous and cynical and to make uncompromising decisions in a corrupt or brutal world. Tough words are matched by tough actions. Detective heroes are detached from society yet have access to every part of it. They are not tethered or hindered by obvious class or social ties (Pfeil 1995). Their intelligence, detachment, and understatement of emotion codes their masculinity as bourgeois-rational, yet when the chips are down they will pull a gun and "roll in the dirt" with the best of them, as no-holds-barred citizen-warriors.[48]

*The Economist*, too, can be seen as such a hero, not only because it cuts through complexity in clipped and terse tones but also because it positions itself as a lone operative, detached from the world (and by implication the rest of the media) by its self-declared superior objectivity, guaranteed by its editorial anonymity. If the detective hero is unhindered by class or social ties, then *The Economist* declares itself to be unhindered by political or commercial ones. Moreover, just as detective heroes can pull a gun if required on their travels through every part of society, so *The Economist* has the "guts" to stick its neck out and routinely make bold and unsolicited policy recommendations at any point on its wanderings through global current affairs, advocating painful reform where this is seen as necessary. For example, on November 9, 1996 (17–22), a reelected President Clinton was challenged to take a gamble and "tell the truth" about both his private financial dealings (the subject of the Whitewater scandal and trial) and the need for public spending cuts in crisis-ridden inner cities. *The Economist* argued: "Forthrightness about his private dealings, if it comes to that, might not doom him, as some suppose; and forthrightness about the country's failings would be a positive service" (November 9, 1996, 18). Meanwhile Russia's ailing President Yeltsin was told he should end conscription and reform the army "as soon as his doctors let him sit up in bed and do a bit of work" (November 9, 1996, 18) even if this would be initially unpopular; NASA was told to scrap its plans for a manned space station as "killing it now would be painful—but not as painful as keeping it" (November 9, 1996, 19); Pakistan's then-new interim prime minister was exhorted to investigate political corruption, conduct electoral and judicial reform, and attack the privileges of the governing class, rather than just hold another election; all countries were urged to "dial C for competition" (November 9, 1996, 22), and Britain's politicians were advised to legalize and regulate mood-altering drugs because "while illegal drugs generally make people boring, alcohol often makes them violent" and "illegal drugs also do less damage to the body," a view that runs counter to public sentiment (November 9, 1996, 22). All this in the space of five pages.[49] In a leader that was originally published in 1988 but whose "timeless message" was reprinted in autumn 1996, we were told that "crunchy" policies, in which small changes have large and unequivocal effects—"leaving those affected by them in no doubt whether they are up or down, rich or broke, winning or losing, dead or alive" (October 5, 1996, 20)—are to be preferred to "soggy" ones that give rise to comfortable uncertainties and moral hazard. In *The Economist*'s eyes, it is clearly more important to be uncompromising than to be right, as "a crunchy policy is not necessarily right, only more certain than a soggy one to deliver the results that it deserves" (October 5, 1996, 20).

The house style of *The Economist*, therefore, manages to embody several forms of hegemonic masculinity in a powerful, if incongruent synthesis; bold, brash, and aggressive, on the one hand, and measured, rational, and logical, on the other, with imperial overtones thrown in for good measure, suggesting superior brawn, brain, and class combined. It is phallogocentric, in that it gives authority and primacy to "the Word" as self-evident "truth" in a "heroic" style that presents language and abstract thought as unified, self-present knowledge.[50] This works to privilege a hegemonically "masculine" subject position (always active, linear, rational, austere) and to limit the play of meaning. When the reader enters the world of *The Economist*, that reader is addressed as a fellow hero and superior brain, perhaps a successful entrepreneur or politician, and certainly an individualist who is capable of being tough-minded. For example, in the "crunchiness" editorial mentioned above, readers are exhorted to "run your country, or your company, or your life as you think fit. But whatever you decide, keep things crunchy"(October 5, 1996, 20). Readers are also positioned as privileged insiders: the journalists are encouraged to write "as if they were sitting by the fireside, talking to an intelligent friend" (December 22, 1990, 34).[51] Readers, then, are invited to share and identify with the elite masculine credentials of Economese, which are far from subtly signaled by the exaggeratedly masculine, phallocentric codes of the house style.

However, one might argue that this style is so incredibly crude and clichéd that few self-respecting, educated Western male readers would "buy" it (and it clearly does irritate some readers).[52] As readers of popular culture, we are now extremely sophisticated in comparison with, say, thirty years ago, and are well attuned to all the ploys and strategies of gendered codes and conventions. What saves the exaggeratedly masculine style of *The Economist* from our potential ridicule, however, is the very fact that it is clearly and self-consciously exaggerated. This fits in with the whole tone of the paper, which is one of ironic sophistication. On one level, the subject matter of *The Economist* is very serious (often deadly serious when it comes to war, civil war, famines, and so forth), but on the other hand, the slightly ironic tone makes all this grim reality more palatable, less tragic, more distant, more of a game.

While the exnomination of *The Economist*'s editorial puts an emotional distance between the paper and its subject matter, so irony puts emotional distance between the reader and the subject matter—emotional distance and control being a central feature of bourgeois-rational masculinity (Seidler 1989). Gentle humor is used in jokey headlines, cartoons, and photograph captions.[53] Irony is used in the text to brighten up the subject matter. For example, a 1991 article on multipolar power balancing started: "Nice to have got rid of communism. Pity the result will be anarchy" (21 December 1991, 65). Irony lapsed into full-blown sarcasm in the ludicrous "improvements" to the U.S. constitution recommended in July 1995, such as prohibition on "rolling a person in the flag when he/she is on fire, except in a manner to be prescribed by law [because] it is no fun passing an amendment unless . . . it stops people doing something they often and happily do. Besides, the prisons are not full enough" (July 8, 1995, 16).

As readers, if we are willing to accept the exaggerated realist conventions at face value, and are prepared to take on board the heavily signaled masculinity without even noticing it, then so much the better, as it is the naturalization of gender that gives it a great deal of its force. However, if the exaggerated masculinity of the house style is a joke, then we are a party to that joke—sophisticated and elite insiders who can both see through and at the same time enjoy the macho rhetorical style. As with the "top cats" billboard slogan, irony saves the masculine message and at the same time positions the readers as part of the educated, intelligent elite. It is a dangerous game, however. If the balance of subtle irony is tipped over into outright parody, then this may have subversive implications. Condemned to replaying culture's tropes, parodying them in the process can undermine their credibility, depending on circumstances.[54] The ironic deployment of the codes of hegemonic masculinity is therefore not as unambiguously reinforcing to the gender status quo as replaying them in a straight, naturalized fashion.

Another realist convention in reporting news and current affairs is the use of metaphor, one of the few literary devices (another is analogy) whose liberal use is permitted in masculine-coded "factual" discourse, perhaps because it reduces the need for long explanations and keeps the language terse. Metaphor affects narrative closure by placing material in clichéd slots, or categories of behavior, as a shorthand way of making (ideologically laden) common sense (Fiske 1987). Although one of the aims of Econometese is to "squeeze out unnecessary metaphors, adjectives and other argument-obscuring figures of speech" (*The Economist* December 22, 1990, 34), *The Economist* is in practice little different from other newspapers and journals in its heavy use of metaphor (often, mixed metaphor). Apparently, mixed metaphors are "the curse" of *The Economist*, such as when it was reported that the Republican Party had been called "a port in a storm for blacks. Fine words, but they buttered few parsnips when the numbers were added up" (December 22, 1990, 32).

Metaphors often carry gender connotations. In current-affairs reporting, the metaphors of sport, games, and war routinely help fix the meaning of politics, economics, and public events as masculine. Indeed, the metaphors of sport and war are virtually interchangeable, with wars often being reported in terms of game or sports strategy and sports being seen in terms of battle plans, not least because sports talk helps legitimize political policies and mobilize citizens for war through its appeal to nationalism and piety.[55] *The Economist* makes liberal use of these masculine-coded metaphors. For example, competition between large companies was characterized as a "clash of the titans" with only some "survivors" (November 2, 1996, 122); competition between airlines became a "battle for the skies"; and the extension of VAT was presented as a "VAT attack" (November 27, 1993, 6). International retailers had entered Asia "armed with an arsenal of high tech inventory management systems," but in 1996 were now "in retreat" with "plenty of casualties" after a local "counterattack" (September 28, 1996, 99). An attempt to control vehicle emissions was a "zero-sum game" (November 27, 1993, 7) and a presidential election was a "presidential race" (November 2, 1996, 61) in which to win one needed to play by "the rules of the game" (November 2, 1996, 68). In these cases, war and battle metaphors allude to and promote a citizen-warrior masculinity, while sports and gaming metaphors can also carry more gentlemanly or bourgeois overtones.

More disturbingly, metaphors of aggressive (hetero)sexual conquest and rape were not unknown in the pages of *The Economist*. For example, an article on Myanmar headlined "Ripe for Rape" included the following: "Asia's businessmen have had their eyes on Myanmar's rich resources for a while. Unlike most of its neighbours, it still has teak forests to be felled and its gem deposits are barely exploited. Its natural beauties and its astonishing Buddhist architecture make it potentially irresistible to tourists. . . . Businessmen are beginning to take the first steps toward exploiting this undeveloped land" (January 15, 1994, 65). Meanwhile, the government was "increasingly welcoming" to foreign businessmen. While it is difficult to imagine many *Economist* readers identifying themselves as either actual or potential rapists, at least metaphorically the reader may identify with the foreign (read *Western?*) businessmen hoping to rape this pubescent ("ripe") girl with her unexploited gems and irresistible natural beauties. The metaphor of territorial conquest as rape or sexual conquest has been in wide circulation in the West for so long that it has become "naturalized," nothing to pass comment on or even to notice (if you are a privileged white male reader who identifies with hegemonic masculinity, that is). This aggressive sexual imagery draws on colonial discourse about white, male exploration and adventure in "virgin territories." It derives in part from the early modern "conquistador" masculinity that is rather more warrior than citizen, mentioned in chapter 3 as one of the masculinities sustaining European colonialism (the other main one—involved in conversion and administration, being patriarchal—see Connolly 1989).

But perhaps the continuing real-life salience of this type of account can be seen when one remembers that Myanmar is next to Thailand, where the internationalization of the economy has led to one of the biggest sexploitation industries in the world (Enloe 1990). No doubt Myanmar would be "ripe" for the same experience. The only thing holding back such an eventuality was apparently another feminine presence, this time coded as strong and resistant: "The opposition leader, Aung San Suu Kyi, is still locked up in her home after more than four years. . . . They have yet to find a way of dealing with Aung San Suu Kyi: an invisible, silent, powerful presence" (January 15, 1994, 65).

It seems *The Economist* wanted to support, at the same time, both the raping businessmen and the resistant Aung San Suu Kyi. *The Economist's* general support for democracy and Aung San Suu Kyi's importance in the Myanmar democracy movement, together with their description of her as powerful, partly mitigated against the rape imagery. On the other hand, apart from the "rape" rhetoric proving offensive and alienating to potential female and Asian male readers (Asians of course, coded as effeminate in colonial racist discourse) at the level of metaphor, in this context it clearly signaled a tacit acceptance, promotion even, of international sex tourism that does in fact often involve forced prostitution, rape (often of minors), and even slavery in some cases, as *The Economist* itself has admitted only too readily (August 31, 1996, 15 and 35; September 21, 1996, 73).

The Myanmar quote may have been an extreme and particularly nasty example of the use of the rape metaphor, but it was not the only one that appeared during this period.[56] Only the following week, another reference was made to rape, this time in the headline of an article on wind farms in Wales. "A New Way to Rape the Countryside" (January 22, 1994, 26). This time it was the "masculine" rape of "feminine" nature, ironically effected by misguided environmentalists. In the context of such overt references to rape, numerous seemingly innocent phrases such as (in the same issue) the suggestion that changes are "forcing open the over-protected economy" of Israel began to carry aggressive sexual overtones (January 22, 1994, survey p. 4).

Other explicitly sexist metaphors and allusions have also been in evidence. For example, from later that year, "after years of watching Intel build its brand at IBM's expense, Big Blue must have found this as emotionally satisfying as a long-suffering sugar daddy cancelling an errant mistress's credit card" (December 17, 1994, 73). The rhetoric here invited the reader to identify with the sugar daddy—not least with the wealth and power over women that the expression implies. In another, similar, example, the sugar daddy was France, when Tahiti was described as "a kept woman," both "prosperous and protected [by her benefactor]" (July 15, 1995, 61–62).

Such sexually aggressive imagery serves to bolster the heterosexual credentials of *The Economist* (its stated attitude to gay sexuality notwithstanding). It also equates heterosexual masculinity with power, performance, and control, boosting the masculinist credentials of both the paper and its readers.[57] Without such aggressive markers of heterosexuality, such a homo-referential world as *The Economist* would automatically carry homoerotic connotations that, given subordinate status of homosexual masculinity, would undermine its "top cat" pretensions.

## Advertising

One can only assume that the "World Profile" proved successful in its aims since the advertising content of the paper in the following years faithfully reflected its themes. An analysis of the full-page display advertisements (excluding recruitment, academic courses, and classified advertising) in the October 7, 1995, edition of *The Economist* found a fairly typical mix of advertisements split between banks and financial services (twenty-one advertisers);[58] computing (hardware and software) and telecoms (fourteen advertisers);[59] airlines and hotels (thirteen advertisers), plus an ad for the purchase of executive jets;[60] exclusive gents' clothes and watches (nine advertisers);[61] major corporations (eight advertisers);[62] executive cars (seven advertisers),[63] and a number of miscellaneous advertisements, including full- and half-page ones for newspapers and journals, business conferences and courses, luggage, Eurostar rail travel, the British army, commercial radio, and government-sponsored export zones.[64]

Some of this advertising overlapped with advertisements published in the British quality daily press—such as advertisements for cars, men's clothes, and airlines, while other advertisements were less widely circulated, particularly ones for investment banks and such items as gents' Swiss watches and executive jets.[65] Display advertising is clearly a way in which a variety of models of masculinity in wider circulation get inserted into the pages of *The Economist*, models that may either resonate with or contradict the editorial line. The next chapter will explore particular display advertisements and the variously nuanced gendered meanings they contain in more detail. However, virtually all display advertisements in *The Economist* are up-market, and in many cases their styles and content reflect, reinforce, and complement the signs and codes of hegemonic masculinity in the editorial pages.

In the fairly typical issue mentioned above, several types of masculinity

ALCATEL
ALSTHOM

Paris, September 27, 1995 - Three months after his appointment as Chairman and CEO of Alcatel Alsthom, Serge Tchuruk presented to the Board of Directors both his analysis of the Group's situation and the results for the first half of 1995. The Board approved the strategic direction and the action plans proposed.

The deterioration of the Group's situation observed in 1994 has continued during the first half of 1995, in which a net loss of FF 1.2 billion was recorded, and no improvement is expected in the second half of the year. The Telecom Sector and, to a lesser extent the Cable Sector, have seen their results significantly deteriorate in a difficult period, but one in which the Group's other activities have resisted well.

## A bad 1995 and a vigorous program of recovery

The Board of Directors took note of the commitment of the new management team to progressively re-establish the situation in order to reach a good level of profitability for 1998, as well as the need to reflect in the year-end 1995 balance sheet future restructuring costs and a write-off of excess goodwill.

Dynamic action plans have been launched. They aim to achieve a rapid recovery through an improvement of FF 7 billion per year in productivity based particularly on the restructuring, to be completed in 1998, of the sectors in difficulty. Simultaneously, aggressive strategies are being implemented in a number of sectors, in particular in the Telecom Sector. These should materialize, in terms of activities and results, the massive investments in technology of the last several years.

The Chairman emphasized that Alcatel Alsthom, which has leading positions worldwide and many technological assets, is a coherent and balanced Group and does not require any major divestments in its core businesses.

### Results at June 30, 1995

With net sales stable at FF 78.3 billion for the first half of 1995, the Group's operating income was FF 1.8 billion, compared with FF 4.4 billion for the first six months of 1994. A loss of FF 1.2 billion in net income was recorded, compared with a profit of FF 2.0 billion for the corresponding period in the preceding year.

**KEY FINANCIAL DATA**

| (in FF millions) | June 30, 1995 | June 30, 1994 | Dec. 31, 1994 |
|---|---|---|---|
| Net Sales | 78,333 | 78,079 | 167,643 |
| Income from operations after financing | 1,797 | 4,376 | 9,492 |
| Net Income | (1,231) | 2,022 | 3,620 |

The decrease of FF 2.6 billion in income from operations results from a decrease of FF 2.2 billion for the Telecom Sector – which recorded an operating loss of FF 0.6 billion – and of FF 0.4 billion for the Cable Sector. The Telecom Sector has been particularly affected by a decrease in equipment prices resulting from an aggressive environment exacerbated by competition among operators. In addition, the European markets have suffered from an unfavorable economic climate.

Furthermore, several other factors of a structural nature have impacted the financial results:

- The strategy for external growth, which has reinforced the Group's position, today affects the results, because of the market downturn that followed the acquisitions;
- the Group's productivity efforts have not created sufficient cost savings to compensate for the decreases in prices;
- the organization, particularly of Alcatel Telecom, based on a geographical segmentation of activities and a proliferation of independent subsidiaries, did not evolve sufficiently to allow an effective response to increasing market globalization.

### Actions for recovery

To correct the Group's current situation, the Chairman proposed a major action program of which the principal outlines are set out below. This program should permit annual productivity gains of FF 7 billion to be realized by 1998.

**Reorganizations**

In addition to the creation in July of an Executive Committee of Alcatel Alsthom – a decision-making body for the Group – a major reorganization will occur inside Alcatel Telecom as of January 1996. In order to better respond to the globalization of its markets, Alcatel Telecom has been reorganized along product lines into eight Divisions having worldwide responsibility for profit and loss, as well as for strategy, research and development, manufacturing and marketing.

To reinforce the efficiency and coherence of its commercial undertakings, Alcatel Telecom's actions will henceforth be coordinated by a single interface for each geographic market and each large client account.

Additionally, at the Alcatel Alsthom group level, the management of treasury, foreign exchange, and financing is now centralized, and the human resources and communication functions have been strengthened in order to favor a greater openness.

**Restructuring**

New restructuring plans will be implemented to permit the Group to benefit from the economies of scale that its size and world-wide position make possible. Based on the current state of analyses in process, their total cost will reach FF 10-12 billion, resulting in the establishment, at the end of 1995, of a restructuring reserve to cover the period 1996 to 1998.

During the next two years, non-core assets will be disposed of for approximately FF 10 billion.

**Readjustment of Balance Sheet Asset Values**

The Group will re-estimate the value of its intangible assets in order to take into account the change in profitability outlook of certain acquisitions. This review should result in a goodwill write-off of FF 10-12 billion.

### Revision of Industrial Strategy

Alcatel Alsthom's revision of its industrial strategy is focused principally on the Telecom Sector. The objective is to strengthen its position as a major player in all segments of the market, while restoring a good level of profitability.

With this in view, three directions have already been defined:

- Pursuing software developments of the E10 and S12 switching systems in order to offer competitive advantages to the Group's large, traditional customers from an installed base of Alcatel equipment that is the largest in the world;
- making a firm commitment to mobile communications,with a reinforcement of its team and an acceleration of developments;
- engaging in more aggressive commercial actions aimed at new operators and at emerging or high potential markets.

Many actions are being undertaken to incorporate into Alcatel Telecom's financial results the technological advances achieved over the last few years in the areas of transmission, subscriber access, intelligent networks and ATM.

In this connection, Alcatel Telecom has today signed with Hermes Europe Railtel (a consortium of 11 rail transport operators) a contract – the first phase of which is valued at FF 1.3 billion – for the supply of an SDH fiber optic data transmission network which will soon link 55 European cities.

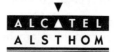

FIGURE 4.1. Ad for Alcatel Alsthom (*The Economist* October 7, 1995, 139). Masquerading as editorial, this advertisement's text-based austerity and lack of visual imagery signify pure bourgeois rationalism.

were on show. At one extreme were the full-page advertisements that presented themselves as if they were editorial, providing business and economic analysis in dry, often closely written, black-and-white text only. Examples include Alcatel Alsthom, which presented its chairman's report (October 7, 1995, 139) (see fig. 4.1); SBC Warburg, which advertised its share-flotation figures (October 7, 1995, 140–41), as did the Mitsubishi Bank (106), and Hughes Electronics, whose "editorial" discussed some of the applications of its products (42). Then there were those advertisements that included small drawings or photographs, along with technical jargon and specifications. Examples include the U.S. Army field jacket (161), IBM's new UNIX system (72–73), and the Meridiana airline (31). Such austere advertisements reinforce and replay the conventions of a bourgeois-rational model of hegemonic masculinity. As an alternative to dry, bourgeois-rational austerity, some advertisements use glossy color to depict the luxury and power of wealth and success. In the October 7, 1995, issue it was particularly noticeable in car advertisements, such as Honda (91), which invited us to "invest in precious metal," and Jaguar (78–79), with "don't dream it, drive it." However, even in glossy advertisements for luxury goods, sepia tones and muted colors can signal a degree of bourgeois-rational restraint, as with the advertisements for Vacheron Constantin watches (122) (fig. 4.2) and Astra executive jets (83). One or two ads deployed crude phallic symbolism, such as Swiss Life (14), with its mountain peak rising out of the sea, resonating with the crasser sexual metaphors that occasionally appear in the editorial pages.

## The Treatment of Women

Women have not been entirely neglected by The Economist, in spite of its masculine readership. The approach to women has not so much been one of exclusion as assimilation. Throughout the period under review, there have been occasional articles analyzing the economic and political situation of women, largely from a liberal-feminist perspective. For example, a special report on women's political and employment status in the European Community, "Europe's Women: How the Other Half Works" (June 30, 1990, 21–24) advocated more reforms to enable equal employment opportunities for women; another leader gave a plug for women's education in developing countries (September 21, 1991, 18); and a third advised that women might avoid the corporate glass ceiling by setting up their own companies

FIGURE 4.2. Ad for Vacheron Constantin watches (*The Economist* October 7, 1995, 122). The advertisement, with its drawing-room scene in the background, invokes the world of the aristocratic gentleman of the eighteenth century. Its muted tones also signify bourgeois masculinity (the real aristocracy would have made more flamboyant use of color) and nostalgia. Ads such as this one for a luxury Swiss watch help to establish *The Economist*'s elite credentials.

(August 10, 1996, 61). Meanwhile a schools brief examined women at work (March 5, 1994, 96–97). Of course, such articles only serve to highlight the fact that the majority of the paper is about men, although this has not generally been explicitly recognized. When individual women have played an unmistakable part in the normal coverage of politics and current affairs, they have tended to be treated as "one of the boys." For example, Mrs. Thatcher was regularly regarded as the embodiment of "warrior" masculinity. In "Thatcher v. Europe," *The Economist* argued that "Battle is joined. Europe must win—for Britain's sake," while "Mrs Thatcher publicly gave warning that, for her, this battle was different" (November 3, 1990, 17).[66]

The explicit reporting of gender issues noticeably increased in 1995–96. Two articles on employment, for example, one from 1994 and one from 1995, showed contrasting approaches to gender. In 1994, a discussion of the movement of low-skilled jobs to the developing world was titled "Working Man's Dread" (October 1, 1994, survey, 16–20) and used statistics on men's wages to back up its arguments. The discussion itself did not raise the different impact of restructuring on women as an issue—indeed, it used the terms *men* and *workers* interchangeably. The following year, in a similar discussion of economic restructuring, "Whistling While They Work" (January 28, 1995, 47) workers were no longer conflated with men and the impact of economic restructuring was analyzed separately for each sex. Reports such as one on Russian feminists (August 12, 1995, 34–35), female indentured laborers in California (August 12, 1995, 39), and South African feminists (October 5, 1996, 123) started to appear.

There was also a noticeable increase in the reporting of women who appeared to depart from the bounds of "normal" politics and economics. Such women were often reported on in sidebar anecdotes, separate from the main story. Anecdotes boxed in sidebars have covered such topics as British women in prison, "Jailbirds" (July 15, 1995, 18), a black female basketball coach "Looking Down on Tall White Men" (August 5, 1995, 46), and the Swedish minister of parliament who telecommuted from home to her "Log Cabinet" while changing her baby's nappies (diapers) (February 25, 1995, 52). Sometimes sidebars have been used to give negative verdicts on feminist demands. One was used to chide Nordic entrants to the European Union for being overly concerned about the balance of the sexes at the commission (February 25, 1995, 51).[67] Other such displays provide amusement, as when Japanese "office ladies" holiday spending money was reported to damp the rise of the yen in "Ladies to the Rescue" (May 6, 1995, 114) and when Swedish women finally made it into the fire brigade in "Sweden's Splashy Women" (September 7, 1996, 42).

To ignore gender issues in contemporary circumstances when they are clearly a part of current affairs would imply a kind of bunker mentality that would be far from reassuring to male readers. The occasional in-depth report on the progress of women in public life plus the use of humorous boxed-in anecdotes can give the paper a false sense of gender "balance" while at the same time legitimizing its main masculinist message, not least by implying that men get on with the serious and important business of life and women provide the embellishment. But perhaps sidebar anecdotes also allow topics that might not otherwise have been included at all to appear in a not-too-threatening fashion, without creating undue discomfort for readers who are otherwise being invited to identify with hegemonic masculinity. Underneath the joking, some serious points have been made. The stories may also be read differently by different audiences, appealing to both New Men and the occasional woman reader as progressive, while providing "male bonding" material for unreconstructed men.

To SUM UP, *The Economist* 1989–96 was thoroughly saturated with the signifiers of masculinity, in its self-promotions, its content, layout, house style, use of language, and advertising. A good deal of these signifiers were elitist, heterosexist, and even imperial. Bourgeois rationalism and citizen-warrior versions of hegemonic masculinity appear to have been woven into the very fabric of the paper, while aristocratic variations played a smaller role. While they may not have had a monopoly on the representation of gender, this triad of hegemonic masculinities, which are well entrenched in Anglo-Saxon spheres, have formed the staple fare of gendered representation in the paper.[68] What makes them all the more potent is that they are constantly signified and resignified in a myriad of subtly and not so subtly different combinations, but are rarely referred to directly, so that the world is viewed from the exnominated perspective of hegemonic masculinity. In the context of such a wealth of signifiers of masculinity, even apparently gender-neutral copy and advertisements are likely to be interpreted as referring to a masculine world (and therefore actually contribute to the discursive construction of that world, regardless of intention), unless women are specifically re-ferred to.

The 11 percent of readers (in 1990) who were women may have been pro-fessional, but it is clear they could never be "top cats." They were constant-ly invited to take up masculine subject positions by the imagery and rhetor-ical strategies, which as argued above constitute *The Economist's* masculine credentials. Although women may read papers such as *The Economist* as if they were honorary men, and are probably used to seeing the public world through the eyes of hegemonic masculinity, such subject positions are al-ways liable to be disrupted when women become clearly "the other," as in the rape rhetoric discussed above.[69] Thus female readers find it hard to take up stable subject positions.[70] Reading or subscribing to *The Economist* is therefore always likely to be a more ambiguous pleasure for professional, en-trepreneurial, and managerial women, and less bolstering of their identities *as women*, than it is to elite or would-be elite men.

# CHAPTER FIVE

# The Economist, Globalization, and Masculinities

A dynamic element needs to be introduced into this hitherto static analysis. So far I have been concerned to demonstrate how constructions of masculinity in *The Economist* form a mutually reinforcing and apparently seamless web. This web legitimates hegemonic masculinity and, while actually made up of a number of shifting ingredients, gives it a sense of continuity. However, there is also an important competitive aspect to the construction of masculinities in *The Economist*, a competitive aspect that provides a dynamic atmosphere that can accommodate change fairly easily. This chapter—continuing chapter 4's textual analysis of the paper by seeking to examine the relationship between changes in hegemonic masculinity and the topic of globalization as it was presented in *The Economist* during the period under study—concentrates on the dynamic aspect. In addition to mapping the actual changes that have taken place in the construction of hegemonic masculinity, this chapter also provides a clear illustration of the proposition made in chapters 2 and 3, that would-be hegemonic masculinities compete, drawing on strategies of masculinization and feminization in the process.

The chapter is divided into two parts: a preliminary section that briefly explores the historic development of masculinities in business and shows how they are articulated in *The Economist* in a way that gives rise to a competitive, hothouse atmosphere of rivalry between different masculinities; and a second, more substantial, part that focuses on globalization and change. This second part starts with a general discussion of globalization and its relationship to gender, then returns to *The Economist* to examine the discourse of globalization and the accompanying changing constructions of masculinity that are produced and reproduced in the paper in confusing profusion. These, often contradictory, changes, each interpreting the relationship between globalization and gender in a different way, are identified. Some of them reflect competition between different gendered interests and some may also reflect short-term developments in the world outside, such as economic downturns and upturns.[1] However, certain trends can also be observed, trends that point toward the modernization of hegemonic masculinity in conjunction with the development of technocracy. I draw together my various observations and arguments in a short conclusion.

## Masculinities in Business

Until now the analysis has focused on exposing the established models of hegemonic masculinity in circulation in both *The Economist* and in IR. The emphasis in this section shifts to examining the competitive relationship between these models, a relationship that in *The Economist* is at its clearest in the business and economics sections. As one might expect, the portrayal of masculinities in business in the pages of *The Economist* reflects their wider history.

According to Peter Stearns, early businessmen saw themselves as warriors, rather than rationalists:

> War and the Darwinian jungle were the moral analogues of modern business. Not a few of the early businessmen had military experience in the wars that spanned the 1770s to 1815. Still more thought of business organisation in terms of military chains of command, with themselves as generals. Business was hailed as the modern substitute for war, with none of the bloodshed and devastation (only rising prosperity) but with all of the male virtues. "Henceforth there shall be business centuries, as in the past there have been military centuries" (Jules Burat, Paris 1845). To a middle-class

world tired of war, this was appealing. Certainly it made the businessman no whit less a man (Stearns 1979, 83).

Rationality as a prized quality arrived only in late-Victorian times with the rise of the professions and bureaucracy. Stearns argues that World War I dealt a death blow to the glorification of the warrior, so that in the twentieth century the "Darwinian jungle" became a rat race instead, with commercial survival and self-justification as family provider the only goals of more rationalist businessmen.

Connell, too, argues that the two world wars killed off versions of hegemonic masculinity organized around the heroism of violence, leaving a conflict between the masculinity of domination (patriarchal, or at least paternalistic) and one of expertise (meritocratic and thoroughly bourgeois-rational) in the postwar corporate world (Connell 1993). By the 1970s, hegemonic masculinity was organized around technocratic rationality and calculation sustained by the hypermasculine myth of toughness, power and strength, competitiveness, confidence, and ability to face down opponents (Carrigan et al 1985).

The business world portrayed in *The Economist* reflects this heritage. It is largely one of a Darwinistic struggle, and while in *The Economist*'s rhetoric these struggles are often conducted through the metaphors of war and sport, evolutionary metaphors are equally common.[2] The international business world is portrayed as a basically evolutionary one where competition in the marketplace ensures the survival of the fittest.[3] For example, in October 1996 financial firms that were not adapting to new opportunities created by technological advances were warned that "today's insurers, bankers and brokers could turn out to be dinosaurs, with new technologies playing the role of the destructive meteor, and only a few surviving in unpredictable new forms. More technologically adept creatures may take over, remaking the industry along entirely different lines" (October 26, 1996, survey, 5).

What counts as fittest is not necessarily force, strength, or size but rather an eclectic range of traits—never stable but always changing to whatever the market requires at any given moment. At the heart of survival, therefore, is intelligence and strategy—bourgeois-rational traits rather than overtly military ones. In terms of the editorial line, at least, bourgeois-rationalism, with warrior trappings, rules the corporate world.

However, within the competitive framework formed by a master discourse of social Darwinism, more specific and contradictory constructions
of masculinity have been inserted into the paper, both through advertising
and through discussion of competing strategies for business success. Indeed,
in an atmosphere of relentless competition, styles of hegemonic masculinity become grist to the mill of business success. Specific elements of hegemonic masculinities are played and replayed in a variety of combinations
and with different emphases. For example, aristocratic constructions have
had a mixed press. Some advertisements have shown status in a positive
light, particularly those advertising status goods and services such as exclusive watches and first-class air travel (see fig. 4.2). Other corporate advertisements have preferred to stress technocratic expertise to status. Nomura
Bank, of Switzerland, managed to combine both when it offered "Nomura
knowledge" as "a priceless privilege for the very few" (November 17, 1990,
17). In the same edition, less status-conscious but nevertheless paternalistic
forms of masculinity vied with the entrepeneurialism of Young Turks, so
that while AEtna Investment stressed "true wisdom" and "over a century of
successful investment experience" (November 17, 1990, 100), showing a
close-up of a wise pair of eyes under greying, shaggy eyebrows (fig. 5.1), a few
pages later Knight-Ridder went for youthful energy with the following:
"You've met the competition? Now let's talk about us. We're not fat cats.
We're fast cats" (November 17, 1990, 136–37). A recurrent theme in business
competition was the threat of a kind of symbolic patricide (normally associated with patriarchal social systems), where size and experience competed
with youth and entrepreneurial chutzpah: "The business heroes of the recent past have not been multinational company men, but entrepreneurs
who have turned start ups into money machines. . . . Anybody with a
bright idea and a rented garage, it seemed, could take on the giants and
win" (June 24, 1995, survey, 3).

It is here, in the detail rather than the overall editorial outlook of the paper, that competition between different forms of masculinity takes place. Although the staple images of hegemonic masculinity in *The Economist* discussed here continued to be reproduced in the paper throughout the period
under review, there were also some interesting changes. Established models
of hegemonic masculinity, loosely organized around bourgeois-rationality
with various degrees of paternalism and warrior trappings, were increasingly
challenged by newer constructions of corporate masculinity, but in a

FIGURE 5.1. Ad for AEtna Investment (*The Economist* November 17, 1990, 100). This advertisement offering "wisdom" identifies financial services with a benevolent paternalism. Produced in black and white, it signifies bourgeois-rational restraint rather than a display of wealth and luxury.

process that was neither simple nor straightforward. It is this process of change, which in the paper has been associated with an increasing emphasis on globalization, that the rest of the chapter will focus on. This starts with a general discussion of the relationship between gender and globalization.

## Gender and Globalization

Contemporary globalization can be seen as an open-ended process involving political, economic, technological, and institutional change and is closely related to the social, psychological, and aesthetic changes associated with the "condition of post-modernity" (Harvey 1989). It is a complex condition in which, through increasing linkages and ever-more-instantaneous communications, the world is being reconstituted as a single social space (although not necessarily a single society), as time and space are shrunk. The nature and extent of contemporary developments is highly controversial and as yet unclear. Globalization has been characterized both as a long-term trend with a number of phases (Robertson 1990) and as a discontinuous phenomenon (Harvey 1989; Gilpin 1987). Its causes have variously been identified as technological progress (Rosenau 1990); developments in capitalism (Harvey 1989); and power politics in the presence of a liberal hegemon (Gilpin 1987). Robertson (1990) and Giddens (1990) name multifactorial causes. Globalization and postmodernity together either represent a dramatic break with the modern era, heralding a neomedievalism, or an intensification of various aspects of modernity (Harvey 1989; Smart 1992).

The intention here is not to get involved in academic controversies about globalization and its causes but rather to characterize it as a developing and open-ended contemporary discourse (in the full-blooded, constitutive sense of discourse — that is, involving material and institutional processes as well as rhetoric) and thus emphasize political process rather than cause and effect.[4] The overall outcome of this open-ended process will depend on the interacting suboutcomes of a "thick" interconnecting web of ongoing political struggles, processes, and decisions in many diverse arenas of life (transcending the various divisions between private, public, and international) and in many geographical locations. Seeing globalization at least in part as a broadly political process allows one to examine the ensuing struggles over direction, nature, and scope of developments between differ-

ent interests, including power struggles between different gendered interests. In the jostling for position between would-be hegemonic groups, different "elements" or ingredients of masculinity are co-opted in new or old configurations to serve particular interests, and particular gendered (and other)
identities are consolidated and legitimated or downgraded and devalued. It
is important to examine such struggles, not least because they help to steer
and influence more traditionally studied social, institutional, economic,
and "political" developments in particular directions, as well as to reflect
them.

In terms of political economy, global economic restructuring—associated with the introduction of new technologies, global capital mobility, the
new international division of labor, and new forms of regionalism—has
set in motion a complex set of economic, political, and social changes.[5]
Gender relations form an integral part of this restructuring, not least
through the casualization and feminization of the workforce, as women's
participation in the cash economy, already increasing on a long-term basis,
has accelerated in recent years. This has been accompanied by the erosion
of welfare provision, the collapse of the family wage system, and a corresponding increase in female-headed households in metropolitan countries.
Overall, it appears that, although women's work is playing an increasingly
central part in both productive and reproductive spheres, and while some
women have gained more autonomy from men in their personal lives and a
few have even benefited from expanded opportunities for women at the professional level, this has been accompanied by a dramatic shift toward the
feminization of poverty (McDowell 1991; Runyan 1996). But the feminization of the workforce has also killed the old compact between male workers,
industrial capital, and the institutions of welfare Keynesianism in developed
countries; it has also in many cases undermined men's personal authority
in the family and has reduced the value of so-called masculine attributes in
the labor market. Linda McDowell goes so far as to argue that "gender is being used to divide women's and men's interests in the labor market in such
a way that *both* sexes—at least among the majority of the population, are
losing out" (1991, 401). While media attention has been focused on the loss
of manufacturing jobs in developed countries and the challenge to blue-
collar masculinities predicated on the male breadwinning role, there
are other links between global restructuring and changes in hegemonic
masculinities.

The gradual softening of hegemonic masculinities in the West (noted above in chapter 2) coincided with the start of global capitalist restructuring, which began after the collapse of the Bretton Woods currency system in the early 1970s (McDowell 1991). Other indicators also support the idea that this softening of hegemonic masculinities is linked to, or is even an integral part of, the processes of globalization. First, the decline in conscription means that military service is no longer a universal rite of passage for men, undermining the ties between hegemonic masculinity and the military.[6] Second, activities and qualities that were previously defined as feminine or effeminate are being increasingly integrated into hegemonic masculinity as the global economy is restructured. Men in the developed world are now positioned as consumers, a traditionally feminine role (Mort 1988; Barthel 1992).[7] Anglo-American mainstream culture is becoming increasingly, if subtly, homo-erotic, as exemplified by the narcissistic display of male bodies in advertising imagery (Mort 1988; Simpson 1994; Bordo 1999); a new "soft boiled," killing-but-caring type of white hero has appeared in popular cinema (Pfeil 1995); and business and managerial strategies are changing to emphasize the formerly feminine qualities of flexibility, interpersonal skills, and team working (Connell 1993). While the feminization of the workforce at first meant casualization at the lower end of the job market as a strategy to reduce labor costs, as global restructuring has gathered pace, such phenomena as delayering, outsourcing, and the casualization of employment practices has started to hit professional and managerial staff. It is argued that this phase of the feminization of working practices and managerial strategies, which might on the face of it offer improved career prospects for professional women, is being accompanied by redefinitions of hegemonic masculinity, so that professional men can stay ahead of the employment game, albeit under less-secure conditions. For example, flexibility in job descriptions and career paths is being reinterpreted as "masculine" risk taking and entrepeneurialism; and computers have lost their feminine associations with keyboard skills, now being marketed as macho power machines (Connell 1995, 146). The techniques of alternative therapy forged in the 1960s counterculture, which were originally used by antisexist men and feminist sympathizers to discover their so-called feminine side, are now widely used in management-training seminars designed to cultivate interpersonal skills and group work and in mythopoetic men's-movement workshops that claim to develop the emotional "wild man" within (Connell 1995, 206–11; Pfeil 1995). According to Donaldson, men's-movement activists criticize hegemonic masculinity in an attempt to colonize women's jobs in an increasing-ly competitive male job market (Donaldson 1993). Since there are different kinds of men's movements, some of which are more sympathetic to femi-nists than others, Donaldson is probably correct with respect to some of the more dubious groups.[8] Such activities are not only socializing white, mid-dle-class men into feminized working practices but are crucially redefining these practices as masculine. As Connell argues, "the larger consequence of the popular forms of masculinity therapy is an adaptation of patriarchal structures through the *modernization* of masculinity" (Connell 1995, 211).

In the struggle to transform hegemonic masculinity, there is a rivalry be-tween New Men and a backlash masculinity supported by disaffected blue-collar males who have lost both their job security and their patriarchal posi-tions in the family. In the United States these are the "angry white males" who disciplined Bill Clinton, the "new style" president, forcing him to rein-vent himself as an "all American man's man" who would keep Hillary, "the wicked witch of the West," out of the public eye, at least until the latter part of his presidency (*Independent on Sunday* February 12, 1995). There is also a complex relationship of rivalry, accommodation, and even synthesis be-tween Western models of hegemonic masculinity and those presented by the rising powers of Asia. Whereas in the past countries such as Japan and China were coerced into adopting Western standards through the treaty-port system, and incorporated them in part in order to qualify for entry into the European-dominated international society of states (Suganimi 1984; Gong 1984), now the prize is a stronger position within a more thoroughly globalized capitalist production system, and perhaps also in international politics.[9]

In all these various struggles between different styles or types of hege-monic and would-be hegemonic masculinities, each variety is being modi-fied by the interest group(s) it represents, in response to the perceived suc-cesses of the others. At stake in these struggles is the pace and direction of global restructuring itself, and the composition of the masculine elite with-in that process.

## Globalization in The Economist

*The Economist* presents itself as a global rather than parochial paper for the political and business elite. With its largely male readership and abundance of masculine signifiers, it cannot help but be heavily implicated in interpretive struggles over masculinity and globalization. Over the period under analysis, changing images in advertisements and changing uses of language in the paper suggest that hegemonic masculinity is undergoing a gradual transformation. But before embarking on a detailed discussion of the presentation of globalization and changing masculinities, it is worth pointing out that the paper has been very "busy" with a confusing range of diverse, complex, and often contradictory new constructions and reconfigurations. There is no simple movement from one kind of hegemonic masculinity to another, but rather a number of gendered moves in different directions. These moves have often been contradictory, some pulling one way and some pulling another, and some even undermining hegemonic masculinity altogether. Thus there is no uniformity of imagery and plenty of room for confusion, unexpected juxtapositions, and even profeminist imagery.

However, there have been at least four main identifiable trends: (1) a decline in patriarchal and paternalistic imagery; (2) in keeping with the theories mentioned above, a softening of hegemonic masculinity toward a New Man construction; (3) in apparent contradiction to the softening trend, an aggressive remasculinization process that is associated with globalization itself and the new technologies that go with it; and (4) a degree of gender anxiety connected with all this flux and change. In the following account of these changes, the material is not neatly divided up into the four categories mentioned here. The account moves back and forth between them, to indicate the cheek-by-jowl nature of these diverse changes and the constant jostling for position between different masculinities.

The transformation of hegemonic masculinity outlined here is inherently unstable, but is nevertheless being articulated through and to large extent steered by a kind of master discourse that sets a clear framework for the interpretation of change. This master discourse is the lens through which the corporate world is viewed: it is the discourse of social Darwinism and of ongoing competition between different styles of masculinity in the pursuit of corporate fitness.

Struggles over the direction of change, outlined below, have taken place alongside a tide of rhetoric about globalization. Globalization itself has been presented as a glamorous process at the cutting edge of progressive capitalist development. It is regarded as a primarily economic force that is causing large changes in every society throughout the world—one that is "enforcing a kind of natural selection between those cultures which rise to the challenge and those which do not" (November 9, 1996, 30). *The Economist* has tracked changes to corporate structure, management strategies, and employment patterns throughout the period in question, focusing on the intensification of competition, which it sees as a principal effect of globalization.[10] Old hierarchies have been challenged, not only by financial deregulation and increased global capital mobility since the 1980s, but also by the widespread introduction of computers and new communications technology, leading to a more integrated global economy.[11] Globalization has been seen as wholly beneficial to developing countries, with multinational companies that were formerly seen as arms of Western imperialism now welcomed as "the embodiment of modernity and the prospect of wealth: full of technology, rich in capital, replete with skilled jobs" (March 27, 1993, survey, 3).

In developed countries, although restructuring problems, which include threats to blue-collar workers and even to highly skilled workers, have been acknowledged, *The Economist* has argued that the promise of new markets and the workings of comparative advantage would iron out any problems:[12] "Fears that low wage economies will eventually pinch many of the rich world's jobs are overdone. . . . In the long run, trade has no lasting effect on total employment in a country providing its labour markets are flexible. Emerging economies will spend their export revenues from textiles and consumer electronics on more sophisticated products from industrial economies" (November 2, 1996, 20). Indeed, globalization and information technology mean that the world economy now works more like the liberal economic textbooks say it should, with increased competition and less distortion of markets: "The theory of perfect competition, a basic building block of conventional textbook economics, optimistically assumes abundant information, zero transaction costs and no barriers to entry. Computers and advanced telecommunications help to make these assumptions less far-fetched" (September 28, 1996, survey, 50).[13] *The Economist* has been resolutely upbeat in its assessment of globalization, arguing that "for the rich world, almost as much as for today's poor countries, the next twenty-five years will be a time of unprecedented opportunity" (October 1, 1994, survey, 3).

There appears to be hardly a cloud on the horizon of this brave new world, except for the threat of beggar-thy-neighbor protectionism spawned by a failure of developed countries to adjust by investing in education to retrain and upgrade their formerly blue-collar workforce (October 1, 1994, survey, 22). As globalization has not been credited with eroding economic sovereignty (this idea was seen as a political smokescreen for introducing unpopular but beneficial changes in policy), it is not regarded as an unstoppable bandwagon, but rather a precious protégé that needs nurturing and promoting (October 7, 1995, 15–16).

### Globalization and Frontier Masculinity

The importance that the 1990s *Economist* attached to the promise of globalization can hardly be overstated. But perhaps the most powerful boost to globalization came not through direct editorial attention to the subject, which tended to be analytical, but rather through the dominant imagery, which integrated science, technology, business, and images of globalization into a kind of entrepreneurial "frontier" masculinity in which capitalism meets science fiction. The "frontier" has historically played a defining part in the creation of a hegemonic WASP (white, Anglo-Saxon, Protestant) masculinity in the United States since the nineteenth century (Kimmel 1987). It has undergone a number of metamorphoses, with accompanying imagery stretching from the cowboys of the old "wild West" to space exploration.

This particular incarnation, a futuristic vision of globalization in which science and business mix to solve all our problems (including environmental ones), has been played out through special surveys with science-fictionalized titles that reflect the increasing role of virtual computer technologies in the global economy: "Telecommunications: Netting the Future" (March 10, 1990); "Artificial Intelligence: Minds in the Making" (March 14, 1992); "Defence in the 21st Century: Breaking Free" (September 5, 1992); "The Frontiers of Finance" (October 9, 1993); "The Global Economy: War of the Worlds" (October 1, 1994); "Television: Feeling for the Future" (February 12, 1994); "The Future of Medicine-Peering into 2010" (March 19, 1994); and "The World Economy: The Hitchhikers' Guide to Cybernomics" (September 28, 1996). These titles have often been illustrated with science-fiction imagery, such as bug-eyed aliens (March 27, 1993) and battling spaceships (October 1, 1994). As can be seen from the topics covered, technology and speed were central motifs in the technocratic rhetoric of globalization that saturated *The Economist* in this period. For example, the survey entitled

"The Frontiers of Finance" (October 9, 1993) devoted twenty-eight pages entirely to the question of computing power and predictions in global financial markets.

At the same time, images of planet Earth from space and corporate advertisements in which *global* was a buzzword became ubiquitous, as in the following illustrative examples taken from the two surveys quoted above: a Bank of New York advertisement featured a picture of the globe from space and mentioned the word *global* three times (October 1, 1994, survey, 17); ABB Group deployed similar imagery of the globe with several instances of the words *world* and *global* (October 1, 1994, survey, 24–25); Singapore Telecom showed a photo of planet Earth taken from the Moon and talked about its "mission" to be at the forefront of technology (March 27, 1993, survey, 9); and Ernst and Young (see fig. 5.2) featured the globe from space, with a satellite in the foreground, while claiming to operate in the "dynamic global marketplace" (March 27, 1993, survey, 15). Although elsewhere "spaceship Earth" imagery often carries environmental connotations, in the images of globalization in *The Economist*, this aspect has rarely been highlighted.[14] Instead, as in these examples, the image of planet Earth from space appeared to signify globalization in general.

This imagery positions globalization firmly in the glamorous, masculine conceptual space of the "international."[15] While "spaceship Earth" images reinforce the view of the world as a single locality—"the global village"—making it appear easily accessible in its entirety (Giddens 1990), at the same time, by the space-mission analogy, globalization is positioned as "out there," and the space of globalization becomes "the final frontier." It is "out there" in the international arena, where only intrepid businessmen dare to tread, as opposed to "in here," in the domestic space of businessmen's homes, where global restructuring has directed a tide of often illegal or under-age female migrants as domestic servants.[16] It is largely presented as a grand, top-down ideology that suits expansive business interests, rather than an as an everyday phenomenon touching domestic lives.[17] It "belongs to" an elite internationalist cosmopolitan culture of males, whom the reader is invited to join, at least in spirit. The world has become the adventure playground of the new, global business elite.

Latterly even the planet itself appears to have been too restrictive a playground in the science-fictionalized world of globalization. In corporate imagery, globalization has moved on to colonize space. For example, a Swiss

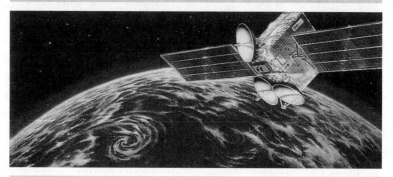

FIGURE 5.2. Ad for Ernst and Young (*The Economist* March 27, 1993, survey, 15). "Space, the final frontier" imagery is linked to the globalization of international business.

Life advertisement asked if the reader had any "extra terrestrial plans" (November 5, 1994, 17), and UniBanco featured an astronaut on a space walk with the slogan "The ground crew was there for him: we are here for you" (September 28, 1996, 82) (fig. 5.3). Hewlett Packard similarly pictured an astronaut in space, with the caption "You never know how far you want to go with your computer. HP PCs give you room to explore" (January 27, 1996, 22). France Telecom had cyclists racing between planets with the copy "Global networking partnerships to keep you in the lead virtually anywhere" (December 16, 1995, back cover), while Inmarsat showed a Mars-like planetary landscape and the slogan "Communicate with travellers in space and time." The Inmarsat copy read: "Long-distance truck drivers can find themselves in places so far beyond the reach of conventional communications, they might as well be on another planet" (September 21, 1996, 32–33). This imagery directly taps into U.S. frontier masculinity as immortalized by the Star Trek slogan "Space, the final frontier."

In its boosting of the brave new world of globalization, *The Economist* promotes what Beverley Burris describes as a "technocratic ideology" (Burris 1989, 458), based on the authority of experts, the legitimacy of science, and the mystique of advanced technology. The belief that technological innovation will solve all our problems is a form of "technological hubris" (Burris 1989, 458). The consequence is that the political and social choices of elite, male, decision makers become masked by an allegedly neutral system of technical imperatives and interests. *The Economist* is often served with a large helping of technological hubris in which the politics of globalization have become obscured in the service of technocratic business interests.

## Globalization, Feminization, and Japan

This technocratic frontier masculinity has not been the only masculinity associated with globalization in the paper. One concurrently running alternative has been characterized as an ongoing rivalry between competitive individualism and a more "feminized" cooperative style of management. This rivalry has often been articulated within a discourse of competition between Western and Asian business practices in corporate culture, pitting the United States against Japan and the "tiger economies" of the Far East.[18] As a regular theme in the paper throughout the period in question, the story took

FIGURE 5.3. Ad for UniBanco (*The Economist* September 28, 1996, survey, 81). Another advertisement that uses space imagery as a metaphor for globalization. Here the businessman is likened to an astronaut out on a space walk—a lone (male) hero at the frontier of human exploration.

various twists and turns. At times it was associated with a decline in paternalistic and patriarchal forms of business management. These were under
siege as globalization and the introduction of information technology
forced corporate change, in which both lifetime job security and numerous
layers of management were swept away: "It all comes down to a change in
thinking about how companies use knowledge. The old view was that strategy should be set by a tiny elite at the top. . . . Now the men at corporate
headquarters realise that decisions are often best taken by those who spend
their lives developing products or dealing with customers" (June 24, 1995,
survey, 5).

In 1990 it was noted that the introduction of computers, previously predicted to further increase the centralization of corporate decision making,
has in fact more often had a flattening effect, contributing to the substitu-
tion of markets for hierarchies (December 15, 1990, 89–90). In 1991, under
the heading "Change, then change again: As markets change, so must managers," *The Economist* survey of management education argued that while
every era has had its business and management fads, the globalization of
markets and the acceleration of technological change were both contributing to the need for more permanent changes in management practices. To
keep up with the pace of change, "western businesses are being forced to
toss old assumptions aside" (March 2, 1991, survey, 7). In this particular survey at least, *The Economist* prescribed a range of feminizing practices: cooperative joint ventures rather than rivalry; flatter companies with less hierarchy and internal divisions; more part-time and temporary workers;
cross-disciplinary and teamwork approaches; and a change in corporate culture as ethics and environmentalism emerge as a new set of "soft" issues
(March 2, 1991, survey, 7–8). Note the "feminized" language in the para-
graph subheaded "Soft to Touch, Hard to Grasp," which stated "the tough-
est challenge facing senior managers (and the business schools charged with
nurturing them) could come from a hard to define set of 'soft' problems"
(March 2, 1991, survey, 8).

Japan was the model for corporate change, although it was argued that
the West might have problems importing the successful ways of Japanese
business giants like Sony because of their failure to adopt Japanese business
culture. For example, "In American and British firms, potential high fliers
tend to be put on the management fast track straight out of University. . . .
Potential Japanese managers spend their 20s learning their company back-

wards" (March 2, 1991, survey, 23). Japanese managers' success was due to on-the-job training, job rotation, vague job descriptions, group learning, and knowledge sharing. A month earlier it had also been reported that the importation of Japanese management techniques to the West was failing to produce the desired productivity gains because relationships between suppliers and manufacturers were too adversarial in the West (February 16, 1991, 87). These arguments about the softening of corporate culture under Japanese influence were reinforced by contemporaneous advertisements that used feminized imagery. For example, a couple of months before publication of the article just quoted, Canon, a Japanese computing and technology corporation, used the slogan "We don't just work together, we co-operate" over a picture of an oriental tunic (December 15, 1990, 112–13) (fig. 5.4); and a month before that, Komatsu, a Japanese construction-machines firm (one with more excuse than most to feature big drills and power machines) depicted a housewife with a patchwork quilt and the slogans "Hello neighbour" and "Co-operation for a better world" (November 17, 1990, 124).

On the other hand, it appeared that the Japanese now had a need for a new "entrepreneur type" of manager who was more innovative and creative. The solution would be a "marriage" in which Japanese MBA students would learn Western analytical skills but with the aggressiveness "mellowed down," while Western students would be taught to "open their minds" and have competitiveness discouraged or even penalized in favor of "team learning" (March 2, 1991, survey, 24–26). Later that year, *The Economist* reported that while for years, American and European firms had mimicked Japanese management techniques, now the Japanese were copying Westerners (August 10, 1991, 57). Consensus-forming rituals and job rotation were being played down in Japan in favor of hiring Western-style entrepreneurial "risk takers" and introducing performance-related benefits.

By 1992, Japanese capitalism was being defended against U.S. critics who saw it as unfair and ruthlessly "predatory" (April 4, 1992, 19–24). The *Economist* argued that Japanese production practices were, largely, more efficient than unfair. It was also observed that Japan's "greying corporate warriors" were being replaced by a new breed: a younger generation who were more competitive, less consensual, and keener on leisure (May 2, 1992, 99).

In March 1993, domesticated language was still being applied to new management strategies in the West. In a survey of multinationals, the usual war and sports metaphors were toned down and replaced by statements such as "multinationalism begins at home" and "when products are more or less equal, the way to compete is to cuddle closer to the buyer" (March 27, 1993, 16). Alliances between multinationals were described as "holding hands," while the reader was told "enemies, friends: who can tell the difference?" (20). On the other hand, technocratic standards of efficiency needed to be reasserted over research and development, which was now becoming "notoriously unruly and profligate" (19).

By the beginning of 1994, the Japanese economic downturn was being attributed to its corporate culture, portrayed this time not as "feminized" or even "predatory" so much as paternalistic and "too stable by half" (January 29, 1994, survey, 7). A debate over "Asian values" and whether they contributed to the success of the tiger economies was now in full swing, with *The Economist* claiming that there is nothing very Asian about strong family ties and the work ethic, and nor would Asian countries be immune to the social trends that have dogged the West (May 28, 1994, 14 and 77–78).

Later that year, Japanese firms, after "decades of cosying up to their subcontractors . . . [were] now discovering the virtues of competition" (May 14, 1994, 107), although Western manufacturers were still adopting Japanese-style informal partnerships and cooperation with suppliers, sharing business information, and in the case of General Motors and BMW even allowing suppliers to help design new cars. By 1995 Japan was seen to be exporting its economic model to developing countries as a distinctive, Far Eastern variety of "non-capitalist market economy" (January 14, 1995, 20), although Japanese multinationals themselves were continuing to "look west" to try to square their "traditional paternalism with the efficiency needed to stay competitive" (June 24, 1995, survey, 20–21). Finally, in 1996 *The Economist* endorsed the view of a United Nations (UNCTAD) world-investment report: "The latest report thinks that 'good practice' is ceasing to mean Japanese production methods, and is becoming Americanised yet again. . . . It also notes the creation of highly successful hybrid management systems, produced by the collision between different cultures" (March 16, 1996, review, 9).

In sum, during this period it seems *The Economist*'s rhetoric offered Japanese business culture as a model for the West that would soften and feminize Western business practices (dismantling paternalistic hierarchies in the process), while offering Western aggression and individualism as an antidote to Japanese paternalism. Whether softer or more aggressive ver-

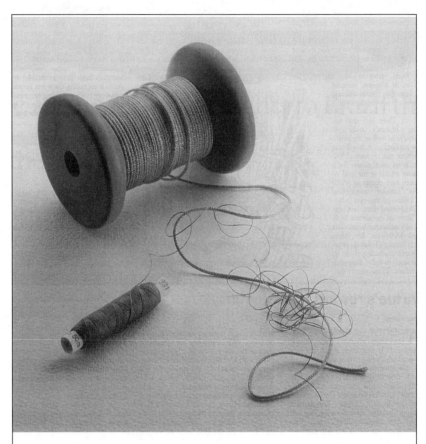

We don't just work together

# We co-operate

It's our belief that people come up with unique ideas
when in a creative work environment. These ideas are then translated
into products intended to serve only one purpose: to enhance
the creativity of the user. *Canon makes it work.*

**Canon**

FIGURE 5.4. Ad for Canon (*The Economist* December 15, 1990, 112–13). Here the advertiser emphasizes cooperation and uses a picture of sewing, an activity often associated with femininity. The ad could be tied in with *The Economist*'s rhetoric on Japanese managerial culture.

sions of hegemonic masculinity were to win out in the end, or perhaps some combination of the two, with the softer elements increasingly incorporated as wholly masculine traits, the reader was left in no doubt that old hierarchies and paternalism were under siege.[19] Underlying this whole debate was the assumption of globalization, which when it was not being associated with "the final frontier" was clearly seen as an important priority in the tiger economies as well as in the West. After the East Asian currency crisis of 1998, the Japanese model unsurprisingly fell out of favor. Nonetheless, the multiple processes of competition, cross-fertilization, and convergence in masculine business styles from East and West witnessed by *The Economist* to that date can be seen as part of the process of forging the culture of a new and potentially globalized hegemonic masculinity.

## Masculinities in Finance

The revolution in financial services has been central to the process of globalization as constructed in the pages of *The Economist*. Nowhere has the collapse of patriarchal and paternalistic imagery associated with globalization been more apparent. More often than not, as paternalistic and patriarchal imagery has declined, financial-services advertisements have filled the gap, not with the softer or more feminized images discussed above but with a variety of remasculinizing images that have helped to reposition the financial-services sector and boost its (formerly flagging) status.

   The nineteenth-century world of the City of London is the world *The Economist* was originally created for. The paper was founded in 1843, as one of the key publications of the financial press that kept the City informed about itself. The imagery in *The Economist*'s "World Profile" (analyzed in chapter 4) still reflects this heritage in its promotion of bourgeois values with aristocratic trappings—the old school tie, the collector's items, the large checks, and so forth. While modern banking in the West grew from unpromising beginnings, by Victorian times domestic banking had become a solidly bourgeois and respectable profession, with the provincial bank manager as an important if unpopular figure in the local community.[20] Popular prejudice against bankers, and particularly international bankers, persisted, however, fueled by a mixture of nationalism and anti-Semitism that peaked in the late nineteenth and early twentieth centuries. In some quarters, international bankers were both demonized and feminized: they were seen as unpatriotic and cowardly, and were also credited with conspiring to take over the world, along with international Jewry, Masonry, and, latterly, Communism (*The Economist* December 25, 1993, 107–9).

The City of London elite largely escaped this negative image, drawing as it did on an aristocratic heritage. According to Will Hutton (1995), the City elite preferred to reproduce empire and the upper-class penchant for land and invisible income from stocks, shares, trading, and merchanting, rather than engaging with or financing British industry. But as Nigel Thrift argues, contrary to received wisdom, top directors and partners of City stockbroking firms were not real aristocrats, but rather formed "a distinct stratum, combining elements of bourgeois and aristocratic cultures but reducible to neither. It was a culture that (despite the trappings of land ownership) was urban rather than rural, functionally progressive rather than reactionary, and combined great dynastic aspiration with an unpretentious devotion to the ethic of work" (Thrift 1994, 339).

Aristocratic trappings were seen as investments, and real aristocrats were considered lazy and effete, in a world that was nevertheless ruled by the narrative of "the gentleman." It was a world with strict codes of behavior and clothing, so that brown suits, for example, were regarded with horror. Trustworthiness was signified and judged by the ability to adhere to these codes, in a culture that was organized through class and sustained and regulated by a network of "men only" social institutions (Thrift 1994, 339–40).

By the mid twentieth century, the social standing of domestic bank mangers and the paternalistic, bourgeois masculinity that went with it was being undermined.[21] In the 1970s, the culture of City banking and stockbroking, too, began to change, as the "gentlemanly code" loosened its hold and finance became gradually globalized, a process that was accelerated by the financial "big bangs" of the 1980s. In the new culture of globalized finance, there has been an increase in risk and the need for risk management, and the traditional ways of working have been swept away. The homosociality has been weakened by an influx of professional and managerial women, particularly in jobs requiring a high level of social interaction. The codes of the English Gentleman have been undermined by the greatly increased presence of foreign firms, bringing expatriate workers with them. With an increasingly cosmopolitan workforce, and a weakening of the traditional rules and hierarchies, formal contracts have replaced word-of-honor agreements. Thrift argues that

In current circumstances the need for reflexivity has been much enhanced . . . leading to a greater emphasis on presentation of the self, face-
work, negotiating skills and so on, because of the increasing need to be
able to read people, as the signs of their social positions are no longer so
foreordained and because of the increasingly transactional nature of business relationships between firms and clients. Thus trust now has to be constituted through work on relationships, not "read off" from signs of trustworthiness. (Thrift 1994, 348)

Meanwhile, in the pages of *The Economist*, banking and financial advertisements at the beginning of the period tended to be formal and austere or
even patriarchal. In 1990 it was still common for banking ads in *The Economist* to feature sober pictures of a bank's chairman or founders, and extracts
from a chairman's statement.[22] Banks tended to stress their strength,
longevity, and solidity. In some typical examples, the Swiss Bank Corporation talked of more than one hundred years of experience and an "excep-
tionally solid capital base" (December 15, 1990, 86); Salomon Brothers
spoke of its eighty-year history as a "leader" (April 28, 1990, 110); AEtna Investment stressed its "wisdom" (November 17, 1990, 100) (fig. 5.1); and First
Chicago's chairman advised that "First Relationships Last" (November 17,
1990, 114). J. P. Morgan capped them all by featuring a photograph of a particularly upright, sober, and elderly former chairman taken fifty years before, together with a boast of 150 years of experience and "sound analysis"
(November 3, 1990, 2–3) (fig. 5.5). These images deliberately invoked the
patriarchal hierarchies and solidly bourgeois credentials of bygone eras. As
such, and coming at least a decade after the global revolution in financial
services had been effected (see below), they represented the last gasp of the
old order and a nostalgic invocation of stability in a world of change. Even
banks that preferred to get on the globalization bandwagon were cautious.
NatWest Bank, for instance, stressed speed, innovation, initiative, and even
adventure, but did so in a restrained format with wordy advertisements and
modest illustrations (April 28, 1990, 117, 119, and 121).

By 1994–95, with only a few exceptions the images of patriarchs and
founders had been largely banished.[23] Expertise was still stressed, but in the
mid 1990s it tended to be a stand-alone bourgeois-rational feature, rather
than being linked to paternalism and elitism, and was presented in a less formal, austere setting. For example, a number of advertisers presented inter-

national finances as complex puzzles to be solved, using colorful and amusing visual conundrums as props;[24] others emphasized insight or intellect.[25] Banker's Trust, in likening investment strategy to a game of chess, managed both (December 7, 1996, 109). Some advertising now also reflected Thrift's analysis of an increasing presence of professional and managerial women, increasing cosmopolitanism, and new emphasis on relationships and interpersonal skills. Non-Western entrepreneurs appeared, such as in the Hong Kong Bank advertisement featuring a Chinese trader on a bicycle (May 13, 1995, 112). Networking and relationships were stressed, for example by Standard Chartered, who showed businessmen and a token woman playing ball or opening doors across the globe (February 11, 1995, 4; August 12, 1995, 2; March 18, 1995, survey, 14–15).[26]

One or two banks even took the opportunity to uncouple their advertising from hegemonic masculinity altogether. For example, J. P. Morgan broke the mold by depicting a white woman banker with a black male client (October 1, 1994, 108–9), and in another advertisement showed intimate conversation between a businessman and a businesswoman accompanied by the "feminine" terms *depth* and *flow* (April 15, 1995, survey, 36).[27] In a similar vein, a long-running and prominent series of Citibank advertisements featured photo stories of a range of bankers and clients presented as business couples engaging in friendly and animated discussion. Between them these advertisements covered virtually every racial and gender permutation,[28] the copy stressing "relationship" or "relationships" (March 9, 1996, back cover; June 29, 1996, 131; October 5, 1996, back cover), "partners" or "partnership" (February 17, 1996, back cover; April 13, 1996, back cover; May 18, 1996, back cover), "commitment" (June 8, 1996, 149), and "understanding" (March 9, 1996, back cover).

This was not the dominant trend, however. In contrast, and in competition with these new, less-masculinist images, there were also the hackneyed images of masculine virility, such as mountain peaks, skyscrapers, big cats, and big drills, and a new emphasis on masculine sport and physical strength.[29] AIG bank showed men engaging in a tug-of-war, (September 10, 1994, 52–53); Peregrine depicted fencing (April 6, 1996, 55); WestLB had rowing (April 6, 1996, 37); and Citibank Personal Banking featured a golfer (June 3, 1995, 38–39). One Morgan Stanley advertisement showed a huge whale surfacing, with the slogan "And the bond market thought you were dead in the water" (April 15, 1995, survey, 18–19). There was also a new em-

# Why the "new" thinking in M&A isn't new to us.

Now that some highly leveraged transactions of the last decade are under scrutiny, there has suddenly been a call for a "return to the fundamentals" of "sound business principles" in M&A and of "relationship banking." At J.P. Morgan, however, we have no such need to get back to basics. We never left them. We will recommend a merger, acquisition, sale, or divestiture only when it is based on a sound analysis of true debt capacity and complements your long-term business strategy in a way that truly benefits your shareholders. For in our 150 years of experience, we've learned that placing our clients' interests before our own is the best way to be successful in the long run. For truly objective advice in M&A, turn to one firm where sound strategic thinking is never out of fashion.

## JPMorgan

Over half a century ago, J.P. Morgan, Jr., said, "The clients' belief in the integrity of our advice is our best possession."

FIGURE 5.5. Ad for J. P. Morgan (*The Economist* November 3, 1990, 2–3). This was one of a number of paternalistic banking advertisements at this time. Such ads often featured chairmen and chairmen's statements; in this case, the image was of a former patriarch, looking stern.

**There's a span of several months until your deal closes. The last thing you want to hear is a rope snapping.**

It's taken months to negotiate your way to this point in your cross-border acquisition. Regulatory approvals will take several months more. Meanwhile, the terms you agreed on are exposed to market volatility.

You need to protect the equity value of your purchase and future funding obligations with hedging strategies that allow you to achieve certainty in an uncertain future.

So you've planned well. And you've selected a firm that won't let those plans fall through.

A team of specialists who actively trade in cash and derivative markets throughout the world. And whose knowledge of structuring techniques and the regulatory environment assures you of solutions that are matched precisely to your risk exposures.

They can design a program that mitigates the risk of rising interest rates by hedging the cost of future financings. Or manage your foreign currency exposure by locking in favorable exchange rates.

They can help you stabilize anticipated cash flows by structuring commodity price hedges. Even shield you against the devaluation of assets in merged pension funds.

A dynamic strategy that can flex with changing events. And deliver you intact to your goal.

*MORGAN STANLEY*

Bombay   Chicago   Frankfurt   Hong Kong   London   Los Angeles   Luxembourg   Madrid   Melbourne   Milan   Moscow   New York   Paris   San Francisco   Seoul   Shanghai   Singapore   Taipei   Tokyo   Toronto   Zurich

FIGURE 5.6. Ad for Morgan Stanley (*The Economist* November 19, 1994, 86). This was one of a number of advertisements in late 1994 that played on risk anxiety. Subsequent advertisements, including ones by Morgan Stanley, put a more robust spin on risk taking.

phasis on speed that had now a become a valuable trait in globalized financial transactions. Another Morgan Stanley advertisement showed an aircraft undercarriage with the slogan "You have to hit the ground running" (November 5, 1994, 82); LTC Bank of Japan argued that "speed is often the difference between success and failure" (March 18, 1995, survey, 22); and Bankers Trust claimed that "speed with accuracy is the foundation of value" (August 3, 1996, 70).

A complementary set of imagery picks up on another of the changes to finance mentioned by Thrift, the increase in "risk."[30] The increasing social relevance of "risk" has also been theorized by Ulrich Beck (1992), Giddens (1991), and Lash and Urry (1994). These writers argue that political conflicts and social cleavages are increasingly organized by the distribution of risks rather than, as in the past, the distribution of goods. Risk societies promote reflexivity, as people reflect critically on the new, less predictable, social conditions of life. Scientific-technical elites are the new "risk winners," the hegemonic partners in an alliance between science and capital (Lash and Urry 1994, 32–35).

"Risk" has certainly become a commonly invoked image in financial advertisements. Indeed, risk of one kind or another seems to have become the principal sign of international danger and uncertainty in *The Economist* in the 1990s. In May 1992, the Bankers Trust, who "lead from strength," warned nervous potential customers that "not taking risks may be the biggest risk of all," and showed a man in an armchair being jolted into the air while pointing out that "you have to leave the cosy and comfortable if you want to move ahead" (February 29, 1992, 2). Another advertisement from Bankers Trust showed a fisherman standing on an island that turns out to be a giant fish, the slogan saying: "Risk, it isn't always where you expect it to be" (May 2, 1992, survey, 2). In the same issue, however, some other banks and insurers were still publishing images and text that invoked the earlier values: ABN–AMRO projected solidity (46); Hong Kong Bank went for longevity (survey, 7); Sun Alliance (34–35) and Barclays (survey, 25–28) presented dry words of wisdom from their chairmen, and the ING Group ran even drier columns of figures from a balance sheet (62). By autumn 1994, financial-risk anxiety had multiplied and was being variously presented as a threatening volcanic eruption (Zurich Insurance Group ad November 19, 1994, 32–33); the cause of a potential nervous breakdown (AXA ad ibid., 57–59); or a rickety rope bridge about to snap (Morgan Stanley ad ibid., 86) (fig. 5.6). Only one advertiser in the November 19 edition saw global financial markets as an opportunity (Matif ad ibid., 113). As Chase Manhattan had stated in an advertisement the preceding week, "in these volatile times, what you want from risk management is a little less risk and a lot more management" (November 12, 1994, survey, 5). Another bank showed a picture of a piece of cloth from a gent's suit caught on a barbed-wire fence, warning that "risk can tear at the corporate fabric" (Chemical Bank ad October 22, 1994, 4). Since barbed wire is often associated with war (and especially with World War I) this picture invokes an image of businessmen engaging in unpleasant and risky trench warfare. In the bourgeois world of The Economist in 1994, risk appeared to be not a challenge to be enjoyed by citizen-warriors, but a necessary evil to be managed.[31]

However, at least one advertiser cleverly offered protection from risk anxiety while at the same time portraying risk taking as heroically and glamorously masculine. Credit Suisse, in a long-running and prominent series of advertisements, featured a series of animated but uninhabited images of protective U.S. sports underclothing, a kind of latter-day armor of helmets, padding, and braces of various descriptions, with the slogan "When you're taking risks, you don't want to take chances." This particular example was of ice-hockey armor, complete with stick as weapon (November 19, 1994, 37). Other examples include American football "armor" (e.g., September 24, 1994, 41; March 18, 1995, 49) and baseball "armor" (e.g., October 1, 1994, 59).[32] Indeed, after the attack of "risk" anxiety in late 1994, a hardening of images of masculinity in banking generally took place through 1995 and 1996, and "risk" became more associated with virility. This reflected an improved economic outlook, but it was also a clear example of masculinization strategies deployed to increase the status of the banks involved, and by association the whole financial-services sector. This remasculinization may also have been a reaction against the encroachment of professional women into the sector. In one example, the Union Bank of Switzerland deployed a series of images from formula-one racing, with the slogan "Master the detail, manage the risk" (October 7, 1995, 108–9). The word risk was repeated no fewer than five times in an advertisement that boasted that "our clients expect fast reactions, technical skill and total attention to detail, continuously, not just for an hour or two. And though the dangers are not physical, they are nevertheless very real. . . . At UBS Global Risk Management, we combine constant attention to detail with coolness under pressure, to help drive your business forward" (October 7, 1995, 108–9).

At the same time, *The Economist*'s editorial increasingly referred to risk and risk management as a route to profit. For example, in its 1995 survey of Wall Street, the paper discussed the risk model of financial intermediation, arguing that "risk has become the organising concept for the entire financial business" as distinctions between banks, insurers and stockbrokers have broken down (April 15, 1995, survey, 21). As risk became a global commodity through derivatives and other new financial instruments, it charted the competition between firms aiming to be one of an "elite of global financial firms set to dominate the business" in "a world-wide gamble" (April 15, 1995, survey, 27–28). This more upbeat approach to "risk" aggressively remasculinized financial services. Relationships with clients also came under scrutiny and were seen to be more important within a risk-management model, with some firms investing in complex conflict-management procedures. For other firms, however, the approach to relationships was baldly instrumental, with one head trader quoted as stating, "You shouldn't expect to get paid to have relationships. Relationships are simply a means by which the firm gets to take risks" (April 15, 1995, survey, 24).

The upbeat approach to risk resonates with the honor code of masculinity in which risk taking is generally admired. In the honor code, bravery and face are also paramount in relationships between men (Morgan 1992). While this code has been generally fairly muted in Anglo-American masculinities in recent years (except perhaps in fiction and the cinema), it is an important ingredient in Mediterranean and Latin masculinities and is still a type that Anglo-American men would recognize and perhaps identify with. Meanwhile, the positioning of financial risk as a sign of international/global danger adds a realist inflection.

The repositioned masculinity of international finance therefore combines elements of bourgeois rationality (instrumentalism and technology) with honor codes (display of competitive risk taking) and citizen-warrior codes (physical strength, heroically facing international danger). In addition, the globalization of finance has resulted in an increased spatial separation of finance from production, with power concentrated in a handful of specialist financial centers (Massey 1994). This is reminiscent of British imperial finances in the nineteenth century, allowing contemporary financial masculinities to draw on this historic status cachet, but with the aristocratic trappings now replaced by technocratic ones.

On the other hand, the increase in the number of images of sports and physical strength in financial services can be partly attributed to an Americanization of financial masculinities in the City of London. Indeed, *The Economist* has itself been subject to increasing Americanization as it became a key player in the increasingly global financial press. This is reflected in its advertising mix, in which U.S. firms are heavily represented, in its large section devoted to U.S. domestic politics, and in its occasional guest articles by leading U.S. economists and politicians, such as Madeleine Albright, the U.S. secretary of state (February 15, 1997, 21–23).

With no long indigenous history of feudal aristocracy behind it, WASP masculinity has always been less secure than that of the English Gentleman, and has therefore been more dependant on "frontier" toughness and the late-nineteenth-century Anglo-American cult of physical fitness and youthfulness for its genesis. Education in colleges such as Harvard and Yale in the late nineteenth century was designed to produce a U.S. aristocracy, but one inflected by a heroic ideal, a kind of (anti-Semitic and generally racist) cowboy philosophy that included admiration for "the rougher manlier virtues," a love of physical strength and courage, of athletic contests, and fighting (Higgs 1987, 165). Education was modeled on the neo-Spartan British public-school system, as it was believed that "the time given to athletic contests and the injuries incurred on the playing field are part of the price which the English-speaking race has paid for being world-conquerors" (Henry Cabot Lodge, quoted in Higgs 1987, 165).

If British "character" was molded through colonial power, then a distinct American "character" was to be formed through the challenges of conquest on the "frontier," with the Western territories seen as a vast internal empire (Mrozek 1987, 226). Although the cult of this "muscular Christianity" has waned, sporting ability and physical fitness continue to be important ingredients in U.S. hegemonic masculinity. Thus through historic connections with earlier manifestations of "frontier masculinity," the imagery of sports and physical strength also resonates with the construction of globalization as a "frontier." As well as representing an Americanization of hegemonic masculinity in *The Economist*, the increase in male-oriented sports imagery, combined with technocratic imagery and the mobilization of "risk" as a sign

# Most providers of information solutions think they reach the finish line when they reach the customer.

## But reaching the customer's customer separates the leader from the pack.

Lately, many companies are racing to demonstrate their customer service solutions. But only Unisys understands that the best way to help customers is to help them reach *their* customers.

Through our unique CUSTOMERIZE process, we offer a pragmatic and disciplined series of steps for helping you turn customer service into a strategic advantage.

Unisys professionals will team with you to evaluate your enterprise from a customer service perspective.

Unisys offers a powerful combination of information services, technology expertise, and industry-specific experience to help enhance your ability to retain customers and win new ones. The benefits speak to your bottom line.

Greater customer-perceived value means greater margins. A competitive advantage in customer service means improved market share. According to a recent independent study, the profit impact of a simple 2% increase in customer retention can be the equivalent of a 10% reduction in overheads.

Not least, Unisys leadership in systems integration and open systems enables us to optimize the value of your existing technology investment at the same time as our CUSTOMERIZE approach produces tangible results for your organisation.

**cus·tom·er·ize** v.t. **1.** To make a company more responsive to its customers and better able to attract new ones. **2.** To customerize an organisation's information strategy, e.g., to extend systems capabilities to branches, booking offices and other points of customer contact and support. **3.** What Unisys does for a growing number of companies and government agencies worldwide. See CUSTOMER SERVICE, COMPETITIVE EDGE, BUSINESS-CRITICAL SOLUTIONS, REVENUE GENERATION.

# UNISYS
### We make it happen.

For more information fax Graham Roberts on (44) 895 862807. And ask how Unisys can help you reach your customers – and serve them better.

FIGURE 5.7. Ad for Unisys (*The Economist* November 5, 1994, 93). One of a number of advertisements in *The Economist* in the mid 1990s that emphasized physical fitness, an important attribute of U.S. constructions of masculinity. This one sought to position computing as masculine.

of international danger, may also be a way of restaking a claim to nondomestic masculinity in arenas where women are now encroaching.[33]

*Meanwhile, in Computing and Telecoms . . .*

In the trend toward invoking masculine physical strength and global imagery and linking them to technology and speed, there has been a clear convergence between financial-services advertisements and computing advertisements. In the latter, such U.S.-inflected masculinizing motifs had been well-established since the mid 1980s (Connell 1995). Illustrative examples from *The Economist* include the following advertisements featuring physical strength: for Oracle—a photo of a coal miner, with the slogan "data mining" (November 5, 1994, 114–15); for Unisys-men's athletics (ibid., 93) (fig. 5.7); for IBM—a weight lifter (June 3, 1995, 103); and for Telia Telecoms—a shot-putter (May 13, 1995, 90). Digital featured power by associating an image of an ocean wave with a flexed bicep (February 11, 1995, 57); signifying both power and speed were Knight Ridder's computer as "power tool"—a large drill—(April 29, 1995, 94) and for $EMC^2$ a fast car (November 5, 1994, 90). That physical strength and sporting imagery should be popular with computing advertisers should come as no surprise, given that the industry is dominated by U.S. firms. But as to why computers should be associated with hegemonic masculinity is less obvious, given that desktop computers, when first introduced in large numbers, were used mostly as word processors by female clerical staff. The association between computing and masculinity has had to be forged through carefully chosen advertising imagery (Connell 1995).

In *The Economist* this association was constantly being reestablished and reinforced. One advertisement featured a baby boy playing on a computer under the slogan "Born in Bell labs" (October 5, 1991, survey, 46–47). More recently, Acer showed a large picture of a man's chest and a smaller picture of a father and son playing with a home PC, using the slogan "No wonder the big guys, and the little ones, choose ACER" (November 12, 1994, 110–11). Meanwhile $EMC^2$ characterized their information storage as a lean and muscular (white) male chest and stomach, opposing it to its fat and flabby rivals (September 28, 1996, 107) (fig. 5.8). The masculinity of telecoms has also been reinforced by such items as an *Economist* survey of telecoms headlined "The New Boys" (October 5, 1991) and the advertising slogan

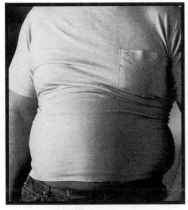
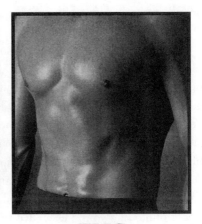

## Ordinary Information Storage.

## EMC Information Storage.

The world's leading companies have put their information at the centre of their growth strategies. Access to that information is critical. And high-performance storage holds the key.

The most intelligent storage solutions come from EMC. Not the computer companies. Their storage holds a lot, but it's slow. And it usually works only with their computers.

At EMC, all we do is create advanced solutions for instant access to enterprise-wide information. No matter which computer platform you use. Our intelligent software lets customers use our storage to do more than just store. They depend on it when defining new markets. To help accelerate product development. And maintain the highest levels of customer satisfaction possible.

To find out more about EMC, call 01372 360000, ext. 381. Or visit us at http://www.emc.com.

**EMC²**
THE STORAGE ARCHITECTS

FreeTo Do More.

FIGURE 5.8. Ad for EMC² (*The Economist* September 28, 1996, 107). Another ad from the mid 1990s that associated computing with both masculinity and physical fitness.

"Man's intelligence leads to ways to communicate" (October 5, 1991, 53). However, later in the period, as with financial services, one or two firms have also used softer or more feminizing imagery: Lotus Notes used the slogan "communicate, collaborate, co-ordinate" (May 13, 1995, 60–61). Hewlett Packard presented a female computer-systems engineer to prospective clients with the slogan "She'll make it work" (November 19, 1994, 25), and followed this image with one of a Latina systems-support engineer (January 28, 1995, 2–3).

Computing and telecoms firms also seem to have been much quicker on the uptake of globalization imagery then banks and financial services. A popular global image from the late 1980s (reminiscent of James Bond films and *Dr. Strangelove*) was deployed by Fujitsu: a darkened control room full of computers and decision makers, with a huge map of the world (October 5, 1991, survey, 10–11). In addition, the new links between the worlds of computing and finance were first made explicit in telecoms and computing ads. The ones described below appeared fairly early in the period, when banking ads were still fairly austere and formal. Fujitsu computers for example featured a photo of a young U.S. investment banker, ready for the fray, with jacket off and braces (men's suspenders) showing (March 10, 1990, survey, 18–19); Northern Telecom boasted about the billions of dollars it shifted a day in financial markets (March 10, 1990, survey, 20–21); and Cable and Wireless displayed a stock-market trading floor (October 5, 1991, survey, 25).

### Increasing Informality

If financial services, computing, and telecoms advertisements between them were dropping paternalism in favor of either an aggressively remasculinized image of hegemonic masculinity and globalization, or, less often, the softer, more feminized imagery discussed earlier, there was also a marked trend toward a relaxed informality in some computing and telecoms advertisements. By 1995 businessmen in smart suits were being replaced by a young computer nerd with long hair and informal clothing (AST computers ad May 27, 1995, 91), a stonemason in sweater and cap (IBM ad February 25, 1995, 40–41), a cool, black U.S. blues musician (IBM ad December 16, 1995, 40–41), and a father telecommuting from home in an open-neck check shirt, accompanied by his daughter and teddy (AMP ad October 12, 1996, 93). A youthful, long-haired and footloose AT&T man was labeled as

"A rucksack, 2 degrees, 3 credit cards and a potential customer" (May 13, 1995, 99).

These images were part of a more widespread trend toward informal depictions of masculinity in the paper. For example, in the October 12, 1996, edition, while Hyundai (154–55) featured a photo of chairman Chung Mong Koo and his mission statement (together with a moonscape and satellite, in a hybrid of patriarchal and technocratic/globalization imagery), this fairly formal advertisement was very much in the minority. It contrasted with relaxed European and American images of masculinity, such as the president and CEO of the Orvis company out fishing in his denim shirt, fleece sweatshirt, and padded fisherman's waistcoat in an advertisement for Chubb Insurance (41).[34] Meanwhile, in the same issue, Hugo Boss men's clothes had jettisoned their usual suits for jeans and a denim shirt, although still with a tie (87), and Armstrong International executive headhunters featured a (male) "managing director" in a casual leather jacket (108).[35] Informality in these advertisements was being constituted as a desirable and "cool" masculine trait.

Airline advertisements had also by and large jettisoned their patriarchal images of formally dressed businessmen being waited on by pretty stewardesses.[36] Some replaced the stewardess with "man meets machine" technocratic images of businessmen (or parts of their bodies) juxtaposed with airline seats and equipment, sometimes complete with measurements and specifications (Qantas ad June 3, 1995, 84; United Airlines ad June 3, 1995, 59; KLM/Northwest ad February 11 1995, back cover; Continental Airlines ad May 13, 1995, 56; Air France ad October 7, 1995, 52–53). Others such as the Meridiana airline stuck to the more traditional image of male hands emerging from the cuffs of a suit and clutching a leather briefcase (March 30, 1996, 59).[37] However, some airlines went in for softer and more informal images. A British Airways advertisement featured a businessman being cradled in his mother's arms like a baby (March 23, 1996, 22)—a businessman image that displayed striking vulnerability when compared to the usual picture of power and privilege. Another "soft" advertisement, for Swissair, pictured a businessman as a daddy kissing a daughter good-bye, with the caption "If you want to get a kiss from someone you love in the morning, pack in a full day's work and be back home to say goodnight, best choose Swissair" (May 27, 1995, 22).[38]

The layout of the paper itself also gradually became more informal. The typeface changed to a more open, rounded style on May 25, 1991. On November 11, 1995, the old-fashioned and rather gentlemanly "Arts, Books, and Sport," a weekly section, was replaced by a shorter one entitled "Moreover," which together with a monthly "Review of Books and Multimedia" that includes reviews of CD ROM titles covered a wider range of topics, reflecting the postmodern interest in culture at many levels, low as well as high.

And it was not only through the change of typeface and organization that the look of the paper changed. When cartoons featured on the front cover, they were no longer line drawings with restrained color added (as on November 24, 1990, when "The Tories Choose" was illustrated by a drawing of a ruckus reminiscent of children's comics), but were bold pictures in increasingly lurid colors. The cover on 16 December, 1995, featured a cartoon mock-horror picture of a tombstone and ghoul advertising the resurrection of Communism in movie style: "Communism II. . . . It's Alive! . . . Just when you thought it was safe for democracy"—all this done out in violent mauve, vivid blue, and orange and yellow. After February 1996 the front cover picture was no longer confined to a formal box but was allowed to fill the whole page. Some of these changes reflect the availability of new, cheaper printing techniques, but they also give a less formal, less restrained feel to the paper.

What is striking about all this increase in informality is that it has been constituted as masculine. A breakdown of patriarchy and an increase in informality would at first sight appear to be in the interests of gender equality. The standard feminist critique of masculinist working practices describes masculine management styles as autocratic, overly hierarchical, rational, and focused on efficiency and task orientation. These are contrasted with feminine management styles that are seen as based on relationships, consensus, collaboration, teamwork, and cooperation (Court 1994). These "feminine" management styles have now been introduced on a widespread scale, and are associated with informality. However, with this new informality being constituted predominantly as masculine, it does not undercut hegemonic masculinity as much as one might expect.

Research into informal management practices in computing and high-tech industries suggests that they do not necessarily constitute an improvement for women. Margaret Tierney found that informal working practices are in fact sex discriminating—that formal promotion procedures are replaced by a "laddish" social network that grooms young men to rise up the ladder. Women and those men who do not fit the "lad" culture are excluded from this important source of advice, support, and visibility and are consequently regularly overlooked.[39] Not only that, but in the new informal work culture, old-fashioned patriarchal hierarchies are themselves being increasingly feminized, with "girls" and "wimps" being seen as more comfortable with rules and hierarchy and less able to deal with flexibility (Tierney 1995). The recasting of rules and hierarchy as feminine has been a cultural sea change not confined to the workplace. For example, the same characterization of rules and hierarchy dominates 1990s action films, in which violent and wild but soft and sensitive killing/caring tough-guy heroes are hindered by feminized, domesticated, impotent, and ineffectual bureaucrats in suits (Pfeil 1995). This reversal is powerful propaganda in the struggle to claim previously feminized traits for hegemonic masculinity as it moves into the new territory of globalization.

## Technocracy and Hegemonic Masculinity

Nor need an increase in informality necessarily conflict with the technocratic-frontier masculinity discussed earlier. Indeed, it may complement it. Beverley Burris associates the trend toward informality with the development of technocracy as a form of organizational control. In technocratic organizations, the workforce is divided into "experts" and "nonexperts." Technical complexity replaces organizational complexity in a culture that values "conspicuous expertise," because "in technocratic organizations who you know becomes less important than how knowledgeable you can appear" (Burris 1989, 453). Rigid rules and hierarchies are replaced by flexible, collegiate, collaborative working styles and enhanced communication for largely male "experts." Meanwhile, for the rest, the nonexperts and "paraprofessionals," work becomes increasingly routinized and regimented under computer control, geographically isolated and feminized (done by women). The fact that both experts and nonexperts use the same technology—namely, computers—masks the very different ways in which their work is organized.

The move to technocratic organization reflects a further stage in the gradual breakdown in patriarchy and increase in technocratic rationality observed by Cocks (1989) and Ehrenreich (1995). However, Tierney's analysis clearly supports the idea of a link between technological globalization imagery and the increase in informality, since both would be implicated in the development of technocracy. If this is the case, then much of the new, "softer" imagery in *The Economist* and its advertisements could be mobilized for a new technocratic hegemonic masculinity, at least as easily as it could be mobilized *against* hegemonic masculinity. In terms of *The Economist*, Bill Gates of Microsoft represents the "expert" technocrat par excellence. In the "Battle of Titans" (September 21, 1996, 106)—the competition to dominate the next generation of computers—Gates was pitted against Larry Ellison of Oracle. The two men have very different personal styles, although neither appear to be remotely domesticated. Gates has been characterized as a workaholic for whom "starting a family has made no difference to his famously long work hours. Even his $30m house is portrayed more as a showroom for Microsoft technology than a home" (106). Ellison, by contrast "works out, sails his boats, flies his planes, dates a lot, and meditates in the replica of a Japanese monastery he built" (106) and talks about his feelings for nearly an hour. In contrast to Gates the technocrat, Ellison represents an expansive but touchy-feely latter-day playboy. In this particular rivalry between would-be hegemonic masculinities, *The Economist*'s money was on Mr. Gates: "so far in this industry, obsession has proved more rewarding than reflection" (106).

### Gender Issues Acknowledged

Another development in *The Economist* toward the end of the period under study was a new (although not always serious) interest in masculinity, which paralleled the increasing interest in women and feminism discussed in chapter 4. This may have reflected increasing awareness and anxiety about masculinity associated with the changes discussed above. For example, the paper made a tongue-in-cheek suggestion to tax the sexes differently, since men "impose disproportionate costs on society" through crime (May 13, 1995, 113), and also reported on the activities of gay businessmen and the strength of the "pink pound" (May 6, 1995, 38). Particularly striking was, in 1996, a new-found self-consciousness and anxiety about masculinity. Masculinity had been occasionally mentioned previously, such as when at Christmas/New Year's 1992/93, in the context of a general discussion of the whole nature/nurture debate and new sociobiological research, it was reported that universal dichotomous gender differences existed. These were described along the contrasted lines of competitiveness, roughness, and mathematical and spatial ability in boys and character-reading, verbal, linguistic, and emotional interest in girls. Such differences were evidenced by such things as the bias toward males in crime statistics across the world and were attributed to genetic or hormonal differences between the sexes. Homosexuality was also claimed to be due to brain differences (December 26, 1992, 61–64).

The sociobiological argument resurfaced at Christmas/New Year's 1995/96, but this time it was reported rather more ironically, with "half-playful dread" and the headline "The Male Dodo: Are Men Redundant?/Are Men Necessary?" (December 23, 1995, 121–23). It was jokingly argued that by the middle of the twenty-first century, men will be "marginal" or an "expensive nuisance" (121). After listing men's perceived weaknesses such as more inherited diseases, more troubled childhoods, more death by violence, rising unemployment, poorer health, and earlier mortality, it was argued that these were all due to testosterone (even rising male unemployment was attributed to this hormone, since brain is replacing brawn in work). Testosterone, "the supreme female invention" (123), apparently makes males fight and take unnecessary risks, and weakens the immune system.

The explanation given was an evolutionary pressure toward a more stable and industrious femininity, counterbalanced by the need for genetic diversity, so that Mother Nature conjured up men as "genetic sieves" (122). Those that survive "beating each other up or risking their lives against predators and parasites" in a "deadly jousting tournament" (123) clearly have superior genes and get to impregnate women, ensuring the genetic health of the species. In addition, scientific research has shown that in the growing embryo, the placenta is largely the product of genes from male sperm that "almost viciously set about exploiting the mother's body, not trusting the maternal genes to do so selfish a job" (123) and thus ensuring foetal survival. In this ultracompetitive masculine world, even the womb is a war zone. Thus testosterone-induced risk taking, competitiveness, and aggressiveness are half-jokingly seen as the only thing preventing the extinction of the male of the species, and not a good long-term bet for survival, given scientific developments in biotechnology and artificial reproduction, not to mention the threat to testosterone and the male sperm count posed by ubiquitous oestrogen-mimicking modern chemicals.[40] Anxieties about falling male sperm counts were aired again at greater length six months later, on August 3, 1996 (77–79).

Of course, this analysis of masculinity fits in well with the general outlook of *The Economist*—promoting a super-Darwinistic, survival-of-the-fittest model that serves to explain the workings of international politics, international capitalism, evolution, and the nature of "Man," all in similar terms. "Man," then, thus described, becomes ideally suited to the pursuit of international capitalist enterprises, and his "success" in such a competitive global economic game is seen to reflect his personal survival strategies, the "success" of his genes, the proof of his (superior) manhood. As noted above, Haraway argues that there has been heavy cross-fertilization between theoretical developments in the human and natural sciences—a cross-fertilization that is connected to the development of capitalism. When it comes to sociobiology, "it is a striking fact that the formal theory of nature embodied in sociobiology is structurally like advanced capitalist theories of investment management, control systems for labor, and insurance practices based on population disciplines" (Haraway 1991, 59). Haraway demonstrates how sociobiologists analyze biological objects "in terms of the systems sciences rooted in military combat, competitive sexuality, and capitalist production" (1991, 65). It is therefore perhaps not surprising to find apparently seamless connections between sociobiology, capitalism, and international politics in *The Economist*.

On the other hand, deterministic sociobiological explanations of human behavior are hard to square with a philosophy of free will and personal responsibility. On September 14, 1996, under the banner of "The Genetic Illusion," with a cover showing a man on DNA puppet strings, *The Economist* argued that "man" is not preprogrammed, after all. Man can apparently go against his nature, with the acid test being not whether it is difficult for someone to make a particular choice, but whether it is impossible (13).

In the same edition, the "Lexington" column reported on "the feminisation" of America (60). This was evidenced by such phenomena as an increase in female delegates, tears, and "sob stories" at political conventions, transvestism and role reversal (in both sexes) on prime-time television and in movies, the burgeoning male cosmetics and girdles market, and the involvement of women in offensive combat positions in the armed forces. Lexington briefly mentioned the debate over whether this "represents a success for women or just a devious new form of male domination," but the column's main point was that gender differences are narrowing. The topic came up again just a fortnight later (September 28, 1996), in a five-page special entitled "Men, Tomorrow's Second Sex," accompanied by a leader with the title "The Trouble with Men." Both the feminization and "male as genetic sieve" arguments were rehearsed again, together with a joking fantasy future without men at all, men being now biologically redundant due to sperm banks—and culturally redundant, to boot, as knowledge-based societies "may be safer in women's hands" (September 28 1996, 20). This time, and more seriously, an explicit link was made between globalization, economic restructuring, and the feminization of society and employment in "rich" countries. This was accompanied by a wealth of evidence and statistics to suggest that women perform better at school and are steadily improving their position in the workplace (with some provisos about sex discrimination), mainly due to the collapse of blue-collar work and the unwillingness of blue-collar men to accept what they see as "women's work," even when it is reasonably well-paid. Although professional men were seen to be adjusting reasonably well to social and economic change, by adding some "'new man' attitudes" (25), blue-collar men were not, since "down at the bottom of the ladder where men are men and women change the nappies [diapers] (but also have the jobs), there are troubles of an entirely different order"(20).

*The Economist*'s argument ran that women's move toward equality has been at the expense of blue-collar men and that the price will be testosterone-induced social dysfunction in men that threatens the whole of society. This, it seems, is kept in check only by work, marriage, and the family. All three are linked and were currently under threat, since unemployed men are also unmarriageable, and sons of single parents and stepparents have more social problems. Without the socializing forces of work, marriage, and the family, men would turn to the "fundamentalist masculinity" of criminality and gang warfare. The argument that men can be civilized only through having to provide for and look after the "purer sex" in the breadwinning role, and that professional men are more "civilized" than the rest, runs deep in the West. It was the foundation of the late-Victorian gender ideology that took women and children out of the factories and made the wives of professional men into an imperial symbol of civilization. *The Economist* did not propose "turning the clock back" (30), but the combination of biologism and "breadwinner" ideology in the analysis left little room for alternative solutions and made the stated commitment to the equality of women seem rather lame. The best *The Economist* could offer were piece-meal reforms such as the employment of more male teachers and the de-criminalization of drugs, both of which would be more compatible with a cultural rather than biological explanation of gender difference.

What is striking about all this analysis is not the generally masculinist drift of such cobbled-together arguments, but rather the fact that masculini-ty was no longer taken for granted. This itself could be part of the trend to-ward masculine self-consciousness associated with the positioning of men as consumers (Mort 1988) and an increase in self-conscious presentation and "impression management" as personal reputation replaces hierarchical po-sition in the workplace (Collinson and Hearn 1994). However, the degree of sarcasm and embarrassed self-mockery involved in its treatment of the topic was extreme, even for *The Economist*. The moral panic over the collapse of the family, that bastion of patriarchy, was also uncharacteristic. Together with the rather confused mixture of contradictory ideas drawn from liberal, patriarchal, and biologically determinist perspectives, in a paper that has been generally known for its faith in both individualism and progress and its cool-headed logical analysis, these factors suggest that in spite of all the hype, globalization was provoking a high level of gender anxiety.

This gender anxiety was also reflected in one or two advertisements. For example, two weeks after the "Trouble with Men" special, NCR ran an ad-vertisement (October 12, 1996, 116–17) that, under the heading "Big Con-sumer is watching you," portrayed the image of a huge woman peering through the glass wall of an office, towering over the workers. The copy read: "There's nowhere to hide. The Age Of the Consumer has hit the fi-nancial services industry and consumers know it" (October 12, 1996, 116). Globalization in this case was not so much a boy's game, but rather a very feminine threat.

The appearance of gender anxiety and the increase in self-consciousness about masculinity suggest that hegemonic masculinity has indeed been un-dergoing a transition process that leaves it temporarily vulnerable. In the light of this, the increasing visibility of women and feminist issues men-tioned in chapter 4 may not reflect only a continuing process of assimila-tion, but could be more ambiguous. In a transition period, the increasing appearance of women, however treated, is as likely to undermine the gender order as it is to reinforce it.

THIS CHAPTER HAS identified a hothouse atmosphere of competition between different masculinities in *The Economist* and has then traced a bewildering array of gendered moves that have taken place in association with globalization. These moves involved not the simple replacement of one type of masculinity by another, but complex overlaps and reconfigurations forged from a mixture of elements drawn from different archetypes. Change itself has been presented as an evolutionary battle of styles for economic and political dominance.

The competing imagery includes a collapse in patriarchal and paternalistic forms; a rivalry and synthesis between individualism and feminized Japanese cooperation; the development of a U.S. frontier-expansionist masculinity with science-fiction trappings; a continuing bourgeois-rational emphasis on expertise; some challenges from the positive appearance of women and blacks; "risk winners" in remasculinized financial services; a general increase in informality; an Americanization of masculinity through the use of images of physical strength and sports; competition between expansive, hard-playing, and nerdy hard-working technocrats; some negative images of women as threats; and a degree of gender anxiety.

This apparently confusing array of imagery together amounts to an attempted (re)construction of hegemonic masculinity. As Robert Hanke (1992) argues, changes in hegemonic masculinity are worked through a variety of mechanisms, including negative symbols of masculinity and feminized constructions. In this case, changes in hegemonic masculine imagery linked to the processes of globalization appear to be moving in at least two main directions at once, as old hierarchies are broken down further and there is a move from administrative to fiscal coordination of bureaucracy (Connell 1990). On the one hand, there appears to be a softening of hegemonic masculinity associated with consumerism and a feminization of management styles; on the other hand, there is a cult of even more rationalized technocratic efficiency. This combination of moves allows for previously feminine characteristics to be repositioned as masculine, and for outdated paternalistic rules and hierarchies to be positioned as feminine.

Hegemonic masculinity is being reconfigured in the image of a less formal, less patriarchal, but more technocratic masculine elite that has the whole globe as its playground. This emerging hegemonic masculinity contains elements of both continuity and change. The aggressive deployment of "frontier masculinity" (now tied to contemporary globalization) provides a link to the past, as does the use of imperialist imagery. The need for softer, more informal qualities in business—qualities previously associated with "femininity"—has not been matched by demands for increased women's status but rather has been associated with Japanese business masculinity.[41] Whether Japanese and other Far Eastern businessmen were really being invited to share in the new globalized hegemonic masculinity of technocracy was less clear.[42] Given the persistence of racist and colonial metaphor elsewhere in the paper, and the West's colonial history of absorbing useful traits from other cultures that remained subordinate, it would seem unlikely, in spite of the paper's liberal, race-blind editorial stand. Indeed, coding Japanese business culture as "soft" or "feminine" may be a new twist on the preexisting racist stereotype of the "effeminate oriental" who is "mute, passive, charming, inscrutable" (Mercer and Julien 1988, 108).

What seemed to be conspicuously missing from *The Economist* (and this was in keeping with its liberal values and faith in progress) were positive images of the kind of backlash masculinity, popular among some right-wing groups, that seeks to restore patriarchal privilege in the family and the workplace. In its editorial pages, *The Economist* has endorsed neither social conservatism nor economic protectionism and has been against large bureaucracies and organizational rigidity. *The Economist*'s loyalties are nearly always to the future, creating a permanent atmosphere of threatened patricide. This contradicts and undermines the lingering patriarchal imagery in advertisements and promotional literature.[43]

On the other hand, the process of change has not been smooth. Not only are dichotomized gender ideologies particularly vulnerable during periods of change, when settled patterns of gender difference and gender segregation lose legitimacy, but the process of change has itself been disrupted by other trends that undermine hegemonic masculinity and posit an alternative vision of globalization. It has been disrupted by the increasing representation of women, in both editorial and advertising, by the increasing coverage of feminist and gender issues that have to be reported if *The Economist* wishes to keep its reputation for progressive liberalism, and by bouts of gender anxiety over masculinity itself. The bouts of gender anxiety, as argued above, stretch the usually legitimizing device of irony to its limit. Connell (1990, 534) suggests that what he calls "hysterical tendencies" in the media, together with the cult of the ruthless entrepreneur (so prevalent in the 1980s), may be signs of the unraveling of hegemonic masculinity rather than its transformation. If the masculinist imagery in *The Economist* is typical of a wider cultural shift, then there is room for feminists to exploit the contradictions between the "softer" and "harder" forms of masculinity that are on offer, to contest the coding of informality as "masculine" and "hierarchy" as feminine; and to nurture those alternative relationships, identities, and narratives that will renegotiate the relationship between diverse groups of women, femininity, and globalization.

However, in terms of *The Economist* itself, on balance, those factors that would undermine hegemonic masculinity have played a minor role in comparison with the dominant, science-fictionalized imagery of frontier masculinity and the promotion of technocracy, with its informal, cooperative-style working practices and a "risk winning" technical elite. In conclusion, *The Economist* is itself a prime site where the interpretive wars and symbolic struggles involved in the jostling for position between would-be hegemonic masculinities is played out—a site that is particularly relevant in terms of the construction of a contemporary, masculinist-inflected discourse of globalization. In the next chapter, this textual analysis of the paper is brought together with the earlier discussion of masculinities in IR, to see what light the one can shed on the other.

# CHAPTER SIX

# The *Economist* / IR Intertext

THE relationship between *The Economist* and IR can be examined through a number of intertextualities that are shared between the paper and the academic discipline. My intention in this chapter, in exploring this relationship, is to highlight some aspects of the gender politics of contemporary IR and the culture in which it is embedded. As established in chapter 4, *The Economist* is an important image maker and circulator of ideas between practitioners in international relations, academics in IR, and the wider cultural context of IR. The arguments put forward in chapter 3 about the competing models of masculinity that animate IR theory are therefore brought together with my analysis of masculinities in *The Economist* from chapters 4 and 5.

First, intertextualities between *The Economist* and mainstream approaches to IR are explored with a view to highlighting the way in which both glamorize and legitimate both the "international" and particular models of hegemonic masculinity in the same mutually reinforcing and mutually legitimating way. I then discuss intertextualities in terms of the characterization of globalization and the newer types of masculinity associated with globalization rhetoric. In particular, I make two points with respect to these developments: (1) that the co-opting of realist imagery for business ends and for the promotion of a masculinist version of globalization goes hand-in-hand with a neorealist interest in IPE as opposed to security matters; (2) by considering the intersections between some postmodern interventions in IR theory and newer constructions of masculinity that appear in the paper, further light is thrown on the assertion (made in chapter 3) that such approaches may be implicated in the construction of an emerging, more-technocratic form of hegemonic masculinity.

To keep the argument in focus, I deliberately limit this discussion of intertextualities to those between *The Economist* and academic IR. In many ways, the analysis so far already depends on shared meanings of masculinity and femininity that are themselves generated intertextually, even though their antecedents are not always explicitly referred to. Many other interesting intertextualities could of course be explored to illuminate the changing cultural, political, and economic context in which both *The Economist* and IR flourish. An examination of such intertextualities would undoubtedly shed further light on developments in the changing construction of hegemonic masculinities; so would an exploration of the impact of external influences such as economic downturns and political events. The discussions below should therefore not be read as a comprehensive analysis, or even as a single coherent strand in a larger narrative process; rather, they are to be read as a partial exposition of the relationship between two sites (the paper and the discipline of IR), where hegemonic masculinities are continually being produced and contested in numerous, varied, and often contradictory ways.

### *Intertextualities:* The Economist *and Mainstream* IR

The editorial line of *The Economist*, together with its rationalist approach to science and economics, fits comfortably with the positivist, game-theoretic world perspectives of neorealism and neoliberal institutionalism in IR (see chapter 4). There is also, perhaps less obviously, a close match between the signifiers of hegemonic masculinity that have saturated the paper and those deployed in mainstream IR. This intertextuality clearly illustrates the cultural connections between hegemonic masculinities and the conceptual space of "the international" within which IR operates.

The code of bourgeois-rational masculinity, itself implicated heavily in the methodology of the positivist approach, is replicated and reinforced by the representational realism of the paper. Like the rational actors of mainstream IR, the exonominated voice of *The Economist* appears physically disembodied and socially disembedded, and the prose shares IR's propensity to elevate calculative rationality above emotion, to be instrumentalist, and to be goal-oriented. Because the prose style forms the framework through which international affairs are apprehended in the paper (just as the positivist methodology forms the framework through which mainstream approaches to IR apprehend "reality"), its importance in promoting the worldview of bourgeois-rational masculinity can hardly be overstated. The worldviews of *The Economist* and of mainstream perspectives in IR are thus complementary and mutually reinforcing.

While in this intertextuality between *The Economist* and all mainstream perspectives in IR the same or similar signifiers of bourgeois masculinity circulate in a general discourse of masculinism, there are more specific affinities between the variety of elitist versions of masculinity signified in *The Economist* and the models of masculinity that frame (political) realism and neorealism. Firstly, the house style's code of masculine coherence that is forever threatened by the feminine Other of formlessness is closely related to the "heroic" code of coherence that Richard Ashley identifies at the heart of IR neorealism (Ashley 1986; 1988; 1989). Like the narrative realism of *The Economist*, (political) neorealism makes use of a modernist narrative structure identified as a logocentric monologue, whose sovereign voice imposes a coherent and singular meaning on history (Ashley 1989, 263). This sovereign voice is structured by the interchangeable masculinist binary dualisms of order/chaos and sovereignty/anarchy. In neorealism, the "sovereignty" of the positivist method (itself analyzed by Ashley as a series of textual strategies to impose order, coherence, and narrative closure) is matched by the "sovereignty" of the state. Both are forever defined against, and threatened by, feminine anarchy and chaos—either the anarchy of multiple interpretation or the anarchy of the international system. Thus "sovereignty" is doubly signed in neorealism, both through its method (shared by neoliberal institutionalists) and through its content, which places the sovereignty/anarchy binarism at its center, thus obscuring the "radical undecidability of history" (Ashley 1989, 272). This double signaling of sovereignty in the sparsely detailed and silently affirmed "paradigm of sovereign Man" (Ashley 1989, 300) represents a deeper, even more rigorous application of the code of unilinear coherence than other modern approaches to IR can muster. (Such approaches tend to have more complicated content, as discussed in chapter 3). Similarly, the code of coherence in *The Economist*'s house style, with its imperative to condense, simplify, and exaggerate, appears more extreme and exaggerated than in other branches of the quality press.

*The Economist*'s house style replicates the neorealist predilection for parsimony and abhorrence of theoretical complication. In his elaboration of the goals of neorealist theory, Waltz argues that to attain the status of "elegance," theories must "be constructed through simplifying. . . . Simplifications lay bare the essential elements in play. . . . The aim is to try to find the central tendency among a confusion of tendencies, to single out the propelling principle even though other principles operate, to seek the essential factors where innumerable factors are present" (Waltz 1986, 37–38). These are sentiments that any editor of *The Economist* could only endorse. Waltz's prose style also echoes (and bolsters) his theoretical preference for simplification and masculine economy (see chapter 3).[1] Indeed, Waltz could be following *The Economist Style Guide* himself, so fond is he of short sentences and clipped statements such as "Laws remain, theories come and go."[2] Like *The Economist*, Waltz's prose style combines the bourgeois-rationalism of coherence in representational realism with a punchy, perhaps even aggressive tone, more reminiscent of citizen-warriors. For example, when discussing the role of theory in social science, his arguments are presented as crisp, logically progressing statements of fact: "Theories are qualitatively different from laws. Laws identify invariant or probable associations. Theories show why those associations obtain" (Waltz 1986, 32). His conclusion that "Theories explain laws" (33) is a highly contestable one (Cox 1986), although it is presented as a short statement of fact, reminiscent of *The Economist*'s exaggerated code of coherence in which feminine equivocation is banished. In Waltz's case, at least, the paradigm of masculine sovereignty is thus signified in three ways: through his positivist method and privileging of parsimony (bourgeois rationalism); through the sovereignty/anarchy binarism that structures the content of his theory (bourgeois rationalism); and through his clipped and brusque masculine prose style (citizen-warrior).[3]

Just as bourgeois rationalism forms only one strand of hegemonic masculinity appearing in realism and neorealism, so it forms only one strand of hegemonic masculinity appearing in *The Economist*. A judicious mix of bourgeois rationalism, citizen-warrior, and patriarchal masculinities applies in both cases.[4] If *The Economist* house style embodies a masculinity that is bold, brash, and aggressive (citizen-warrior), yet measured, rational, and logical (bourgeois-rational) as well as effortlessly superior (patriarchal/elitist), as was argued above, then surely this is exactly the kind of masculinity best embodied by princes and statesmen, according to realist doctrine. The heroic tone and the "tough decisions" on what to highlight and what to ignore in a struggle effectively to "grasp" the essence of complicated issues in the text, mirror the "hard choices" required by statesmen and diplomats, who negotiate complicated and treacherous international affairs on behalf of the state (Rothstein 1991, 409).

In another parallel, the occasional lapse into the misogynistic metaphorical language of sexual conquest directly mirrors the kind of language Machiavelli used to resurrect the citizen-warrior model of masculinity from ancient Greece and Rome. Meanwhile, the Machiavellian, antidemocratic requirement of secrecy in the realist conception of diplomacy—in which success depends on only a select elite having privileged access to sensitive information, so that "the enemy" may not anticipate one's moves (Rothstein 1991)—resonates with the way in which *The Economist* interpellates it readers as privileged insiders. "Insider knowledge" is not only implied by the intimate tone of the "fireside chat" and the appreciation of the paper's irony, but has also been deliberately invoked in the promotional literature of the Economist Intelligence Unit, whose publications are produced by the Economist Group of publications and are heavily advertised in the weekly paper. The name of the unit itself suggests that insider knowledge is what it purveys. In a booklet advertising its *Foreign Report* (accompanying the April 29, 1995 issue), the reader was told that "[s]ince it first appeared 48 years ago, Foreign Report has gained an enviable reputation among decision makers and leaders. Now it's your chance to share their inside information" (leaflet April 29, 1995, inside front cover).

Subheadings described *Foreign Report* as "Your private intelligence service" and exhorted the reader to "Join the insiders." The "exclusive information and forecasts" it contained were guaranteed as "intelligence uncensored" (ibid.). The concept of "insider knowledge" clearly carries connotations of elitism and power confined to a few important men at the top, while the masses remain on the "outside." The notion of an "intelligence service" completed the picture—metaphorically presenting a world of diplomacy and spying, which resonates with both the real and fictional

spies of the cold war. James Der Derian has identified an intertextual blur-
ring of boundaries between fact and fiction in cold war spy culture, which
he argues

> represents a field of ideological contestation where national security strate-
> gies, with their endgames of impossibly real wars of mass annihilation, can
> be played and re-played for mass consumption as a simulation of war in
> which states compete, interests clash, and spy counters spy, all in signifi-
> cant fun. . . . In the confusion and complexity of international relations,
> the realm of the spy becomes a discursive space where realism and fantasy
> interact, and seemingly intractable problems are imaginatively and play-
> fully resolved. (Der Derian 1989, 163–64)

Popular fictional accounts of espionage have borrowed heavily from real
life, while real spies have not only consumed vast amounts of spy fiction,
but are known to have also modeled themselves on fictional characters. Spy
culture glamorizes the alienated world of realpolitik, and its popularity
crossed all classes in the cold war period: even U.S. presidents helped to al-
lay their fears of nuclear annihilation and national insecurity by reading spy
fiction: John Kennedy reportedly was a fan of Ian Fleming's James Bond
and Ronald Reagan enjoyed Tom Clancy novels (Der Derian 1989, 172).

This intertextuality between fact and fiction in spy culture has been replayed in the pages of *The Economist*. On the fiction side, James Bond
made an appearance in April 1996, in an advertisement for Omega watches
(April 6, 1996, 4; April 20, 1996, 2). The advertisement showed a still photograph of the actor Pierce Brosnan from the film *GoldenEye*, wearing an
Omega watch, with the caption "James Bond in GoldenEye." Bond, although fictional, was insinuated in with all the other "personalities" in this
series of Omega advertisements.[5] The copy read: "The legendary secret
agent James Bond is back, in a high drama, high-living and high-style adventure." James Bond, suave, sophisticated, and never too busy to frequent
casinos or date women as well as outwit the thinly veiled cold war enemy,
epitomized the *Playboy* lifestyle identified by Ehrenreich: one of conspicuous consumption and heterosexual flight from domesticity (Ehrenreich
1983)—but with the added bonus of an aristocratic English twist. With his
aristocratic background, his unflappable cool, ruthlessness, and superior
brain, Bond embodied all the virtues of an Anglicized version of a Machi-

avellian prince, his intrigues updated for a technocratic twentieth century with electronic wizardry and consumerism thrown in. As an icon, James Bond resonates particularly well with the images of elite masculinity appearing in *The Economist*'s " World Profile" (see chapter 4), which featured a glamorous world of conspicuous consumption, technological gadgetry, foreign travel, and success with women, with gentlemanly overtones. Bond's later, post-1970s appearances may have become more parodic (Ehrenreich 1983, 104), and the Omega advertisement clearly deployed his image playfully, but in the mid 1990s the Bond image was still a potent signifier of masculine power and a glamorous international elitism. Other slightly tongue-in-cheek references to James Bond have included a feature article on a James Bond convention in Jamaica, the former home of Ian Fleming (*The Economist* November 9, 1996, 149). The article concluded: "Bond taught fans less how to kill (himself or others) than how to shop, for Cartiers, Aston Martins and designer clothes." Appropriately positioned on a nearby spread (147) was a Cartier advertisement. The parodic element inevitably attached to Bond's representation in the 1990s fits well with the general irony of *The Economist*, in a kind of replay of cold war hegemonic masculinity for nostalgic half-believers, at a time of great change and uncertainty. The cold war was over, but the emerging new regime of "globalization" was not yet settled.

Turning to fact, the CIA, the U.S. intelligence agency, calling itself "the clandestine service," chose to advertise for new recruits through the pages of *The Economist* in September 1995 and again in an identically worded advertisement in December 1996.[6] On offer was "the ultimate overseas career" demanding "an adventurous spirit . . . a forceful personality . . . superior intellectual ability . . . toughness of mind . . . and a high degree of integrity" (September 9, 1995, 9; December 21, 1996, 157). The advertisement claimed that "these people are the cutting edge of American intelligence, an elite corps gathering the vital information needed by our policy makers to make critical foreign policy decisions." In a further reinforcement of the fact/fiction spies-and-diplomacy intertext permeating *The Economist*, a film/television advertisement for the paper launched in September 1996 featured the former diplomat Henry Kissinger, sitting next to an *Economist* reader on a plane journey. Kissinger is arguably one of a handful of people with the ultimate "insider knowledge" of the cold war and a master at diplomatic intrigue, who in dealing with China and the Soviet Union is widely regarded as having successfully played the two countries off against each other in a sophisticated balance-of-power game.[7] As Peter York argued, in this advertisement, "the casting is utterly right for its targets' private fantasies" (*Independent on Sunday* October 20, 1996, review, 34).

The affinity with (political) realism occurs not only through *The Economist* replaying elements of hegemonic masculinity that happen to be in general cultural circulation, but also through much more specific constructions of hegemonic masculinity, which although cloaked in the language and conventions of bourgeois rationality, often have their roots in Machiavelli's reworking of the citizen-warrior model. Such constructions elevate and glamorize the international connection.

### Globalization, The Economist, *and Mainstream* IR

In examining the intertextualities between *The Economist* and mainstream IR in terms of globalization, I wish to make two main points. The second point will be to consider intertextualities between the paper and mainstream IR on the presentation of globalization itself, but first I will argue that the mobilization of realist imagery in the service of global business has helped promote the recent neorealist interest in international political economy (IPE).

It is worth remembering that the realist constructions of masculinity in *The Economist*, such as the spy/intelligence rhetoric, have been mobilized in the service of business, rather than politics. For example the Economist Intelligence Unit provides business intelligence, not political intelligence. In the glamorized international arena of *The Economist*, the business elite wears realist clothing. This appears congruent, because international politics and business have been constructed as inhabiting very similar Hobbesian worlds. In the spaces of international and market anarchy, at the extremes, war and bankruptcy are an ever-present threat, and success is measured in terms of political or market power. The interchangeability of politics and business in this imagery gives the "low politics" of trade and political economy access to the glamour of "the international." The cold war, which represented a rivalry between giants forced to resort in the main to maneuvering rather than violence, became the model for rivalry between large multinational corporations, with the James Bond playboy image being particularly suited to both worlds. With the cold war over, global business was thriving in the mid 1990s, not only expanding its markets into formerly Communist areas, but also deepening through having the whole planet as its production line. Cold war realist imagery may have met its sell-by date in terms of politics, but its well-established and easily recognized tropes were subsequently mobilized to promote and glamorize globalization as an elite masculine pursuit. Thus the globe became the expanded playground for playboy businessmen and their new gadgets produced by science. If the international world is glamorous, then the concept of "the globe" offers an even wider playing field, where business elites appear to "have the whole world at their feet."

If this interchangeability between business and politics in realist imagery has helped glamorize business and globalization in *The Economist*, then it has also helped to give the neorealist approach to IPE a glamorous appeal to young men that was once reserved for strategic studies. Waltz's neorealism retains a traditional focus on high politics and war, but in this he stands rather alone. Other neorealists such as Robert Gilpin (1987) have concentrated instead on IPE. As cold war realist imagery has been co-opted by business and finance, they have been able to make the move from "high" security politics to the "low" politics of trade and economics without any great threat to their masculine status as realists.

Another affinity between the corporate world of *The Economist* and neorealist IR and IPE is that they all share a social-Darwinist lens on the world. As argued in chapter 5, the corporate world of *The Economist* is one in which the fittest survive, in terms of corporate strategies and styles as well as companies. Through sociobiology, the behavior of men has also been explained in terms of social-Darwinism, giving *The Economist* a super-Darwinist lens on the world. Meanwhile, in the realm of IR theory, there has been a convergence between neorealist theories of IR and neoclassical theories of free-market economics, also around super-Darwinism. A clear example of the confluence of sociobiology, *The Economist*'s rhetorical style, and neorealist IR theory appears in Frances Fukuyama's article "Women and the Evolution of World Politics" (1998). Writing in a curt style reminiscent of both Waltz and *Economist* leader writers, Fukuyama argues that the competitive, war-prone nature of international relations is largely determined by masculine biology and genetics. He states that "female chimps have relationships; male chimps practice realpolitik" (Fukuyama 1998, 25) and that "the line from chimp to modern man is continuous" (27). This is basically a Hobbesian view of the world (albeit one that Fukuyama would like to see constrained) dressed up with scientific explanation. Fukuyama's argument is reductionist in that he equates chimp behavior with human behavior, and the traits of individual men with large-scale, institutionalized social phenomena such as warfare (Ehrenreich 1999). He also makes the classic sociobiological assumption that traits that are "rooted in biology" (Fukuyama 1998, 27) are more difficult to change than mere culture, and that humans are "hard-wired to act in certain predictable ways" (30). His references to recent genetic research, for example, ignore the complex relationship between genes and their environment in which environmental influences may dictate which genes are switched on, or "expressed," and when (Ridley 1999). While the point of Fukuyama's article may have been to discuss the influence of women on international politics (of which more below)—and he displays a self-consciousness about masculinity previously absent in this type of IR theorizing—his analysis of "Man" and his social environment is, if anything, cruder than that reflected in *The Economist* (at least on the paper's science pages) but nevertheless shares the same basic perspective.[8] Man is a creature who is constantly competing for dominance in a status hierarchy.

Fukuyama's article refers to the "evolution of world politics" in its title, and it associates developments in global politics with the evolution of humankind. His brand of evolutionary history echoes the explicit incorporation of evolutionary theory into the neorealist cannon. The stated intention of deploying evolutionary theory is to add a dynamic dimension to analysis, to explain change. In a special edition of *International Studies Quarterly* devoted to evolutionary theory and its impact on both strategic studies and IPE, the "evolutionary analogy" is employed because "[i]n our view, biological and social systems are both subject to evolutionary processes and for that reason share certain similarities. They are complex systems that exhibit selection pressures, and cooperative and synergistic features; and in their transformations they employ innovation and thrive on innovation" (Modelski and Poznanski 1996, 316). Neorealism is deemed to show "a close affinity" with social Darwinism, in which innovation replaces mutation and economic and social competition replaces natural selection (ibid., 319). Haraway's observation that theoretical developments in the human and natural sciences have always been closely linked to technological and theoretical developments in capitalism is again relevant here. Apparently, even Darwin acknowledged his debt to Malthus. Thus it is hard to imagine "what evolutionary theory would be like in any language other than classical capitalist political economy" (Haraway 1991, 39). Both employ the language of progress, scarcity, and competition.

This interchangeability between the concepts of natural selection and the processes of social and economic competition is strikingly similar to much of the globalization rhetoric of *The Economist*, discussed earlier. In both *The Economist* and IR there are apparently seamless connections between capitalism, sociobiology, and international relations in their construction of "the paradigm of Man" (to borrow Ashley's phrase), and their mutual reliance on social-Darwinism. This super-Darwinist worldview tends to promote a bourgeois-rationalist-with-warrior-trappings version of hegemonic masculinity (warrior trappings boost the credibility of the hegemonic masculinity of international business, as bourgeois rationalism on its own can appear rather tame and domesticated). The international—or, rather, global—business arena is perceived to be a ruthlessly competitive environment governed by the "natural selection" processes of economic competition, and permeated by the same aura of danger and uncertainty as is the world of international relations.

Discussions in chapter 5 traced some of the historic connections and affinities between "frontier" culture, "foreign adventure," and "the international," all of which occupy a conceptual position far removed from domesticity and have helped construct certain elitist and expansionist versions of Anglo-American hegemonic masculinity. It is unsurprising, then, that this "frontier culture" can be found in academic IR as well as in *The Economist*. The anarchic world depicted in both academic theory and popular culture necessitates and indeed injects a heroic element into the "frontier" activities of entrepreneurs (and, by association, the academics who study them) as an anecdote related by Ashley (1996) confirms: a female colleague suggested that "you boys in IR . . . always talk as if you're out there on the plains somewhere, on horse-back, galloping alone" (quoted in Ashley 1996, 240).

Moving on to examine the presentation of globalization itself, in *The Economist* it has been characterized as an economic phenomenon, the product of an interaction between market forces and scientific innovation (as discussed above). The effects of globalization have been analyzed in terms of changing management strategies and employment skills, new global divisions of labor, competition between U.S. and Japanese styles of capitalism, and technological wizardry in finance. Although a whole host of meanings have been encoded into the globalization discourse, related to such issues as reflexivity, risk, adventure, informality, and gender, these form a subtext. Ostensibly, globalization has been presented as a largely material phenomenon, and little, if any, direct attention has been given to the politics of subjectivity.

As it is in *The Economist*, so it is, by and large, in mainstream IR and IPE. The term *globalization* has become widely used as a general metaphor for changes in the world economy, such as increased economic integration and interdependence, combined with instantaneous communications (Hurrell 1995; Strand 1996), and as such has been bandied about a great deal in post–cold war discussions of the international order and the contemporary nature of world society (e.g., Luard 1990; Axford 1995; Holm and Sorensen 1995; Hirst and Thomson 1996). Where globalization has been more explicitly theorized in mainstream IR and IPE, it has been seen, for example, as the result of benign U.S. power in the world economy (Gilpin 1987),[9] the triumph of economic liberalism (Fukuyama 1989; Ohmae 1990 and 1995), or determined by technological progress (Rosenau 1990). This type of upbeat theorizing concentrates on technology, economics, and high politics, all staple masculinist fare of *The Economist*.

There are also some more specific connections. For example, Gilpin, like *The Economist*, maps a rivalry between U.S. and Japanese capitalism in terms of corporate culture: "The economic differences between Japan and its economic partners are not merely economic disputes; they result from a cultural clash of societies with different national priorities, social values, and domestic structures" (Gilpin 1987, 377). Later, Gilpin analyzes the competition between the U.S. and Japanese economies in terms of "evolutionary fitness." He argues that whichever country's corporate culture adapts most effectively to the global economic environment—that is, whichever country can achieve the best "fit"—will dominate the global economy (Gilpin 1996, 427). This social-Darwinist argument fits in well with the general outlook of *The Economist* on globalization.

This mainstream IR literature (and the portrayal of globalization in *The Economist*) contrasts with the sociological and social-geography literature on globalization that also examines risk and reflexivity (Giddens 1990; Lash and Urry 1994), the relationship between globalization and postmodernism (Harvey 1989; Giddens 1990; Lash and Urry 1994), and time/space disruptions (Harvey 1989; Giddens 1990). In considering the subjective aspects of globalization as well as the material and political ones, this alternative literature has spawned a new global politics and sociology literature that examines such matters as the dissolution between cultural experience and territorial location (Tomlinson 1997), the decentering of the state and new kinds of citizenship (Albrow 1996), and reflexive connections between individuals and global institutions (Spybey 1995)—all relevant to IR. The impact of globalization on international relations and global political economy is far-reaching. However, discussions are generally confined to a narrow range of topics: economic competition between states, struggles between governments and markets over control of economic policy, a deepening of interdependence, and new opportunities to shrink the "globe" through high-tech warfare. The dominant trend is to stick to the staple fare of economics and technology, together with state and interstate politics.[10] As Julian Saurin (1995) argues, to understand globalization one needs a new mind-set, one that is not focused on territorialism and comparative method but one that, rather, can understand the global reconfiguration of social authority, including principles of identity and representation as well as resource allocation and distribution. The politics of subjectivity connected to globalization have a bearing on IR and IPE, and wherever the politics of subjectivity are to be found, gender constructions are usually heavily implicated. Moreover, wherever this is not explicitly acknowledged, it is likely to be implicitly coded.

## Globalization, The Economist, *and Postpositivist IR*

Postpositivist approaches to IR have generally cast more widely for an analysis of globalization than have mainstream approaches. Feminists, for example, have examined some of the gender implications of global restructuring (e.g., Peterson and Runyan 1993, 1998; Runyan 1996; Pettman 1996; Marchand and Runyan 2000). Critical and postmodern theorists have examined the discourse of globalization itself (Kofman and Youngs 1996) and have related globalization to new local/global relationships (e.g., Walker and Mendlovitz 1990); to inequality (Hurrell and Woods 1995); to the development of global cities (Shapiro and Neaubauer 1990); to an emerging global civilization (Bateson 1990; Brown 1995); to time/space contractions (Der Derian 1990); and to risk and reflexivity (Elliott 1995). A *Millennium* special issue (1995) was devoted to a critical discussion of the relationship between globalization and liberalism.

However, in spite of considering the implications of globalization itself in more critical and varied ways, many of which include a reflexive or subjective aspect, some postpositivist contributions, as was suggested in chapter 3, nonetheless play into the hands of the emerging hegemonic masculinity of technocracy, which in *The Economist* is firmly linked to globalization.

The poststructural obsession with breaking down boundaries and occupying of previously feminized space has parallels with the new informal working practices of the technical elite. As suggested in my analysis of *The Economist*, these working practices were themselves previously coded as feminine but are now being successfully colonized for hegemonic masculinity. Thus the occupation of previously feminized space in postpositivist IR does not necessarily break from the dominant trend in contemporary hegemonic masculinity; rather, in some cases it can be seen to complement it. This trend undermines the claim of Ashley and others who do not explicitly tackle gender issues to "speak from the margins," at least in gender terms.[11]

In addition, as mentioned in chapter 3, postmodern IR theorists such as Der Derian and Shapiro have shown an enthusiasm for new technology that is characterized in playful, science-fiction terms. Just as the rhetorical style of Waltz uncannily paralleled phallogocentric Economese, so does Der Derian's rhetoric echo the science-fictionalized world of technology associated with globalization in *The Economist*. The technophilia is similar. Der Derian's close attention to military and telecommunications hardware, his reference to fast cars, and his general techno-celebratory stance have already been mentioned. Similarly, *The Economist* shows an enthusiasm for technology and has linked globalization to images of fast cars, space rockets (which are themselves associated with military hardware), and machine power. Der Derian deliberately uses language with high-tech, scientific connotations. So does *The Economist*. The mixing of science with fiction is also similar. Der Derian has invoked hidden powers in the "deep black" (Der Derian 1990, 304), and used terms like *cyberspace, chronopolitics* and *simulation sickness* (301), while *The Economist* has borrowed the H. G. Wells title *War of the Worlds* (*The Economist* October 1, 1994, survey cover) and also shown bug-eyed aliens (March 27, 1993, survey cover). *The Economist*, too, has used terms like *cybernomics* (September 28, 1996, survey cover). Der Derian and *The Economist* have both used the imagery of space and speeding into the future. Der Derian praises the futurists, who he argued "burned brightly" (Der Derian 1990, 306). *The Economist* meanwhile deployed its own version of futurism in surveys such as "The Future of Medicine—Peering into 2010" (March 19, 1994, survey title). Both have made references to "the frontier," as in "Speed: The Final Frontier" (Der Derian 1990, 306) and "The Frontiers of Finance" (*The Economist* October 9, 1993, survey title).

In this use of language, Der Derian may be tongue-in-cheek, but then so is *The Economist*. The tone of take-it-or-leave-it sophisticated irony serves to distance the author/newspaper from the rather crude promotion of techno-celebratory masculinity and, at the same time, to (re)produce and promote those very things. More generally, if technocratic masculinity is more reflexive and self-conscious than other varieties of hegemonic masculinity, as Thrift (1994) argues, then so is postpositivist IR more reflexive and self-conscious than other perspectives.

The stylistic intersections between Der Derian's work and the masculinist constructions associated with globalization in *The Economist* are numerous enough to implicate this particular strand of postpositivist IR in the promotion of an emerging, hegemonic, technocratic-frontier masculinity that is heavily Americanized. Indeed, put together, the incorporation of previously feminine elements by writers such as Ashley and the technological "virtual reality" themes of writers such as Der Derian fit in well with the twin-track softening and remasculinizing constructions of globalization in *The Economist*, which, as I have argued, serve just such an emerging global technocratic masculine elite. This does not mean that these postpositivist contributors to IR would themselves be included in such an elite, nor does it even mean that they would meet such a development with approval, but it does show the limits of "the oppositional imagination," to employ the phrase used in Joan Cocks's 1989 title, particularly when it is blind to its own gender constructions.

In terms of the discipline of IR, these stylistic intersections show how those postpositivists who remain gender blind, rather than representing a break with positivist perspectives in IR, may rather provide continuity. They do this by inadvertently adding new constructions of hegemonic masculinity to the pot of masculine rivalries that already animates the discipline. In failing to break from masculinist conceptions of international relations, they may be enabling such rivalries to continue, so that the discipline of IR remains an important site for the symbolic shaping and reshaping of hegemonic masculinity.

## The Significance of Intertextualities

The above exploration of intertextualities reveals a very high level of correspondence between *The Economist* and IR theory, in terms of both the construction of masculinities and the characterization of the international realm, including its latest trend, globalization. This correspondence represents a web of mutually reinforcing influences between IR, *The Economist*, and the wider Anglo-American popular culture that they both tap into. While the basic models of citizen-warrior, patriarchal, honor/patronage, and bourgeois-rational masculinities have been in circulation a long time, and certainly predate both *The Economist* and the founding of IR as a distinct discipline, the particular conjunctions of ingredients taken from these models is constantly evolving.

This analysis has not tried to establish whether particular constructions of masculinity, or of globalization, have appeared first in the theoretical constructions of the discipline, *The Economist*, or elsewhere. Regardless of its origin, for any particular construction to become significant for the production of masculinities on the ground, it needs to be repeated across a variety of diverse media. As a widely read, high-quality newspaper serving the global elite, *The Economist* has political and economic influence. It is therefore very likely that its images of elite masculinities, even if they are created without conscious intent, are equally influential. If this is true of *The Economist*, then it is so much more so with IR, which has the added credentials of academic rigor and the status as the highest form of knowledge on international affairs. Even if the discipline of IR is not the originator of particular models of masculinity, its minimum influence is as an intellectual cornerstone of ideas on gender and masculinities: it endlessly repeats, endorses, promotes, legitimates, and above all naturalizes particular versions of hegemonic masculinity.

To some extent, neither IR theory nor *The Economist* can help but be enmeshed in the power games of the culture within which they are produced and circulated.[12] However, given its authoritative position with regard to the production of knowledge, IR theory both could, and should, be far more mindful of its promotion and endorsement of hegemonic forms of masculinity. The degree to which the masculinities that inhabit IR scholarship actually construct the identities of individual men on the ground depends on processes of identification, which are informed by how the IR/popular culture nexus, partially explored here, interacts with institutional practices and experiences of embodiment. This can happen in various combinations of mutually reinforcing and/or contradictory ways. However—because the discipline of IR constructs a gender-segregated sphere that is thoroughly saturated with masculinities; because it carries the highest status as knowledge; and because, as this chapter has shown, it is closely woven into the wider culture through heavily gendered intertextualities, IR can be seen to play an important part in the symbolic aspect of gender identification. In the case of an expansionist version of Anglo-American hegemonic masculinity, which as this book has argued continues to be partially constructed through a relationship with the international or the global, the role of the discipline may even prove to be crucial.

## Afterword on the Intertext and the Impact of Feminism

In the latter part of the period under study, there were some changes in the representation of gender in the pages of *The Economist*. It was suggested above that the process of globalization and the gendered struggles between would-be hegemonic masculinities associated with this were increasingly accompanied by highly ironic, self-conscious bouts of gender anxiety over masculinity. It was also noted that the coverage of women and "women's issues" in the paper during 1995 and 1996 was increasing, although often confined to humorous peripheral anecdotes that were considerably less serious than the traditionally masculine affairs of the main text. The effect of this was ambiguous—such sidebar anecdotes acknowledged but could have helped contain and neutralize feminist threats to hegemonic masculinity through derisory humor. However, perhaps they also insinuated previously taboo or unsettling material into the paper, in a fashion that would not cause the current readership to turn away. Moreover, advertisements showing women in strategic business roles were also increasing. Although at the end of 1996 the overall effect of *The Economist* was still comfortably masculine, the long-term implications of these trends might prove more subversive.

It is perhaps worth a brief examination of the paper's post-1996 editorial content to search for clues as to where such trends might be leading. A glance at some of the paper's subsequent treatment of women and feminism suggests that, combined with some of the more woman-friendly advertising being included latterly, perhaps irony did have the effect of habituating the readership to a range of threatening topics, which had some potential to undermine hegemonic codes of masculinity.

It has already been noted that the number of articles mentioning women and feminism increased during 1995–96. In the three years following the end of the study (i.e., 1997–99) it is my impression that *The Economist* continued to pay more attention to women and explicit gender issues. The contributions of women (other than major figures such as Mrs. Thatcher, who had always received good coverage) were fairly regularly included, with, for example, a review of women's history books (September 12, 1998, review 13); a review of crime fiction that included female writers alongside male ones (June 19, 1999, review, 5); and occasional obituaries of interesting women, such as Dorothy West (August 29, 1998, 89), Anita Hoffman (January 9, 1999, 96), and Mary Jane Rathbun (April 24, 1999, 124). In 1998, a sixteen-page survey was devoted entirely to the issue of women and work (July 18 1998, survey, "Women and Work"). This contrasted favorably with an article on women's work in 1990 that spanned only four pages (June 30, 1990, 21–24) and a two-page "schools brief" on women at work in 1994 (March 5, 1994, 96–97). Offensive language such as the use of the rape metaphor was also conspicuous by its absence. If material about feminists had largely been sidelined to humorous boxes in 1995–96, by 1999 it was the turn of non-hegemonic masculinity: for example, a story about "Japan's pretty boys" and their increasing consumption of "men's beauty products," appeared in a sidebar (July 10, 1999, 77). Although the occasional leader had always promoted equal opportunities for women, feminism now received some serious supportive coverage in the body of the paper, with for example a favorable review of feminist literature (March 13, 1999, review, 3–4). Feminism was also described as "the most far reaching contemporary struggle for recognition" (June 19, 1999, review, 8) in a critical review of Francis Fukuyama's (1999) book *The Great Disruption: Human Nature and the Reconstitution of Social Order*. Fukuyama's analysis of social change was taken to task for technological determinism, and he was criticized for ignoring the impact of feminism, characterized by the reviewer as the real driving force behind the changes Fukuyama identified (*The Economist* June 19, 1999, review, 7–8).

By 1999, the subject of (hegemonic) masculinity, too, was receiving less hysterical, more evenhanded coverage. For example, a piece headlined "The Trouble with Boys" (May 29, 1999, 35–36) suggested that the "near obsession in officialdom" over the recent poor performance of British boys in literacy and English-language skills and its underlying causes (including the suspicion that this was connected to feminism in the classroom) was misplaced, because "boys' language skills tend to lag behind those of girls' [*sic*] the world over" (35). In the past this was less apparent, not least because educational selection in Britain was "skewed deliberately" (35) to balance the sexes. Far from agreeing with the government's concerns, the article pointed out that there was little talk of extra help for girls who lagged behind in sciences, and that ethnicity and class correlated far more closely with educational outcomes than did gender. Another article, the following month, headlined "Mournful Man" (July 10, 1999, 109–10) reviewed a number of books that discussed the modern complaint that men are increasingly marginalized or at a disadvantage. Again, the article showed little sympathy with this viewpoint, which was "ridiculously exaggerated" (110), at least in the hands of the anthropologist Lionel Tiger. The article mentioned the need to keep things in perspective, and asked "how many men would willingly trade places with women?" (109). It is interesting to contrast this brisk and level-headed coverage of the topic of masculinity in these two articles with the hysterical tone of similar discussions in 1996.

It seems that the initially ironic introduction of material that might be regarded as irrelevant or anxiety provoking, or perhaps both, to an overwhelmingly elite male readership did pave the way for a gradual change in *The Economist*'s mainstream coverage—a change that could eventually undermine the paper's masculinism. There is perhaps a parallel here with a remark Carol Cohn made in a different context. When discussing a flippant and humorous acronym that defence intellectuals used to disguise a particularly unpalatable aspect of nuclear war, she observed: "but it seems to me that speaking about it with that edge of derision is exactly what allows it to be spoken about and seriously discussed at all. It is the very ability to make fun of a concept that makes it possible to work with a concept rather than reject it outright" (Cohn 1987, 713). Having been exposed to the coverage of explicit gender issues for a while in a similar fashion, perhaps *Economist* readers had become habituated to reading about women, feminism, and the contemporary state of masculinity. More serious coverage would then appear relatively unremarkable.

Although these examples are not a systematic study of the whole period, they point to the increasing integration of women and gender issues into the general fabric of the paper, admittedly on a small scale and on a generally Eurocentric basis. While previous reference has not been made to the status of contributors to the paper, it is interesting to note in this respect that throughout the 1990s, although the readership was overwhelmingly male, the paper had a number of women journalists in senior positions, such as economics editor, diplomatic editor, and environmental editor. The chief executive from spring 1992 to summer 1996 was also a woman, Marjorie Scardino. Subsequently, in 1996, Scardino was promoted to the position of chief executive of Pearson (a media conglomerate that part owns *The Economist* Group), thus becoming the first female chief executive of an FT-SE 100 company. Clearly there is no glass ceiling for women at *The Economist*. However, the presence of women in newspaper publishing has so far done little to change the culture of work in the field, which involves long hours and unexpected demands that are fairly incompatible with child-care responsibilities. Scardino has children, and a profile of her published in the *Independent on Sunday* revealed that she apparently got around such problems by having a model New Man husband, who while working part-time was "now firmly established as 'principal carer' for the children" (Peter Popham, *Independent on Sunday* October 20, 1996, 19).[13]

The article also stated that Scardino was personally responsible for the increase in humor and irony in the paper during her period as chief executive, with jokes latterly appearing even in its annual reports (*Independent on Sunday* October 20, 1996, 19). Without imputing any particular motives to this promotion of irony and humor, and while not wishing to overstate the effect of the changes that it has been associated with, the increase in visibility of feminism and explicit gender issues that have come in its wake have at least tempered if not undermined the relentless competition between masculinities that has otherwise characterized the paper.

Since *The Economist* offers a representational window onto more general gender power struggles, and given how closely the gendered imagery of *The Economist* and IR theory mirror each other, change in one may coincide with or presage change in the other. So, as a corollary to the changes in *The Economist* in the latter half of the 1990s, perhaps students of IR can also expect a more serious treatment of gender issues in mainstream academic literature. Fukuyama's (1998) article "Women and the Evolution of World Politics," mentioned above in connection with its sociobiological underpinnings, is notable in this respect. Fukuyama's point is that, on the whole, women are different, and that the feminization of politics with its concurrent shift toward "a less status and military-power-oriented world," at least in the "democratic zone of peace" (Fukuyama 1998, 35), is a good thing, although limited in scope by the presence of competitive, aggressive males. He also refers to demographic changes, in which elderly women are predicted to form powerful voting blocs in democratic countries by the mid twenty-first century. Although Fukuyama's article completely ignores feminist literature (as does his 1999 book, also criticized above), and instead relies on dubious and hackneyed sociobiological theories to underpin its claims, this is an interesting argument—and one that does not have to depend on faulty sociobiological reasoning. It also does at least indicate that women are no longer "invisible" to mainstream male academic theorizers. It is a mainstream article by a mainstream male author in a mainstream journal, for whom women and women's demographic power are no longer invisible but are regarded as having a potentially profound influence on the shape of international relations. Such developments suggest that while feminists and mainstream IR theorists may continue to talk at cross-purposes, as a frustrated Ann Tickner has pointed out (Tickner 1996b), perhaps they will not always appear to inhabit entirely different disciplines.

# IR and the (Re)Making of Hegemonic Masculinity

ASKING the question "What role does international relations play in the shaping, defining, or legitimating of masculinity or masculinities?" entails making a shift from the standard practice of taking identities (whether gender or otherwise) as givens—which might then inform international relations, toward a more sophisticated, constructionist view that sees cross-cutting influences in both directions. The simple answer to the question is that international relations has played an important part in not only reflecting and legitimating specific masculinities, but also in constructing and defining them. In particular, this book has argued that the discipline of IR is heavily implicated in the construction and promotion of Anglo-American models of hegemonic masculinity—and that this role continues in connection with globalization. Particular models of masculinity are hidden in the methods; they inhabit the theories as shadowy subtexts to the stated subject matter, and rivalries between different masculinities inform paradigmatic and methodological debates—all in a glamorous international arena that is symbolically separated off from the rest of society as an all-male sphere.

Like other feminist approaches, this perspective has refused to accept international/domestic and public/private boundaries to politics as relevant. In this case, it is because they obscure the relationships between the international and the private, and render the question of gendered constructions of identity outside the remit of international relations. Such boundaries both construct international relations as a masculine space and then hide the crucial role that its theory and practices play in the construction of specifically masculine identities.

The approach taken here has also refused to accept that academic discourse and popular culture are discrete areas of life. It has explored some intersections between the two to illuminate their mutually reinforcing role in constructing the symbolic dimension of the gender order and gender identities. This is not to overplay the influence of academic discourse (or popular culture), or to suggest that academic discourse determines gender identities. The outcome depends on the degree of congruity between the discursive fields of academic IR and popular culture, on the one hand, and the institutional processes and embodied practices that they inform and reflect, on the other. It also depends on varied readership strategies and processes of identification and negotiation. Although these are not explored in any detail here, the ubiquity of the constructions of hegemonic masculinity that have been revealed, and the congruence between their representations in academic discourse and popular culture, point to an extremely influential, culturally hegemonic role for the representation of elite Anglo-American masculinities with glamorized international or global connections.

While deriving insights from feminism on the construction of gender identities and the nature of masculinism, masculine gender identities have been theorized here in a more fluid way than is generally found in feminist literature. Relationships between masculinities have been characterized as not only hierarchical, but also as involving much rivalry, jostling for position, change, and synthesis. In the micropolitics of masculinities, multiple interpretive wars are waged using strategies of masculinization and feminization, a few of which have been mapped above. Thus masculinism can be seen to involve not just the elevation of masculinity over femininity, but also the elevation of some types of masculinity over others. This type of theorizing has the advantage of capturing some of the complexity of gender politics. It avoids both an overly static picture of what is actually an ever-changing reality and the dualism that has dogged much feminist scholarship. It can also avoid the pitfalls of voluntarism, on the one hand, and cultural determinism, on the other, through careful attention to historical context and an awareness of the ongoing interplay between all three dimensions of embodiment, institutional practices, and discursive formations in the construction of gender identities. It is to be hoped that future feminist theorizing of gender identities will continue to move away from static conceptions and toward more open-ended analyses of the processes of gender identification. The perspective developed here is hopefully a step in this direction, and although the focus of this book has been on the relationship between masculinities and international relations, the approach is intended to have more widespread applications.

## Mapping Anglo-American Hegemonic Masculinity

A contribution to the project of exploring the politics of masculinities is the mapping of Anglo-American hegemonic masculinity. The ideal types of citizen-warrior and bourgeois-rational man, and to a lesser extent Judeo-Christian patriarch and honor/patronage aristocrat, first encountered through a fairly brief examination of some of the literature on gender and masculinity, have proved useful guides to the various constructions of Anglo-American masculinities in both IR and *The Economist*. Indeed, they have matched so well the various representations of masculinity that have been discussed here that it seems clear that Anglo-American hegemonic masculinity is indeed largely made up of shifting combinations of elements from these particular ideal types. While the bourgeois-rational model may be in the ascendant, it is important not to underplay the influence of the others, which continue to provide an elitist element to contemporary constructions, even as the twenty-first century opens.

As well as being constructed out of elements from various historically produced ideal types, contemporary Anglo-American hegemonic masculinity continues to be shaped by an encounter with the "international" realm beyond the borders of the state and/or "civilization." In the past, this encounter, in the British case, took the form of colonialism, wherein the identity of the Victorian English Gentleman was defined in relation to a global hierarchy of racialized masculinities. In the case of the United States, it took the form of internal colonialism and life at the "frontier." The particular point that this book has made (reinforced by the textual analysis of *The*

Economist) in connection with this history is that encounters with the "international" continue to play a crucial part in shaping Anglo-American hegemonic masculinity. In the era of the cold war, spy culture and the iconic figure of James Bond—an international consumer playboy—drew on notions of aristocratic leisure to provide a reincarnation of the English Gentleman and to promote the world as an "exotic" consumer playground. The racial hierarchy of colonialism was replayed in a more muted and subtle form. In the post–cold war context, it is "globalization" that takes the place of colonialism and the "frontier." The discourse of globalization as it appears in The Economist continually borrows and recycles "frontier" imagery. Such a discourse has tipped the emphasis further toward the U.S. rather than English inflection of this hegemonic masculinity during the period under investigation. In the pages of The Economist, the "frontier," together with competitive fitness and informality of style, were by the mid 1990s invoked more often than patriarchal privilege or gentlemanly codes. This partly reflected a reconfiguration of Anglo-American hegemonic masculinity in conjunction with economic restructuring, workplace changes, and new management styles, but also reflected a more local phenomenon (given that The Economist was and is a British publication): the Americanization of the City of London and of the culture of international finance.

The analysis of Anglo-American hegemonic masculinity offered here has not covered in depth the extent to which its relationship to women and subordinate masculinities may also be reconfigured through globalization. In the textual analysis of The Economist, some contradictory trends have been noted: the colonization by masculinity of what was previously regarded as feminine and the concurrent feminization of hierarchy; a cross-fertilization between Anglo-American and Japanese cultures of masculinity; the appearance of progressive advertisements that show Asians and blacks and women in powerful positions; and an ambiguous, although apparently improving attitude to both women and feminism. These are questions that merit further research. The only safe conclusions that can be drawn from the observations made here are that both hegemonic masculinity and gender relations in general remain in a state of flux and confusion. However, if, as in the past, Anglo-American hegemonic masculinity can successfully incorporate new elements while retaining its elitist international connotations and connections to the past, then any changes in the form of relationships with women and subordinate groups of men are likely to remain peripheral or relatively insignificant in terms of removing substantive gender inequalities.

The analysis of contemporary changes to hegemonic masculinities made here has also focused exclusively on the challenges of global economic restructuring. This is largely as a result of the choice of *The Economist* newspaper as the representative of popular culture and its cross-fertilization with the academic world, and also reflects the dominance of the theme of economic restructuring in IR discussions of globalization. This is perhaps unfortunate, if it gives the impression of a perspective founded on economic determinism, where changes in the gender order are seen as purely reactions to economic stimuli. It is perhaps worth mentioning that economic change is just one strand in the flux over hegemonic masculinities with international relevance. Others, which have not been pursued here, include global environmental issues and environmental movements that have produced some deliberate attempts to reform or transcend hegemonic masculinity (Connell 1995) and responses to the pressures of four decades of second-wave feminism (Segal 1990).

A third strand, suggested by cyberfeminists, is that the conceptualization of the relationship between man and machine is undergoing a profound transformation; this is in connection with the spread of computer networks. It is argued that while men, viewed as autonomous, separate and self-contained selves, previously wielded tools and machines to refashion nature, now, operating computer consoles, men are as nodes inserted into computer networks and are no longer individually the sole and separate instigators of action (Plant 1997). Meanwhile, developments in biology, biotechnology, and medicine are also challenging the traditional inside/outside and self/not-self boundaries of Anglo-American hegemonic masculinity (Haraway 1991; 1997). If these and other developments represent a cultural shift as large and significant as cyberfeminists suggest, then it has important implications for the bourgeois model of hegemonic masculinity and its analogous "state as rational actor" model. Given that coherent worldviews cross disciplinary boundaries, if men are no longer seen as autonomous rational actors it will not be long before states are also viewed differently. On the other hand, bourgeois-rational masculinity has undergone a number of alterations over the last hundred years or so, such as dropping the nineteenth-

century emphasis on sexual continence. It may merely be being reconfigured in a new variation, as biotechnological developments and the internet
are used to further enhance the fantasy of disembodiment (Hooper 1999b).

Meanwhile, cyberfeminists themselves make liberal use of postmodern
technostrategic language in their attempts to subvert new technologies for
feminist ends. As Carol Cohn found in another era, using technostrategic
language can be very enjoyable, as "talking about nuclear weapons is fun. I
am serious. The words are fun to say; they are racy, sexy, snappy. You can
throw them around in rapid fire succession. They are quick, clean, light;
they trip off the tongue" (Cohn 1987, 714). Such language offered distance,
feeling of control, and escape from victimhood with regard to nuclear
weapons. In the case of cyberfeminists, postmodern technoscientific language could provide similar pleasures, and detract from the fact that, as
Donna Haraway (one of the leading promoters of the feminist use of such
language) herself admits, new technologies are being fashioned in profoundly masculinist ways (Haraway 1997). Cyberfeminists are trying to subvert technoscientific language to feminist ends. Nonetheless, the language
they use is not so far removed from the type of postmodern technolanguage
that I have criticized James Der Derian for reproducing (see chapter 3), although the ends to which it is put are very different.[1]

### Postpositivists and Masculinism

The continuing salience of the encounter between Anglo-American hegemonic masculinity and the "international" or the "global" signals the importance of international relations as a site for the examination of contemporary changes and challenges to this type of masculinity. As this book has
argued, the predominantly Anglo-American discipline of IR has a role to
play, not least in helping to construct and promote the new forms of hegemonic masculinity associated with globalization. It seems ironic that some
postpositivist approaches to IR, which are otherwise critical of the discursive
role of mainstream IR in constructing elitist and exclusionary boundaries,
could be at the forefront of such developments.

The overall perspective of the book is generally sympathetic to postpositivist approaches. Like other postpositivists, I have argued against the view
that given identities go on to construct international relations in any

straightforward way. Rather than adopting the scientific language of cause and effect that is so common in IR discourse, the emphasis throughout this book has been on the micropolitics of power and the cross-cutting influences between IR, popular culture, and gender identities. Positivist methodologies are incapable of capturing such cross-cutting influences, because if gender identity is simultaneously a *cause* and an *effect* of the practices of international relations, then it cannot be treated as a "variable" whose influence can be isolated.[2] If, furthermore, as argued here, academic theories are themselves implicated in the production of masculine identities, then standard historical methods that aspire to academic objectivity are also inadequate to the task. The diffuse conception of power; the interest in the power/knowledge nexus; the view that theories are implicated in the worlds they purport to describe; the refusal of disciplinary boundaries; the acknowledgement of indeterminacy; the interest in popular culture—all these are characteristics of the perspective adopted here and are recognizable as aspects of postpositivist thinking.

However, postpositivist contributions to IR still tend to perpetuate the abstract rationalism of Western philosophy, and many remain gender-blind. Through the examination of some of the intersections between academic discourse and popular culture, some postmodern scholarship has also been shown to resonate with a masculinist discourse of globalization that promotes a new, informal, technocratic form of Anglo-American hegemonic masculinity. This is an important point because it undermines some poststructuralist claims to be radically undermining the disciplinary power structures of modernity. Clearly, a number of nonfeminist poststructuralists are failing to disrupt, effectively, one of the major disciplinary power structures of modernity—that of gender difference and gender inequality. Not only are they in fact failing to challenge the gender order, but in the case of contributors such as Der Derian and Virilio, their playfully ironic technolanguage games are probably actually helping to update and reinvigorate an Anglo-American hegemonic masculinity. What is being challenged, in gender terms, is not the overall disciplinary effect of modern IR discourse, but rather the specific, arguably outdated, models of hegemonic masculinity that inhabit modern perspectives within the discipline. This challenge merely perpetuates existing masculinist rivalries, albeit with a new twist, and offers continuity with modern perspectives in IR, rather than the promised radical upheaval. This has implications not only for the unequal position of women, but also does little to help marginalized groups of men and subordinate masculinities.

Postpositivists are attuned to the discursive role of language, and claim to be reflectivist. Der Derian and Shapiro have themselves explicitly discussed intertextuality and the cross-cutting influences between IR and popular culture (Der Derian 1989; Shapiro 1989a; 1989b). Therefore, they could easily reflect a little more on the gendered implications of the language they choose to use, and on its intertextualities with a popular masculinist discourse of globalization. It is a testament to the entrenched masculinism of the discipline that this would probably adversely affect their careers.[3] Nonetheless, it is a grave disappointment to find that at a time of considerable flux and change in gender terms, a number of postpositivist contributors to IR are either continuing in a disembodied rationalist tradition or even helping to forge new versions of hegemonic masculinity, rather than taking the opportunity to challenge gender inequalities between women and men.

## Feminist Challenges

The arguments put forward here suggest that the masculinism of IR is even deeper and more entrenched than feminist commentators have so far revealed: the discipline has constructed an all-male space for the production of masculinities, and it is involved in embodying and promoting particular constructions of Anglo-American hegemonic masculinity, which have wider cultural relevance and influence. Even some postpositivist critics continue in the tradition of masculine rivalries and promoting new forms of hegemonic masculinity. If the Anglo-American dominated discipline of IR so thoroughly represents and helps to construct the hegemonic masculinity of the sole remaining superpower, reproducing all the elitism and internal complexities and rivalries of that hegemonic masculinity, then it could appear futile for feminists to try to reform the discipline—and a demoralizingly uphill task to transform it into something else.

However, this pessimistic view may underestimate the impact that even apparently marginal attention to gender issues could have on the constitution of IR as a masculine space, and consequently on its role in the production and reproduction of hegemonic forms of masculinity. While the masculinist edifice of IR might seem more complex, more comprehensive, and even more mutually reinforcing than before, perhaps it is also more vulnerable to disruption than some feminists have supposed, and the main focus of this book has implied. The vulnerability of hegemonic codes of masculinity to a feminist challenge may be underestimated. Although I have concentrated on the representation of masculinities and their links to masculine identities, changes in the representation of women and feminism could help transform the environment within which struggles between different masculinities are played out. The power of such struggles over masculine identities, as I argue, depends to some extent on their taking part in a space that has been naturalized as a masculine space. If the environment is no longer so clearly a masculine one, then some of the imagery loses its gender-specific connotations, while the rest loses the power of naturalization. Cracks in the edifice of masculinism are appearing, not only with the arrival of feminist scholarship and a number of postpositivist fellow travelers who take gender seriously, but also in that gender issues are beginning to be addressed, however crudely, by more mainstream IR contributors.

This possibility undermines the easy assumption, made on both sides of the feminist/masculinist divide, that liberal and empirical feminist approaches are relatively nonthreatening to the status quo. Critics of liberal feminism have argued that it challenges too little to be effective in bringing about meaningful change (e.g., Brown 1989; Sylvester 1994). As if to echo this, some traditional male academics have found aspects of liberal and standpoint feminism to be acceptable supplements to mainstream theorizing. Both Keohane (1991) and Jones (1996), for example, have ranked feminisms on the basis of their "usefulness." They both dismiss poststructuralist feminism, preferring empirical (Jones) or standpoint-feminist scholarship (Keohane) that can be more easily adapted to supplement preexisting IR scholarship rather than challenge it. Clearly, they find some varieties of feminism more threatening than others, although their particular interpretations do not do justice to any of them, or to feminism as a whole (Weber 1994; Carver et al 1998).

However, just as liberal feminism, if carried to its conclusion, would of necessity involve the transcendence or transformation of liberal domestic politics (Eisenstein 1981), perhaps even relatively mild, apparently reformist, feminist contributions to IR might have radical potential. Molly Cochran argues that even highly empirical feminist IR scholarship, such as that produced by Cynthia Enloe, cannot easily be used to supplement analysis in the "classical tradition," because, in spite of being interested in the "real," it is nonetheless epistemologically incompatible. Its central problematic is widened from traditional concerns to incorporate questions of inequality and oppression, which it is at pains to redress. As Holsti recognized, changing the central problematic in effect triggers a paradigm shift with potentially radical effects (Carver et al 1998). Steve Smith also concludes that "feminist concerns, even liberal feminist concerns, may make IR, as currently defined and practiced, untenable" (Smith 1998, 60).

Perhaps feminist contributions to IR cannot, and should not, be divided so easily into reformist and transformist varieties. Changes in the representation of women and feminism in *The Economist* in the latter half of the 1990s, and a recognition by academics such as Fukuyama that women matter to international relations, may mark the beginnings of an epistemological shift. These—albeit as yet minor—influences occurred after the introduction of feminist imagery at the margins of the newspaper and the recognition of feminist issues at the margins of IR discourse. Habitual exposure to feminist ideas, however critically or derisorily received, may of itself result in eventual changes to the accepted parameters of discourse.

In the same fashion, empirical and historical analysis of the relationship between (masculine) gender identities and international relations could also prove ultimately transformative, even where overtly reflectivist approaches are rejected. The narrow focus of part 2 of this book on the symbolic dimension of gender identity construction reflects my own particular interest in exploring the relationship between apparently abstract theoretical perspectives and the cultural and historical circumstances and political interests that sustain them (and that they sustain). It is not to downgrade the importance of institutional and embodied practices, or the construction of subordinate masculinities. The approach developed in part 1 of this book could be used to explore the gendering of specific groups of men through the practices of international relations in a way that builds on, rather than undermining or eclipsing, existing feminist insights into gender constructions, gender relations, and gender inequalities.[4] Moreover, far from providing sociologically determinist explanations, it would allow for the micropolitics of such gendering processes to be exposed. By transcending the levels-of-analysis problem and transgressing the private/public/international divides, not to mention introducing voices from outside the Anglo-American world, empirical research on this subject might severely disrupt the all-male, largely Anglo-American space of IR, and thereby interfere with the production of hegemonic masculinities therein.

It may prove harder for mainstream male academics to dismiss such research as irrelevant, as it has a more obviously direct bearing on their own involvement in IR than does general feminist scholarship, which is (incorrectly) assumed to be about women. On the other hand, discussing masculinities is bound to awaken personal insecurities for male academics. As Craig Murphy argues, men would "have to let our masculine identity(ies) become the basis for research" (Murphy 1988, 105). Examining the construction of masculinity at the microlevel, "where all of us know something about the construction of masculinity . . . [we] would have to face very real fears . . . and those fears are exacerbated when they are placed in the context of the masculinist drive for competence and control" (Murphy 1998, 105). In this respect, the explicit study of masculinity may meet with even more resistance than feminist scholarship in general (Smith 1998).

*Feminist Praxis*

Finally, I would like to make one or two brief comments about the implications for feminist praxis of the arguments put forward in this book. First, beware: hegemonic masculinity comes in many guises and is extremely resilient and inventive. It has weathered many apparent crises, undergone many transformations, and survived many upheavals. However, this is a time of tremendous change that has unsettled naturalized gender constructions. History tells us that such times are propitious for feminist interventions. Contemporary struggles between groups of men over different and contradictory would-be hegemonic masculinities, some of which incorporate formerly "feminine" traits, could be exploited by feminist activists. Pointing out the contradictions within so-called masculinity highlights the multiple indeterminacies of an apparently stable gender order. Keeping such contradictions visible could help in very practical struggles. For example, women in the workplace who wish to contest the employment implications of the recoding in the business world of informality as "masculine" and of "hierarchy" as feminine need to be able to demonstrate the hypocrisy and inconsistencies of this trend. They could also strategically reclaim informality as a feminine trait in the propaganda war over gender difference.

Second, if hegemonic forms of masculinity are neither monolithic nor consciously imposed from above by a small coterie of elite individuals, but are rather produced and reproduced in the micropolitics of everyday life in local situations, then there should be multiple openings for feminist intervention at the local level. Lots of local, small-scale feminist interventions, armed with knowledge of the gendered micropolitics of particular situations, may have a cumulative effect as powerful as larger-scale campaigns. They would certainly be a useful adjunct to such campaigns. Being aware that a number of different models of masculinity are in play could also help feminists decide when to engage in and when to pull out of strategic short-term alliances with groups of men who oppose particular forms of hegemonic masculinity. Although men who embody subordinate masculinities are more likely to be fellow travelers, politically speaking, even some hegemonic groups' political power could prove useful to certain feminist causes.

Some forms of hegemonic masculinity are likely to be more uncompromisingly masculinist than others. The masculinism of bourgeois rationalism, for example, with its formal commitment to equality, is rather more ambiguous than that of traditional patriarchy. In the past, bourgeois rationalists have at times found common cause with feminists against traditional forms of patriarchy, and the further erosion of traditional patriarchal forms of power and male privilege can only be welcomed by feminists. This is not only because traditional forms of patriarchy are in themselves odious to feminists. The narrowing of socially acceptable forms of hegemonic masculinity to bourgeois-rational and New Man varieties would reduce their overall flexibility and resilience. Stand-alone, bourgeois-rational masculinity, deprived of warrior or patriarchal trappings, would be vulnerable to feminist arguments for equality. In spite of the social contract as historically constituted being problematic for women, bourgeois-rational masculinity alone may not be able to underpin the sexual division of labor for long (MacInnes 1998).

Third, while the main thrust of this book has been to show how resilient and sophisticated hegemonic masculinity is, a counterthread, running through the discussions, has emphasized the potentially disruptive encroachment of gender issues into the previously naturalized masculine institutions of both The Economist and IR. Institutions that are defined as masculine, or are exclusively male, are important arenas for the production, reconstruction, and naturalization of masculinities. Masculinity appears to have no stable ingredients and therefore its power depends entirely on certain qualities constantly being associated with men. Masculine spaces are precisely the places where such associations are cemented and naturalized. Therefore, even the marginal appearance of women (particularly if they refuse to play the part of honorary men), together with feminist ideas, and/or other self-conscious references to gender issues, may sufficiently alter the overall ambience of such spaces that their masculine associations become weakened. Under such circumstances, the power of such institutions to underpin institutionalized gender differences (whether intentional or otherwise) would be diminished, even if the majority of their practices remain masculinist. The setting within which such practices take place is as important as the practices themselves, in that it is the setting that naturalizes the practices as masculine. Feminists and feminist sympathizers, therefore, should perhaps continue to try to enter masculinist environments and then keep gender somewhere on the agenda, even if only through humor. In spite of apparently limited gains, and regardless of marginalization or even derision, such actions may yet prove effective in the long run.

# Notes

## Introduction

1. In this book I refer to both the theory and the practice of international relations. I have used the same form (*international relations*—lowercase initial letters) for both the discipline and for the practices and issues that have formed the discipline's subject matter. Where clarification seemed to be needed, I have used IR to refer to the discipline.

2. For example, see Enloe (1993) on masculinity and soldiering; Weber (1990, 1993) on the representation of masculinity in Latin American politics, and Zalewski and Parpart (1998) on the whole question of masculinity and international relations.

3. This question has occasionally been asked by feminists before, most often specifically in relation to soldiering and war. See for example Ehrenreich (1987), Enloe (1993), and Bourke (1996; 1999), discussed in chapter 3. See also Zalewski and Enloe (1995), discussed below. However, it remains a relatively neglected question, and as yet has not been given a great deal of consideration in general terms.

4. Hoffman (1977) argues that IR has developed as a U.S. discipline, shaped by the needs of superpower policymaking. While this may be disputed, it is a fact that most scholarship that is self-identified as within the discipline of IR is in the English language, and most university departments of international relations have, until very recently, been in the English-speaking world, with the United States dominating scholarly output. This is not to suggest that international affairs are not researched

elsewhere, but they have rarely elsewhere been considered as part of a distinct and separate discipline, which has become rather insular (see introductory chapters in Holsti 1985 and Olson and Groom 1991). The boundaries of IR and its emergence as a distinct discipline is significant in gender terms (see chapter 3 below).

5. If theories are not just tools, or even critiques, but are everyday practices, as Zalewski (1996) argues, then perhaps they help construct the identities of the theorists as well as the theorized. See chapter 3.

6. What is particularly interesting from the perspective of this book is that their choice of examples is drawn largely from studies of the relationship between masculine identities and international relations. Drawing on the work of Cohn and Hartstock (among others), they argue, for example, that strategic identity has been inflected with a kind of masculinity that allows no discussion of death, pain, and destruction and that leads to the dehumanization of strategic thinking. Meanwhile, military identity, in the case of the Vietnam War, was so heavily built on ideas of manhood and masculinity that the principal U.S. war aim became not to aid the Vietnamese, nor to protect U.S. strategic interests against regional Chinese influence, but simply to avoid a humiliating defeat. That their examples of two-way influences between international relations and particular identities should so readily draw on examples of specifically masculine identities suggests that there are in fact a wealth of strong connections of this type to be explored, and that international relations forms an important site for the production of masculinities.

7. As I argue below, these dimensions are interconnected in practice and have been separated for analytical convenience only. Similarly, the two-way relationship between masculine identities and international relations has been split into completely separate strands for the purpose of highlighting the direction of influence that has been relatively neglected by academics. In any given practical situation in which men engage in international relations, the influence is likely to run both ways.

8. This covers a period of rapid political, social, technological, and economic change after the relative stability of the cold war, a period in which the term *globalization* came to the fore.

### 1. The Construction of Gender Identity

1. The concept is still vigorously defended, and widely applied in modified forms in, for example, rational-choice theory in politics, neorealism and institutionalism in international relations, and neoclassical economics.

2. For a history of the treatment of women in Western philosophy, see Coole (1993).

3. For a discussion of the critical literature and one formulation of this argument, see Benhabib (1992).

4. I have tended to skate over or even ignore large areas of feminist theorizing on gender in which there is no specific focus on gender identity as opposed to structural

inequalities or other issues. Therefore this is a very inadequate and lopsided account in terms of the overall development of feminist theory as such.

5. In this they shared the functionalist approach of "sex role" sociologists such as Talcott Parsons, viewing sexual differences as developing because of the functional needs of social life, although Parsons placed considerably more emphasis on patterns of socialization, rather than inherited psychobiological programming (Haraway 1991, 32). The justification for sex differences and inequalities was the same, but the relative contributions of nature and nurture were disputed. However, even in sociological sex-role theory, the assumption was that biological differences underpinned and structured the processes of socialization (Connell 1987, 47–53).

6. To give a simple example, grabbing a child forcefully might be interpreted as an aggressive act when done in the playground, and as a protective one when the child is in front of an oncoming car.

7. An early and influential exploration of the sex/gender system was provided by Rubin (1975), and gender as a category in history was later explored by Scott (1988). A history of the feminist use of the sex/gender distinction can be found in Haraway (1991).

8. A highly selective list of contributors to postwar feminist institutional analysis includes, in the radical feminist camp, Millett (1970); Greer (1970); Daly (1979); and MacKinnon (1987) on patriarchy and male power; Rich (1979) on the institution of motherhood; Brownmiller (1977) and Dworkin (1981) on sexual violence. For a liberal feminist approach, see for example Friedan (1963) on equal rights. Socialist feminist approaches include Mitchell (1971); Rowbotham (1973); Kuhn and Wolpe (1978); Eisenstein (1979); Barrett (1980); Young (1981); Phillips (1983, 1987); Burton (1985) on socialist feminist theory; Oakley (1974) and Hartstock (1983) on domestic labor; Wilson (1977) on women and the welfare state and on problems with Marxist feminism. Institutional analysis with an international dimension includes Folbre on the political economy of development (1994); Enloe on the armed forces (1983) and international politics (1990).

9. There is large literature on this in the sociology of education. For Britain, see for example Whyld (1983) and Kelly (1985); Arnot (1986). Steinham summarizes the U.S. findings on the differential treatment of girls and boys in the U.S. educational system (Steinham 1992, 118–30).

10. Selective examples include, on purchasing "femininity" through advertising, Williamson (1978) and Myers (1986); on the representation of women, Pollock (1977), Winship (1981), and Gamman and Marshment (1988); on the relationship between gender identity and media images, Coward (1984) and Betterton (1987). Cultural-studies and media-studies literature has both developed in parallel with and has regularly criss-crossed mainstream feminist theorizing on gender identity, absorbing feminist psychoanalytic theory and promoting semiotic and discursive approaches. It has also been at the forefront of debates about masculinity (see for example Chapman and Rutherford 1988).

11. Freud's basic theory on the Oedipus complex was that all infants have a polymorphous sexuality with diverse desires that are basically narcissistic and contain the possibility of bisexuality. Boys and girls are equally active in exploring their environment and their bodies, and both desire their mother as their primary love object. The psychological development of the infant as it progresses through childhood depends on the repression of some desires and the displacement of others in ways that are structured differently for boys and girls because of the different positions of the father and mother in family dynamics. The crucial change is during the Oedipal phase, where the child has become aware of its sex, and a triangle of desire and rivalry is set up between the child and its parents. In the case of the boy, his desire for his mother is repressed because he fears castration by his rival, his father. The ensuing mixture of guilt, desire, and fear structures an incest taboo, but allows for a displacement of his desire onto other women in later life. He renounces the maternal bond and chooses to identify with the powerful father instead. This identification with male power and activity may include a homoerotic element, which, unless successfully repressed, may result in homoerotic desires in later life. In the case of the girl, the progress through this phase is more difficult, because her desires have to switch from one sex to the other. During the Oedipal phase, she is forced renounce her desire for her mother and replace it with one for father and men, and at the same time renounce her active sexuality in favor of a more passive and receptive one. This is achieved through the effect of her disappointment in discovering her lack of a penis (her "castration"), which prompts her to redirect her attraction to her father, who possesses the magic item and sets up a passive desire to possess a penis by proxy—that is, through sexual intercourse with a male lover and the subsequent fulfillment of having a baby. While men repress their passive, feminine side, women repress their active, masculine side, so that gender identity and character is formed as a part of psychosexual development. It is the layering of desires and prohibitions in the unconscious, and the possibility of the eruption of previously repressed feelings or patterns in later life, that provides the complexities, contradictions, and frailties of gender identity and adult sexuality (Freud 1953a; 1953b).

12. Although Freud's explanation of often-ambivalent relationships between men has been used by radical gay theorists to analyze homoeroticism and homophobia (e.g., Simpson 1994).

13. For example, Connell (1987, 152) observes that in Ancient Egypt intrafamilial royal dynastic marriages would have made Freud's hair stand on end.

14. Feminist appropriations of Foucault include work on the relationship of women to the fashion and beauty industries (Bartsky 1990) and anorexia nervosa (Bordo 1989; 1993b).

15. This contrasts with the feminist analyses of patriarchy and capitalism cited above that understood power to be an oppressive force that some people or institutions wield over others. This oppressive conception of power was given depth by psychoanalytic theories that showed how oppressive power in society was converted into repres-

sion in our psyches. Emancipation from gender inequalities and socially produced gender differences would come from political empowerment of the oppressed, psychotherapy, or some combination of the two.

16. Although it would be fair to say that the relative strength of class divisions between women has long been an intrinsic part of socialist-feminist debates since the turn of the century (Phillips 1987).

17. A similar argument is made by Mouffe (1994).

18. Mouffe also regards different forms of identity as the stake in a power struggle (Mouffe 1994, 110).

## 2. Masculinities and Masculinism

1. See below for discussion of "hegemony." In synthesizing Foucauldian and Gramscian influences, I am roughly following authors such as Said (1978); Cocks (1989); and Laclau and Mouffe (1985).

2. Butler's inattention to historical context (criticized in chapter 1) owes much more to the influence of French feminist poststructuralists on her theory of gender identity than it does to the influence of Foucault.

3. For a radical feminist analysis of patriarchy, see for example Daly (1979). On dual-systems theory, see Kuhn and Wolpe (1978); on capitalist patriarchy, see Young (1981). For a later defence of the concept, see Walby (1990).

4. See, for example, Grant and Newland (1991); Tickner (1992); Peterson and Runyan (1993); Sylvester (1994).

5. The epistemological debate is between empirical, standpoint, and poststructuralist feminisms. For discussion of feminist epistemology and successor sciences, see for example Harding (1986); Nicholson (1990), and Haraway (1991).

6. As Carver (1995) argues, *gender* is not a synonym for *women*. Jones (1996), writing in an IR context, also criticizes feminists for paying too little attention to men and masculinities. Perhaps it is unsurprising that feminist accounts of gender generally tend to focus more on constructions of "femininity" and the exclusions of "women" than on masculinity or masculinities. However, this is not an excuse for deploying crude and monolithic constructions of "masculinity," particularly when care is taken to provide nuanced and contextualized accounts of women and "femininity" (Carver 1995).

7. I use the term *men's studies* very broadly to indicate a body of literature concerning men and masculinity that has been written by men. This literature is extensive and varies in its sympathy with or opposition to feminist insights. It coexists, sometimes uneasily, with contributions to the subject from feminist cultural studies and queer studies (a branch of gender studies that refuses the categories heterosexual/homosexual), and the term *men's studies* is itself contentious. Examples include Hodson (1984); Metcalf et al (1985); Abbott (1987); Brod (1987); Seidler (1987, 1988, 1989, 1990, 1991); Kimmel (1987b); Kimmel and Messner (1989); Mangan and Walvin (1987); Jackson

(1990); Hearn and Morgan (1990); Gilmore (1990); Roper and Tosh (1991); Middleton (1992); Rutherford (1992); Morgan (1992); Hearn (1992); Brod and Kaufman (1994).

8. See the introduction in Brod and Kaufman (1994).

9. Similar dualisms may also occur in other philosophical traditions such as Taoism, but here I am concerned with the Western tradition.

10. She went on to try to transcend binarism and recuperate such a space through "ecriture feminine," an alternative style that can in fact be produced by both sexes (discussed in Moi 1985, 105–8).

11. Some feminists go so far as to argue that the masculine/feminine dichotomy is the primary one through which other dichotomies receive their status by association, because they are so readily "mapped onto" gender (Peterson and Runyan 1993, 23). This argument stretches the point too far, in my opinion.

12. This happens regardless of the actual participation of women, but of course the association of science and politics with masculinity also helps to perpetuate the underrepresentation of women in these fields.

13. For further discussion on the role and limits of phallocentric imagery, see below.

14. This is not explicitly argued by Peterson and Runyan, but is rather my reading of their work. At any rate, they make no reference to psychoanalytic discourse.

15. This is the of argument made by Grant (1991) and Tickner (1992) on behalf of international relations, and also Keohane (1991), who sees an affinity between such "feminine" qualities and his own interdependence approach.

16. As Enloe argues, large numbers of women are currently engaged in international politics but are the hidden support workers—army wives, diplomatic wives, prostitutes, nurses, and so forth (Enloe 1983; 1990).

17. See for example Hodson (1984), Metcalf and Humphries (1985), and Abbott (1987).

18. Much of the men's-studies literature produced before the 1990s was derivative of earlier feminist or role-model theories (Cornwall and Lindisfarne 1994).

19. As McMahon (1993) argues, much of this literature overpsychologizes gender politics.

20. Jackson's answer is to adopt a personal autobiographical style of writing as a radical strategy to make public such emotions and decenter the unified masculine subject. However, it is not clear that this in itself undermines masculine power. It depends on the context.

21. A number of feminist theorists have recently tried to transcend dichotomous thinking by the use of unorthodox language. An example in international relations can be found in the work of Sylvester (1994).

22. In my view, this argument parallels a discussion by Anne Phillips (1993). Although Phillips discusses feminist political strategies for change rather than the existing gender order, she argues that feminists need to pay attention to both the politics of ideas and the politics of presence, rather than always championing one over the other.

23. See, for example, the discussion in Nicholson (1990).

24. Examples include Carrigan, Connell, and Lee (1985); Brod (1987); Kimmel (1987b); Kimmel and Messner (1989); Seidler (1989; 1990; 1991); Jackson (1990); Hearn and Morgan (1990); Gilmore (1990); Middleton (1992); Rutherford (1992); Morgan (1992); Hearn (1992); a special edition of *Theory and Society* (vol. 22, 1993); and Brod and Kaufman (1994). Many of these contributors dislike the term *men's studies* and identify themselves as involved in profeminist men's writing or in critical studies on men and masculinity, to distinguish themselves from the mythopoetic men's movement exemplified by authors such as Bly (1991, 1992).

25. Some contributors continue to place a good deal of emphasis on pain and emotional denial as the price of power. Kaufman (1994) argues that men's power is now being undermined so that the rewards of emotional alienation are undermined and the pain highlighted. Seidler (1987, 1989, 1990, 1991) also retains a concern with rationalism and emotional repression, albeit historically contextualized. His work is a good example of the development of more sociologically sophisticated and historically contextualized accounts of masculinity within men's studies, but which nevertheless maintains a narrow focus on the gender styles and concerns of white, middle-class heterosexuals.

26. There is also the problem that the contributors are themselves in a position of privilege, which is hard to undermine from within. For example, contributors such as Jackson (1990) and Rutherford (1992) deliberately transgress the public/private split by using autobiography and their own emotional history as material for academic reflection. But given that social positions of the contributors and the power relationships in which they are enmeshed affects the degree to which emotional disclosure indicates vulnerability, it is unclear how genuinely radical such productions might be. Some have argued that it is impossible for men to be feminist or contribute effectively to the undermining of their own power. For a discussion that problematizes men in feminism, see Jardine and Smith (1987) and a counterargument by Boone (1990).

27. For example, ecofeminists have appropriated and renegotiated qualities such as "nurturing" and women's connection to nature to challenge unsustainable development (Mies and Shiva 1993). In contrast, cyberfeminists have embraced the new technologies in an attempt to forge a new relationship between "femininity" and technology (Haraway 1991).

28. Constructions of homosexuality have by and large proceeded along the same dualistic lines as sex and gender. Thus homosexuals have been understood as either feminized men or virilized women, and their relationships have been characterized in terms of active and passive partners.

29. Until the mid nineteenth century, the prevailing view was that this racial hierarchy was the result of cultural differences and degrees of "civilization." However, by the end of the nineteenth century and the advent of social Darwinism, it was seen as the result of differing biology and natural selection. Hall (1992b) documents the change of attitude and its consequences in imperial administration in Jamaica. For fur-

ther discussion of the relationship between hegemonic and subordinate masculinities, see below.

30. See, for example, Segal (1990); Roper and Tosh (1991); Cornwall and Lindisfarne (1994). In recent years there has been a small explosion of interest in masculinities in the field of cultural studies, some of which explicitly draws on Connell's theory. This is partly because it is readily compatible with the existing neo-Gramscian framework of British cultural studies (Best and Kellner 1991, 294).

31. In the Gramscian understanding of cultural hegemony, the dominant ideology is constructed from a range of preconstituted elements that can be arranged and rearranged in a thousand different ways. It is pervasive enough to be redundant, instantly recognizable—a part of what we know already (Hall 1973). In IR, the term *hegemony* often signifies a much-less-subtle form of power and dominance. See for example Gilpin (1987).

32. Even when it comes to sexuality, phallocentric discourse fails to offer the only possible interpretation of either the functioning of male genitals or of conventional heterosexual intercourse, let alone other kinds of sexuality. For alternative views of heterosexual intercourse and nonphallic masculinity, see Cocks (1989, 150–73) and Segal (1994, 136–40). For an alternative metaphor of male sexuality based on the testicles rather than the penis, see Flannigan-Saint-Aubin (1994), who illustrates this with reference to the movie *Superman*. He counterposes Superman's active and invincible phallic masculinity with Clark Kent's vulnerable, nurturing, testicular one. In the 1990s *New Adventures of Superman*, phallic masculinity was eclipsed as Clark Kent was now the hero and Superman became the difficult alter ego.

33. Ehrenreich (1995) identifies a further postwar decline in patriarchy (and see below). Competition between patriarchal and bourgeois values existed throughout the 1980s in Britain's Conservative Party, where the belief in competitive individualism (phallic) undermined and contradicted the belief in "family values" (patriarchal).

34. Cornwall and Lindisfarne (1993) treat masculinity as a totally flexible concept that is not necessarily even to be associated with males. In this they go further than Connell (1987), who sees masculinities as culturally and historically defined, but nonetheless always associated with men. Masculinity need not *always* be associated with men, but it must *generally* be so to be recognizable as masculinity.

35. An interesting argument is put forward in this context by John MacInnes (1998). He argues that masculinity does not as such exist but has been invented to explain the contradictions between a traditionally patriarchal sexual division of labor and the egalitarian thrust of capitalism and market economies, which are associated with equal rights.

36. This might also indicate a change in the status of homosexuality, which, while still being subordinate, may not be quite so far down the pecking order of masculinities as before. See above and below for further discussion of homosexuality and its subordinate status.

37. Three discussions on the problems of reproducing rather than challenging gender symbolism in the study of masculinities include Morgan 1992; Rogoff and Van Leer 1993; Coltrane 1994.

38. Foucault used the term *genealogy* to mean a method that was designed to excavate patterns of the exercise of power, starting from a question posed in the present and without having to make reference to a transcendental subject (McNeil 1993, 149).

39. As both Seidler (1988) and Morgan (1992) point out, Weber's seminal work *The Protestant Ethic and the Spirit of Capitalism* can be fruitfully read as a discussion of modern bourgeois masculinity.

40. Notably the waning of personal violence and heroism associated with the honor code and dueling after World War I (Connell 1993).

41. For a smaller group of profeminist men, the liberation of women implied the liberation of men from the restrictions of traditional masculinity.

42. For discussions, see for example Mercer and Julien (1988), Staples (1989), and Segal (1990).

43. One strand of anti-Semitism earlier this century saw Jews as a "third gender," the males, whom it was considered had broad hips and narrow shoulders, being predisposed to homosexuality, while the "masculinized" females had narrow hips and broad shoulders—and, worst of all, relative social equality (Gilman 1995).

44. The term *hypermasculine* is used in the contemporary literature to mean exaggerated displays of physical toughness (which in terms of the archetypes mentioned above would belong to the warrior and honor traditions of hegemonic masculinity) and has close connections with the concept of machismo. It is possible to imagine *hypermasculinity* being applied to extreme examples of other forms of hegemonic masculinity—for example, an extremely cold, ruthless and calculating rationality. Therefore, like masculinity itself, the term has no ultimately stable meaning.

45. For example, in the NAFTA negotiations of the early 1990s, the feminized and indigenous image of Mexican workers worked against Mexico's inclusion in the deal (Marchand 1994). Meanwhile, Chicanos in California have the opposite reputation—one of excessive machismo and participation in gang violence, a reputation that descends from the North European view of the conquistadores (Zinn 1989).

46. Class, sexuality, and race are not the only criteria dividing grades in the hierarchy of masculinities. As Brod argues, such categories fail to encompass anti-Semitism, which creates a cultural or religious divide (Brod 1994). Edwards (1994) stresses age as a factor, while Hearn and Collinson detail a long list of divisions: age, appearance, bodily facility, care, economic class, ethnicity, fatherhood and relations to biological reproduction, leisure, marital and kinship status, mind, occupation, place, religion, sexuality, size, and violence (Hearn and Collinson 1994, 109).

47. Mercer and Julien explore the contradictions of being gay and black (Mercer and Julien 1988).

48. Connell makes a similar argument in respect of the tattoo- and motorcycle-

style of white, working-class, protest masculinity, which coexists with a contemporary breakdown in the gender division of labor, an acceptance of women's economic equality, and an interest in children (Connell 1993).

49. Hypermasculinity is not just projected onto subordinate groups but is also associated with a more generalized backlash against changing divisions of labor, particularly in popular culture (Connell 1993).

### 3. Masculinities in International Relations

1. A more conventional way of looking at the relationship between men and international relations is through the "levels of analysis problem" (Hollis and Smith 1990). See below for a discussion of why this is problematic in gender terms.

2. Before the creation of Israel, anti-Semites regarded the Jews' lack of a warrior caste as proof of their status as a dubious effeminate "third gender." Their lack of physical involvement in soldiering was supposed to make them believe that their bodies were "merely extensions of the psyche." Therefore psychosomatic illness was a deemed a distinctly Jewish phenomenon and psychoanalysis dubbed a "Jewish science" (Gilman 1995, 187).

3. Not for the first time. The earlier Boer War had provoked similar anxieties about the physical quality of recruits (Bourke 1996).

4. A contemporary example is of Arab citizens of Israel and of Palestinians in many other Arab countries.

5. For a discussion of the dominance of Western values in international society (for which one can read "the values of Western hegemonic masculinities"), see Bull and Watson (1984: parts 3 and 4). While many postcolonial leaders have been directly or indirectly influenced by Western standards of hegemonic masculinity, there remain considerable cultural contradictions and tensions between such standards and other cultural forms. I disagree with Hedley Bull's (1984) view that Western values have come to form a universally acceptable common standard of international society.

6. This feminization of undesirables echoes the Nazi constructions of feminine Others documented by Theweleit (1987, 1989) and discussed above.

7. Spies who defected to the other side were associated with deviant sexuality and therefore tainted with deficient/subordinate masculinity—both in fiction and reality.

8. As Richard Ashley has argued, Waltz's systemic theory, produced in his book *Theory of International Politics* (Waltz 1979), has not been entirely successful in this project, as it contains an uneasy tension between systemic causation and methodological individualism (Ashley 1986).

9. As Robert Cox (1986, 212) argues, although its roots are in historical enquiry, a good deal of IR theory has thus been transformed into an ahistorical form of "problem-solving theory" in which current parameters and power relations are taken as permanent. The mode of thought ceases to be historical, even though the materials used are derived from history.

10. See for example Axelrod and Keohane (1986) for a vision of "cooperation under anarchy" and Buzan (1993a) and Buzan et al. (1993) on "structural realism" and "mature anarchy."

11. Waltz's (1979) neorealism is an influential contemporary example of this approach.

12. This assumed difference still underpins theories of moral development. See Benhabib (1992) for a discussion of these issues in relation to gender.

13. Thus there are three uses of the word *private:* (1) as in *civil society* (private enterprise, rather than the public state); (2) as in *familial* or *domestic;* and (3) as in *privacy.* There are also two uses of the word *domestic;* it can mean either within the family or within the state.

14. It has been argued that in societies where there is greater segregation of the sexes, there are generally more marked gender inequalities (Gilmore 1990).

15. Coincidentally, it was only after women had made inroads into the public sphere of politics through gaining the vote that IR became institutionalized as a separate discipline in the academy. See Grant (1991).

16. In a reversal of my argument above, the gendered subtext of realist discourse (handed down from Machiavelli) inscribes the anarchy of the international realm as a feminized space, contrasting with the masculine realm of sovereignty within states. However, it is this very characterization of the international as full of feminine danger that in part excludes women from participating in its affairs. Feminine dangers need to be tamed by men—women could only multiply them. See Tickner (1992) and below for further discussion of the gendering of realism.

17. As feminist security theorists have argued, this model falsely attributes a condition of safety and security to the inside of states, where women tend to face their greatest dangers (Tickner 1992).

18. There is not only a journal of that name, but it has also been used in book titles such as the Smith et al (1981) edited volume *Perspectives on World Politics.* The view that IR should not be separated from politics and political theory is also gaining ground. For example, in the mid-1990s edited volume *International Relations Theory Today* (Booth and Smith 1995), five out of fifteen chapters were explicitly devoted to this theme.

19. For example, the British International Studies Association subgroup on international political economy (IPE) has renamed itself after global political economy (GPE).

20. This book includes the words *international relations* in its title to indicate that the discipline of IR is the subject under discussion, although the approach is one of gender politics.

21. The ten categorizations are international theory versus political theory; communitarian versus cosmopolitan thought; the three Rs (realism, rationalism, revolutionism); the three waves or great debates (idealism, realism, behavioralism; the inter-

paradigm debate (realism/neorealism, liberalism/globalism/ pluralism, neo-Marxism/structuralism); state centrism versus transnationalism; neorealism and neo-liberalism; the postpositivist debate; constitutive versus explanatory theory; foundationalist and antifoundationalist international theory. In my view, the three Rs and the interparadigm debate are loosely parallel, and realism, state centrism, and neorealism are fairly closely related, as are transnationalism, liberalism, pluralism, and neoliberalism. In the postpositivist debate, constitutive versus explanatory theory, and foundationalism and antifoundationalism cover similar ground.

22. Steve Smith gives the examples of Little and Smith (1991); Olson and Groom (1991); McGrew and Lewis (1992); and Viotti and Kaupi (1993), whose books are schematically organized by the debate. Smith cites a number of theorists for whom it has also been a starting point: Holsti (1985); Hoffman (1987); Whitworth (1989). He attributes its first use to Michael Banks in 1984. However, while Banks may have coined the phrase *inter-paradigm debate*, this was predated by the first edition of *Perspectives on World Politics* (Smith et al, 1981), which introduced the idea that the discipline could usefully be divided into these three contemporary perspectives, which provide not only alternative ideologies but also alternative accounts of the relevant actors, processes, and outcomes of international affairs.

23. In the great bulk of North American output, the main division is between neo-realists and neoliberal institutionalists, but the more substantial disagreement is between both the positivist schools, on the one hand, and the postpositivists, on the other (Lapid 1989; Smith et al 1996).

24. An examination of Tickner's (1992) detailed account of realist masculinity shows how mutually incompatible elements have been shamelessly combined, although she does not stress this herself.

25. It would be worth noting whether this change occurred at the same time as the appearance of a nuclear capability that could to all intents and purposes annihilate nature.

26. References are too numerous to mention, but for discussions of the theory see for example Keohane (1984); Jervis (1985); and Axelrod and Keohane (1986).

27. Seidler views socialism as having been hampered by this legacy, and also views poststructuralism as a part of the rationalist tradition (as do some feminists—see below).

28. This has been extensively discussed in the liberal/communitarian debate in political theory, where John Rawls (1972) uses a rational-actor model to underpin his theory of universal justice, and critics argue that his model contains implicit norms (Sandel 1984).

29. There is also much use of heavily sexualized language and banter—perhaps more in keeping with the citizen-warrior model of masculinity than the rational-bourgeois one, although the effect is much the same—to sanitize and provide emotional distance from the subject matter (see Cohn 1987).

30. Although my preferred reading of the word *patriarchy* relates to a specific historic type of gendered hierarchy (see chapter 2), I am here following the more general use of the authors cited in this section.

31. As Eisenstein suggests, this may mean that, in the end, liberal feminism has a more radical potential than it intends, in that the achievement of women's equality in the public sphere would of necessity involve the transcendence or transformation of liberalism.

32. Susan Strange, arguably the founder of IPE as a subdiscipline, denounced this trend as one of "imitating economists" (Strange 1995, 167).

33. This in itself highlights the fact that while the liberal/communitarian debate in political theory, and latterly in IR (see Brown 1992), is presented as a huge divide, in practice their outlooks are very similar (see Taylor 1989b).

34. More recently, Francis Fukuyama (1989) has replayed a version of this argument, suggesting that realism has become dangerous and irrelevant with the end of the cold war. He likens realism to chemotherapy, which is harmful to the patient if it is continued after the cancer has been killed.

35. This was indeed a time when more and more complex models of international decision making were being produced. See, for example, the numerous complex diagrams mapping U.S. foreign-policy making, produced by Alger (1991; originally published in 1977).

36. See chapter 6 for further analysis of Waltz's prose style.

37. In a similar vein to the discussion here, Lucian Ashworth and Larry Swatuk trace the history of IR as a masculine contest between two types of masculinity—warrior realism and rational liberalism—with emasculation as the crucial weapon (Ashworth and Swatuk 1998).

38. Since these concerns were expressed, some edited volumes on IR theory have taken to including a token chapter on feminism (e.g., Booth and Smith 1995; Smith, Booth, and Zalewski 1996; Burchill and Linklater 1996) but feminist analysis has still not been thoroughly integrated into other postpositivist perspectives.

39. The analogy between man and state is a central plank of the masculinism of IR. The model for masculinity here is the bourgeois-rational model discussed above.

40. This is also the case in Waltz's later *Theory of International Politics*, where "man" has been banished, but states as rational actors are incompatible with the argument that systemic forces alone explain war (Ashley 1986).

41. The indiscriminate projection of oppositional characteristics onto disparate groups may account for the apparent affinities between marginalized perspectives, such as the similarity between the so-called African worldview and the feminist standpoint perspective. See Mohanty (1991).

42. This is particularly ironic, since Derrida's aim was to decenter "logocentrism," rather than reinforce it.

43. Linklater's earlier work tended to ignore both women and the gender issue— hence, titles such as *Men and Citizens in International Relations* (1982).

44. This is not the case in some other social sciences, where such perspectives are rapidly becoming the new orthodoxy.

45. There is also the thorny question of to what extent male academics can legitimately speak for feminism. While there is plenty of room for them to speak for feminism as in supporting it, speaking for feminism as in representing it is more tricky. For a discussion on whether men can be feminists, see Boone (1990). It is also worth noting that there are problems of representation within feminism, even when all the participants are female.

46. In Baudrillard's usage, simulacra are repetitions without originals, in an age where the opposition between original and copy has been lost; hyperreality is the result of the real being continually manufactured as an intensified version of itself (Baudrillard 1983; Connor 1989, 151).

47. Der Derian's academic output can be divided into two categories (see Huysmans 1997): his earlier genealogical work (e.g., *On Diplomacy* 1987) and his later "symptomological," or semiological, works (1989 onward). It is the latter type of analysis that I want to discuss here.

48. It is an "intertextual" method outlined in more detail in the volume *International/Intertextual Relations* (Der Derian and Shapiro 1989). For a discussion of *intertextuality*, see also chapter 4.

49. For the U.S. forces, the glamour of the simulation technology obviously competes with the need for tough heroes to engage in "realistic" action. This perhaps represents a struggle between a masculinity based on World War II heroism, which lasted through the cold war, and a newer one, organized around "virtual" skills.

50. My thanks to I. R. Douglas for drawing my attention to this point.

51. The fear that new technologies would be appropriated for masculinity is one factor behind cyberfeminist attempts to develop a constructive rather than critical feminism-technology relationship (see Haraway 1992).

52. Not that earlier strategists did not have their own rhetorical games. These were organized around highly sexualized imagery, which itself served to reduce anxiety by translating deadly nuclear war into mischievous boyish games (Cohn 1987). Such rhetoric was commonplace in cold war strategic circles, but by and large was excised from the more formal academic writings that aspired to "objectivity."

### 4. *The Economist's* Masculine Credentials

1. *The Economist* identifies itself as a newspaper, although it is published in the format of a weekly journal. Its content is more like that of a newspaper than a journal or magazine. It has a number of other unusual characteristics, such as the anonymity of its authors (there are no by-lines). It also always refers to itself, and is convetionally referred to by others, as *The Economist*, rather than, as would be more usual for a newspaper, the *Economist* (this convention is followed here, and is discussed below).

2. Circulation details published in *The Economist's* "World Profile," an in-house document made available to would-be advertisers in the early 1990s (source: *The Economist*). By September 1993 circulation had reached 534,000 (*The Economist* September 4, 1993, 26). In 1995, *The Economist* claimed to reach "our world-wide readership of over two million businessmen [*sic*] in more than 175 countries" (April 15, 1995, 112), although it is not clear whether these were all subscribers. It is very likely that many copies are read by more than one individual through institutional subscriptions.

3. During the period studied, weekly sections were devoted to politics and current affairs from Britain, Europe, the United States, and Asia, plus other "international affairs" coverage, and to business news, finance and economics, and science and technology. In addition, special surveys were conducted on topics such as the European Community (July 3, 1993) the world economy (October 1, 1994 and October 7, 1995), "the future of cities" (July 29, 1995), the internet (July 1, 1995); defence technology (June 10, 1995); the software industry (May 25, 1996), and international banking (April 27, 1996). A series of briefs entitled "Face Value" profiled various business leaders and entrepreneurs (e.g., Marc Andreessen, August 5, 1995, 72; Peter Tsang, February 3, 1996, 62). Special reports also regularly featured a selection of IR topics such as the United Nations (June 12, 1993 and October 21, 1995), the future of Europe (August 7, 1993), "peace in the Middle East" (September 18, 1993), "dealing with China" (November 27, 1993), "the new world order" (January 8, 1994), foreign aid (May 7, 1994), democracies and war (April 1, 1995), Iraq (April 8, 1995), Japan's relationship with Asia (April 22, 1995), nuclear proliferation (March 25, 1995), ethnic cleansing (September 23, 1995), Northern Ireland (February 17, 1996), Bosnia (January 20, 1996), terrorism (March 2, 1996), and Israel and Lebanon (April 20, 1996).

4. Examples, again chosen from the period under study: "Economics Focus" features regularly examined theories and research produced by academic economists (e.g., "Inflation," May 13, 1995, 122, and "Development," April 27, 1996, 116). "Management Focus" features examined contemporary managerial strategies and new managerial theories (e.g., "Transformation," May 6, 1995, 91, and "Trust," December 16, 1995, 83), as did a comprehensive survey of management education (March 2, 1991). Newly published scientific research formed the main source for weekly science features (e.g., "Downsizing Genes," February 10, 1996, 105, and "The Superconducting Tease," April 29, 1995, 129). Academic sources in politics and IR were used for special features such as "The Covert Arms Trade" (February 12, 1994, 21–23), which drew on the work of Michael Klare in the *World Policy Journal*, Ed Laurence in *Political Science Quarterly*, and Chris Smith in *London Defence Studies*. "The Left in Western Europe" (June 11, 1994, 2123) cited Geoff Mulgan and Robin Murray of the Demos think tank; "Islam and the West" (August 6, 1994, survey, 1–3) discussed Samuel Huntington's well-known 1993 *Foreign Affairs* article that predicted a clash of civilizations; "America and Japan" (April 13, 1996, 21–25) quoted a debate on U.S. foreign policy sparked off by Joseph Nye in the IR journal *Foreign Affairs*; and "Democracy and Technology" (June 17, 1995, 21–23) referred to the theories of Alvin and Heidi Toffler. In addition, a special 150th-

anniversary edition (September 11, 1993) included commissioned articles by Ali A. Mazrui (director of the Institute of Global Cultural Studies, New York); Henry Louis Gates (head of Afro-American Studies at Harvard University); Lawrence Freedman (head of war studies at King's College, London); Michael Waltzer (a professor at Princeton).

5. For example, an article on Europe by John Major, the former British prime minister (September 25, 1993, 23); one proposing a new international economic regime by Jeffrey Sachs, professor of economics at Harvard University (October 1, 1994, 27); one on U.S. foreign policy by Raymond Seitz, former U.S. ambassador to Britain (May 27, 1995, 23); and one on "reforming Japan" by Ichiro Ozawa, Japan's former opposition leader (March 9, 1996, 19).

6. For example, Barry Buzan and B. A. Roberson cite five different issues of *The Economist* in their discussion of the relationship between Europe and the Middle East in the 1990s (Buzan and Roberson 1993, 132, 141–42); while in the same volume, Carlton cites two issues when discussing civil war and terrorism (Carlton 1993, 172, 175). In another example, contributors to the *Review of International Studies* (Halliday 1994, 117; Crystal 1994, 147; and Grieco 1995, 25, 37) have all cited *The Economist*. These are merely illustrative examples; there are numerous others.

7. In the past, free trade has been the paper's religion. The founder, James Wilson, was convinced that it would "extend civilisation and morality throughout the world" (*The Economist* September 4, 1993, 26). For more recent support for free markets, see for example the leader "The Modern Adam Smith" (July 14, 1990, 11–12) and "Gatt: Remembering the Unthinkable" (November 7, 1992, 15). For an application of liberal economic theory: "Zero Inflation" (ibid., 21–24). On democracy and the rule of law, see for example "Democracy Works Best" (August 27, 1994, 11–12) and "Democracy and Growth: Why Voting Is Good for You" (August 27, 1994, 17–19).

8. On liberal feminism see "Europe's Women: How the Other Half Works" (June 30, 1990, 21–24). Admittedly, *The Economist* may be more extreme in the degree of its social liberalism than the majority of IR readers—for example, it supports the legalization of heroin and other drugs (May 11, 1996, 14) and also supports homosexual marriage (January 6, 1996, 17).

9. See, for example, editorial support for the United Nations on its fiftieth birthday (October 21, 1995, 18) and support for European Monetary Union (September 30, 1995, 16).

10. For discussions of the degree to which liberal institutionalist goals have been hampered by the requirements of political realism, see the following articles that appeared in Christmas double issues: "The State of the Nation State: She Is My Country Still" (December 22, 1990, 73–78); "A Multipower World: The Great Dance Resumes" (December 21, 1991, 65–67); and "The Shape of the World: The Nation-State Is Dead. Long Live the Nation-State" (December 23, 1995, 17–20).

11. As evidenced by the following quote: "A quarter of a century ago, when multi-

national firms suddenly loomed large on the radar screens of pundits and politicians, they aroused a mixture of awe and fear . . . [but] global enterprises have not taken over the world" (March 27, 1993, survey, 5).

12. See for example "Survey of the World Economy: War of the Worlds" (October 1, 1994) and also the leader "The Myth of the Powerless State" (October 7, 1995, 15–16) and the accompanying "Survey of the World Economy: Who's in the Driving Seat?" (October 7, 1995).

13. For example, "Rational Economic Man: the Human Factor" (December 24, 1994, 96–98) examined the rational-actor model and the theoretical modeling of rationality. "Evo-Economics: Biology Meets the Dismal Science" (December 25, 1994, 97–99) discussed game theory and evolutionary theory as they apply to political and economic competition and cooperation. Almost any issue of *International Studies Quarterly* will contain at least one article that applies game theory or rational-choice theory, while a recent special edition entitled "Evolutionary Paradigms in the Social Sciences" (40, no. 3, 1996) was devoted to the confluence of game theory and evolutionary theory in IR.

14. For example, the well-known and distinguished political economist Robert Gilpin characterizes himself as a "liberal in a realist world" (Gilpin 1986, 304), a description that also aptly fits *The Economist*.

15. Published in *The Economist*'s in-house "World Profile" (see note 2). The survey consisted of a mailed eight-page questionnaire, sent to a sample of 10,811 subscribers, with a response rate of 64 percent. It was conducted by Research Services, Ltd., and Erdos and Morgan, Inc. (USA).

16. The following is a selection of the international academic IR and related jobs advertised in 1995: professor of European politics, European University Institute, Florence (January 7, 86); senior lecturer in politics (international relations), University of Hong Kong (January 7, 90); lecturer in development studies, LSE (January 7, 85); executive director of the Institute of Policy Analysis and Research (January 21, 12); assistant director, International Institute of Strategic Studies (February 4, 9); head of European Programme, the Royal Institute for International Affairs (February 4, 115); and editor of *The World Today* (April 22, 134); director of the Foreign Service Programme (February 18, 122) and director of the Refugee Studies Programme (March 18, 135), both at Oxford University; ethnic conflict analyst (March 4, 132) and lecturer in international relations and European studies, Central European University (March 25, 156); professor of South East Asian Studies, John Hopkins University (March 25, 159); lecturers in European integration (April 1, 125) and contemporary European studies (September 30, 156), Queen's University, Belfast; professorships in European politics and IPE at Warwick University (April 22, 135); chair and lectureships in international relations and politics, University of Sussex (May 6, 138); research project managers in IPE at the Catholic Institute for International Relations (June 10, 121); director, the Mershon Center for National and International Security, Ohio State University (July

1, 12); professor of the history of international relations, at the Graduate Institute of International Studies, Geneva (July 8, 118); professor of politics and international relations, University of Reading (July 15, 104); lecturer in Iberian politics, Loughborough University (July 15, 105); chair in development studies at the University of Wales, Swansea (July 29, 84); six posts in European integration and North-South relations, University of Bonn (August 26, 92); academic officers, development and peace and security studies, United Nations University, Tokyo (October 14, 168); lectureship in European studies, University of Bradford (October 21, 159); research associates for *Adelphi Papers*—international security issues (December 9); chair of politics, reader in comparative European politics and lecturer in international relations, University of Nottingham (November 4, 170); and associate professors of international political economy of Latin America and the Pacific Basin, Boston University (November 25, 155).

17. Selected academic courses and research fellowships in the field of IR advertised in 1995 include midcareer fellowships in international affairs/development, Princeton University (January 7, 92); senior research fellow on the Middle East, Royal United Service Institute for Defence Studies (January 7, 85); various studentships in regional security, King's College, London (February 18, 123); postdoctoral fellowships in the political economy of European integration, Bremen University (March 11, 146); M.A., international studies and diplomacy, University of London (April 1, 130); courses on international peacekeeping and mediation, Lester B. Pearson Training Centre, Canada (April 8, 125 and July 8, 113); M.Sc in international policy, University of Bristol (May 6, 133); international summer school, London School of Economics (May 13, 141); fellowship in gender and development, Institute of Development Studies (June 10, 119); fellowship in international relations of Northeast/Southeast Asia, Australian National University (August 5, 100); senior fellowships in international peace and conflict resolution, U.S. Institute of Peace, Washington (August 12, 93); M.A. in international relations, International University of Japan (August 19, 86); Ph.D. internships in peace, multilateralism, and governance, United Nations University, Tokyo (September 2, 126 and December 2, 137); short courses in EU development, Oxford European Centre for Public Affairs (September 30, 154).

18. UN agencies advertising for staff in *The Economist* in 1995 include the ILO—the International Labour Office (e.g., February 18, 11); UNESCO—the Education, Scientific and Cultural Organisation (e.g., April 22, 12); UNDP—the Development Programme (e.g., April 22, 13); UNEP—the Environment Programme (e.g., May 13, 11); UNPF—the Population Fund (e.g., May 13, 10); UNOPS—the Office for Project Services (e.g., May 20, 130); UNFAO—the Food and Agriculture Organisation (e.g., June 17, 9); UNICEF—the Children's Fund (e.g., August 5, 13); UNHCR—the High Commission for Refugees (e.g., August 26, 9); ESCAP—the Social Commission for Asia and the Pacific (e.g., October 14, 12); IFAD—the International Fund for Agricultural Development (e.g., October 21, 12); WIPO—the World Intellectual Property Or-

ganisation (e.g., November 11, 158); IAEA—the International Atomic Energy Agency (e.g., November 18, 14).

19. Including, in 1995, USAID—the U.S. Agency for International Development (March 18, 134); the Commonwealth Secretariat (e.g., April 22, 13); the Inter-American Development Bank (May 6, 10); the European Commission (e.g., May 27, 11); European Monetary Institute (e.g., June 17, 7); OECD—the Organisation for Economic Cooperation and Development (e.g., June 17, 10); the World Bank (e.g., August 12, 9); British ODA—the Overseas Development Administration (e.g., August 26, 94); the CIA—the U.S. Central Intelligence Agency (September 9, 9); OSCE—the Organisation on Security and Cooperation in Europe (e.g., November 4, 172); WTO—the World Trade Organisation (e.g., November 18, 164); and the British Foreign and Commonwealth Office (December 9, 129).

20. For example in 1995, Amnesty International (January 7, 10–11); Human Rights Watch Africa (March 4, 134); East-West Consulting (April 15, 129); International Council of Voluntary Agencies—a forum for NGOs (May 6, 11); the Great Britain–China Centre (June 17, 10); Transtec (July 1, 109); the European Movement (September 16, 161); and Parliamentarians for Global Action (November 18, 164).

21. See Fiske (1982) for a concise summary of the methods of analysis used in cultural and communications studies and a fuller explanation of the terms used here. Hartley (1982) also covers similar ground, but with particular reference to news reporting.

22. For a discussion of the general application of textual and intertextual approaches to IR itself, see Shapiro (1989a).

23. Black British viewers with Caribbean roots may have a very different relationship to such an image: they may instead conjure up nostalgic feelings for "home," or they may associate the image with employment such as subsistence fishing or plantation labor, or perhaps even slavery itself.

24. Cultural theorists have made use of Louis Althusser's (1971) concept of "interpellation," a form of hailing or invitation through which ideology constructs or recruits individuals as subjects. Texts, it is argued, "interpellate" the reader, inviting them to take up particular ideologically inflected subject positions in relation to the material being presented via a number of rhetorical and/or visual strategies. See discussion in Fiske (1987, 53–58). In the case of the clichéd palm tree/tropical beach advertising image example above, the viewer is assumed to be white, British, and dissatisfied with the drudgery of daily life. Viewers are invited by the images to positively identify with a bourgeois subject position of a more leisured class, enjoying luxury in paradise.

25. Women are used to having to adopt a masculine reading or viewing position in relation to media output.

26. Although *The Economist* has an international readership, it carries (some) different advertising material in different parts of the world, and also has in recent years

produced minor editorial variations (such as a smaller section on U.K. politics and current affairs in the U.S. edition). The edition I examine in this study is in all cases the one read in the United Kingdom.

27. For example, in the palm tree/tropical beach example discussed above, a "wild reading" would be one that associated the image with subsistence fishing.

28. This is similar to the phenomenon where the appropriation of Western status symbols, such as the business suit, by non-Western peoples, can, when translated into local cultural contexts, result in incongruous juxtapositions that appear absurd or ridiculous by Western standards, and merely confirm the wearer's subordinate status in Western eyes.

29. This is not to say that some mischievous readers may not deliberately make wild readings in order to gain pleasure in subverting what they regard as the intended effects of the authors. In the palm tree/tropical beach example discussed above, a subversive reading would be one that deliberately refused the expected subject position and connotations and instead perhaps associated the image with neocolonialism or environmental degradation. How subversive alternative readings might prove, whether intentional or unintentional, is a question that has exercized contributors to cultural studies in recent years (see for example Fiske 1987, 18–20 and 62–83; and Bordo 1993, 260–63 for a critique of Fiske).

30. The bias toward men of course realistically reflects the fact that most of the international business and professional elites *are* men, but also has the effect of reinforcing and helping to (re)produce the associations between such elites and masculinity.

31. Of course, it may well be that subscribers falsely inflated their status in replies to the survey, or that lower-status subscribers were heavily represented in the 36 percent of subscribers who failed to respond to the questionnaire.

32. Women's handbags have never, to my knowledge, been advertised in *The Economist*, and perfume advertisements are extremely rare (although Ralph Lauren have advertised a men's fragrance—November 19, 1994, 4). The figures for purchases of perfume and women's handbags may have been included to promote the paper to would-be advertisers of such products (perfume advertisements, at least, appear regularly in such men's magazines as *GQ—Gentleman's Quarterly*, and *Arena*). On the other hand, they may have been included to guarantee an image of heterosexual success, stated in terms of buying presents for women (this interpretation is reinforced by the accompanying pictures, discussed below). It may be important to include such signals in this overwhelmingly masculine world, which could otherwise carry homoerotic overtones, rather as Hugh Heffner put centerfolds in *Playboy* magazine (Ehrenreich 1983). (An altogether more mischievous reading would be to interpret such figures as evidence of a high level of cross-dressing among the masculine elite, who in Britain at least have long had a reputation for minor deviations from the sexual "norm.")

33. *Active* may be a code word to signal health and virility, as *affluent* alone might indicate old duffers in their dotage.

34. Nelson Mandela appearing here probably signified a liberal interest in current

affairs—although another reading might suggest that the reader could be an elite black, perhaps with an upper-class education.

35. As with the figures for purchase of perfume and women"s handbags, these items are most likely to have been included as guarantors of heterosexuality and heterosexual "success." However, jewelry has occasionally been advertised in the paper, as in the series of Garrard advertisements appearing in late 1996 (e.g., December 7, 1996, 36), trading on its royal connections as "the Crown jewellers." *The Economist* does deliver a readership that would be able to make frequent duty-free purchases in international airports, so perhaps there was also a commercial logic at work here.

36. The annual Richard Casement internship offers a young, would-be science correspondent three months internship at *The Economist* (see, for example, January 28, 1995, 95). Special science and technology survey topics included science (February 16, 1991), artificial intelligence (March 14, 1992), telecommunications (October 23, 1993), medicine (March 19, 1994), earthquake engineering (April 22, 1995), and biotechnology (February 25, 1995).

37. Until late 1995, the paper reported the arts in a section entitled "Arts, Books, and Sport." The section reviewed books, mostly with a scientific or political content, although some novels were included, and carried short pieces aquainting the reader with recent developments in the arts, such as opera, music, and theater, together with pieces on architecture, sport, and other cultural topics. See, for example, "Art, Books, and Sport," May 14, 1994 (131–36), which had reviews of books on diplomacy, Latin American affairs, and industrial decline, as well as a "novel of the month" and articles on American composers, films made in India, Chinese culture, and cricket. Throughout most of the period under review, science and technology was given a higher profile than the arts. However, on November 11, 1995, the "Arts, Books, and Sport" section was replaced by a shorter weekly section entitled "Moreover" and a monthly pull-out supplement, "Monthly Review of Books and Multimedia," thus changing and also boosting the relative importance of arts coverage (see chapter 5).

38. This does not seem to deter them, however. See Waltz (1979) for an IR-inflected defence of the scientific method in the social sciences, and Hollis and Smith (1990) for a discussion of the merits of scientific explanation versus (historical) interpretation in IR.

39. Psychometric tests do show a small but consistent male advantage in spatial ability (recall and selection of shapes, mental rotation and identification, geometric skill) *from adolescence* onward. However, contrary to popular belief, such tests show no reliable gender difference in either general mathematical ability or verbal skills (Archer and LLoyd 1985, 30–38). As Connell argues, small overall differences between the sexes should be seen in the context of a huge overlap and a large variation within each sex group, which is far greater than any difference between the sexes (Connell 1987, 170). As to the cause of such differences, as they appear in adolescence, one might speculate that they are related to the deliberate gendered choices that adolescents make regarding subject interests (mentioned above).

40. The average time devoted to reading each issue of *The Economist* in 1990 was one hour and fifty minutes, spread over four occasions, with 88 percent of subscribers reading more than three-quarters of the paper (World-wide Subscriber Survey, Source: *Economist*).

41. Realism as a genre or narrative style is not to be confused with political realism, the IR perspective, or philosophical realism (although clearly there is some affinity between the three).

42. Examples of the literature are Watt 1957, Barthes 1973, Williams 1977b, Belsey 1980, MacCabe 1981.

43. For further discussion of the deployment of masculine and feminine representational codes and conventions, see Fisk 1987 and Betterton 1987.

44. Indeed, Fiske characterizes TV news as essentially "masculine soap opera" (Fiske 1987, 308).

45. This may have been different in the past—apparently Sir Walter Layton, editor in the interwar period, added the words "time alone will tell" to the end of articles to soften the opinions therein (*The Economist* December 22, 1990, 34).

46. This is a general observation. Clearly there are many specific differences between the conventions of these different genres, and between them and the conventions of *The Economist*. Although in the detail such distinct genres may diverge a good deal, nonetheless I think there are enough similarities and echoes to make general intertextual comparisons.

47. Fictional detectives and spies make rather more use of understatement than does *The Economist*, which as I argued above, prefers exaggeration, although irony is used liberally in all three cases (see below).

48. Western heroes are not always required to be superintelligent, and so are perhaps more wholeheartedly in the citizen-warrior mold, although they are often loners, individualists who operate at the margins or "frontiers" of society. See chapter 5 for a discussion of "frontier masculinity" in *The Economist*.

49. Another randomly chosen example: October 12, 1996 (19–22). *The Economist* told the South African government to give Inkatha more power and to be nicer to whites to consolidate post-Mandela democracy; told Britain to keep its options open on the single European currency and to resist French pressures to extend the Eurotunnel concession; told the United States to leave the question of euthanasia to each individual state; and told Cambodia's prime ministers to be tough with their former friends in the Khmer Rouge.

50. The term *phallogocentrism* is derived from the concepts of phallocentrism (privileging the masculine in language) as used by feminist theorists (see chapters 2 and 3 above) and logocentrism (privileging "the Word"), as used by Derrida. See for example Grosz (1989) for a discussion of the relationship between these two terms. Flax (1990) defines phallogocentrism as the fantasy of control and omnipotence associated with "the Word."

51. The "fireside chat" is the strategy of radio journalism, with its combination of intimacy (the domestic setting) and authority, with the spoken word effortlessly and commandingly floating out of nowhere/everywhere. As a written paper, *The Economist* can never fully achieve this quality.

52. See the epithets mentioned above, from *The Economist's* discussion of its own house style (December 22, 1990, 34). Also discussed is the fact that some readers find the style patronizing. I expect they do not like being lectured at in words of one or two syllables.

53. For example, the cover of the September 7, 1996 issue sported the headline "Saddamned if You Do, Saddamned if You Don't," with a cartoon of Saddam Hussein's head emerging from a jack-in-the-box. Inside, cartoons depicted a diminutive Tony Blair facing up to a huge trades-union horse (19) and a huge fat businessman (20). A photograph of a rugby scrum was captioned "Scrambling for money" (21); a photograph of Bob Dole, the U.S. presidential candidate, pointing upward with his index finger, was captioned "Isn't that a vulture?" (46); and a photograph of two children reading a book accompanying an article on literacy was captioned "The day the TV broke" (47). Such examples were typical and ubiquitous.

54. See discussion of Judith Butler's account of the subversive potential of parody in chapter 1. Kroker and Kroker (1991) also argue that "masculinity" has been taken to such hysterical extremes that it is "imploding," although their thesis seems overoptimistic in the light of previous episodes in history (see Kimmel 1987a, for example).

55. A successful example of this was Douglas Hurd's announcement that the British should "punch above our weight" in foreign affairs, as a way of mobilizing support for military spending and intervention in Bosnia. See Shapiro 1989b on the genealogy of the sport/war intertext and its representational uses in world politics. In the academic world of IR, the metaphorical use of sport and gaming to represent war and politics has developed into a full-blown epistemology in "rational choice" and "game theory" approaches.

56. In subsequent years, however, the use of this type of metaphor has been avoided. This may reflect increasing editorial sensitivity to the possibility of offence.

57. This is by no means the only way in which heterosexual masculinity need be characterized or interpreted. See Cocks (1989) and Segal (1994) for alternative, more women-friendly, constructions of heterosexual masculinity.

58. Banking advertisements may have been especially heavily represented in this issue (October 7, 1995) since it contained a survey of the world economy. They consisted of the following advertisers (in order of appearance): Swiss Life (14); J. P. Morgan (23); Bank of America (86); Deutsche Kommunalbank (survey, 10); Citibank (survey, 13); Jardine Fleming (survey, 17); Banco Bozano Simonsen (survey, 19); Komercni Bank (survey, 20); Polish Development Bank (survey, 25); Gulf International Bank (survey, 35); Sakura Bank, (survey, 36); Rossiyskiy Kredit Bank, (survey, 40); Credit Suisse (survey, 48); Mitsubishi Bank (106); Union Bank of Switzerland (108–9); Flem-

ings Save and Prosper (111); Geneva's Private Bankers (125); New York Stock Exchange (131); ABN-AMRO (136); SBC Warburg (140–41); West LB (184).

59. In order of appearance: Texas Instruments (October 7, 1995, 20); Microsoft (35); Unisys (45 and 47); Canon (60–61); CODA (64); IBM (72–73); J. D. Edwards (80); GE Information (survey, 4); AT&T (survey, 46–47, and 105); Hewlett Packard (117); Odyssey (126); NTT (144–45); Nokia (152); Royal Mail (181).

60. Ads are listed in order of appearance. Airlines: Singapore Airlines (October 7, 1995, 24–25); Meridiana (31); Iberia (39); Air France (52–53); Lufthansa (67 and 69); Cathay Pacific (95); American Airlines (102); and Swissair (149). Hotels: Holiday Inn (51); Hotel Schille (77); Imperial Hotel (111); Okura and Reed Continental, (survey, 30); Palace Hotel (survey, 40). Executive aircraft: Astra Executive Jets (83).

61. Ads are listed in order of appearance. Gents' clothes: Thomas Pink, (October 7, 1995, 4); Giorgio Armani (29); Holland and Holland (48); Hugo Boss (71); Army Field Jackets (161). Watches: Omega (2–3); Audemars Piguet (19); Seiko Kinetic (32); Vacheron Constantin (122).

62. Ads listed in order of appearance. Bayer (October 7, 1995, 26); Hughes Electronics (42); ABB (survey, 2–3); Arab Petroleum Investments Corp. (survey, 14); LG Group (100–101); Alcatel Alsthom (139); Samsung (112–13); Hyundai (182–83).

63. Ads listed in order of appearance. BMW (October 7, 1995, 40–41); Jaguar, (78–79); Honda, (91); Samsung (112–13); Vauxhall (120–21); Toyota (132–33); Saab (150–51).

64. Advertisements for newspapers and journals (October 7, 1995, 54; 85; 99; 118 and 154; and survey, 39, 45); business conferences (74; 84; 88; 89; 134; 143; 146; and survey, 9); British army reserves (36); luggage (57); Eurostar (58) and commercial radio (114). Export zones and government promoters include Pakistan (22 and 26); Taiwan (29); Dubai (96); and Malta (146).

65. Other exclusive watches, mostly Swiss, advertised include Rolex (e.g., May 1, 1993, back cover); Blancpain (e.g., April 29, 1995, 16)); Breitling (e.g., April 29, 1995, 79); Movado (e.g., June 3, 1995, 10); Patek Philippe (e.g., June 3, 1995, 45); Willabee Ward (e.g., May 6, 1995, 129), and International (May 6, 1995, 32–33). Executive jets are also regularly featured, with no fewer than three different brands being advertised in one single edition (September 7, 1996): Learjet 60 (24); Galaxy (35); and Gulfstream (60).

66. See discussion in chapter 2 and also Peterson and Runyan (1993) on the double bind that prominent political women are placed in with regard to gender.

67. This provoked a letter of protest from one (male) reader (March 18, 1995, 8).

68. Such constructions of hegemonic masculinity were not the only ones on offer, and I shall discuss alternative, perhaps even destabilizing images of masculinity in chapter 5, together with a more detailed analysis of the competitive and sometimes contradictory relationships between these various models.

69. Similar experiences may apply to black male readers, whose ability to identify with elite masculinity may also be disrupted.

70. Indeed, women are invited to take up masculine subject positions a great deal of the time by the narrative structures and conventions of films, books, and television programs. The instability of such subject positions may result in unstable, schizophrenic identities (Mulvey 1975). Whether there is room for a specifically "female gaze" is hotly debated (Fiske 1987; Gamman and Marshment 1988).

## 5. *The Economist*, Globalization, and Masculinities

1. As this is intended as a primarily textual analysis, I have not explored such inter-textualities with short-term changes and events in the outside world.

2. Although military metaphors were routine in the period studied (as in all news and current affairs reporting—see above), warriors themselves were rarely explicitly invoked, and when they were, they were distinctly sanitized. For example, an ad recruiting British army reserves talked in terms of how military service could improve one's management techniques—"as recommended by leading management consultants" (October 7, 1995, 36). Military-style clothing was on offer in the same edition, with the "genuine leather U.S army field jacket" that, the ad stated, "millions of fighting men swear by" (October 7, 1995, 161).

3. The market is also deemed to ensure the delivery of consumer satisfaction and widespread economic progress in a largely benign process.

4. A similar discursive approach to globalization is adopted by Kofman and Youngs (1996).

5. While I concentrate on economic changes here, I do not mean to endorse the view that globalization can be reduced to, or is wholly driven by, political economy. See my concluding chapter.

6. This is not necessarily the same as a decrease in militarism itself. Women as soldiers may be relegitimizing the military. See Enloe (1993, 60).

7. Although men may have made purchases in the past, their identities were more bound up with production than consumption. Through the 1950s and 1960s, consumers were equated with housewives. Now "lifestyle" purchases that help to define one's identity and personal products are aimed equally at men and women. David Evans takes the view that the enormous amount of energy focused on sexuality and the proliferation of sexual identities in the West over the last few decades needs to be understood in relation to the material interests of the market and state. Evans views them largely as the product of a shift of emphasis away from relations of production to the promotion of new forms of commodification through a differentiated marketplace (1993).

8. The mythopoetic men's movement popularized by Robert Bly (1991; 1992) among others has been heavily criticized in the men's-studies literature as an anti-feminist, backlash phenomenon with rituals strikingly parallel to nineteenth-century masonry. It allows privileged white men to see themselves as gender "victims." See, for example, Kimmel and Kaufman (1994); Connell (1995); Yudice (1995); and Pfeil (1995).

9. See "Japan: The New Nationalists," (*The Economist* January 14, 1995, 19) and further discussion below.

10. See "Survey of Financial Centres: Can the Centre Hold?" (June 27, 1992); "Survey of the World Economy: Fear of Finance" (September 19, 1992); "Survey of Multinationals: Everybody's Favourite Monsters" (March 27, 1993); "Survey of Wall Street: Other People's Money" (April 15, 1995); "Survey of the World Economy: Who's in the Driving Seat?" (October 7, 1995).

11. Between 1986 and 1989, currency trading doubled, and then increased one-third again by 1992, to $900 billion a day (September 19, 1992, survey, 9). By 1995 it approximated $1.3 trillion. The stock of international bank lending rose from $265 billion in 1975 to $4.2 trillion in 1994, while in 1992 total cross-border ownership of tradable securities stood at $2.5 trillion. McKinsey estimated that the total stock of financial assets traded in the global capital market increased from $5 trillion in 1980 to $35 trillion in 1992, twice the GDP of OECD countries, and forecast a total of $83 trillion for the year 2000 (October 7, 1995, survey, 12).

12. "The share of low skilled labour has fallen to only 5–10% of total production costs in developed economies, from 25% in the 1970s" (October 1, 1994, survey, 29), while data processing, accounting, computer programming, and the like was also being increasingly farmed out to workers in developing countries (30).

13. See also the special leader "Technology, the Future of Your Job and Other Misplaced Panics" and the special "Technology and Unemployment" on February 2, 1995 (front cover and 23–26).

14. Garb (1990) explores the widespread use of "whole Earth" imagery. He argues that such images privilege a single external viewpoint and thus provide a "univocal model" (269) of the world that appears singular and whole (in contrast to the multiple, multisensory world of experience and premodern narrative). It also carries connotations of a historic transcendental quest associated with the masculine ego and a patriarchal God. In the light of Garb's analysis, it is quite easy to see why the one Earth image has been used to promote globalized business.

15. As Doreen Massey argues, *global* is already coded as masculine through its other meaning, as in global/universal, rather than local/particular (Massey 1994).

16. One of the largest exporters of female domestics is the Philippines. Filipinas with good education and qualifications still often end up as migrant domestics. They remit income home, thus keeping their families fed, and collectively play a crucial role in their country's economy and balance of payments. This is the less glamorous underside of globalization (Ling and Chang 2000).

17. This contrasts with feminist discussions of the globalization of production that concentrate on the implications for the everyday lives of ordinary people (McDowell 1991; Runyan 1996).

18. This discourse was by no means confined to or even initiated by *The Economist*. Economic rivalry between the United States and Japan was generally topical from the late 1980s, when the two economies became intertwined through the U.S. budget

deficit. It has also permeated academic IPE discussions of globalization. See below for discussion.

19. Rivalry between management styles had also been reported in Europe, where the need to cooperate in the single market in order to compete globally has been hampered by a clash of managerial styles, with patriarchal "Napoleonic" bosses in France pitted against flexible but secretive Italians, ageing technocratic experts in Germany, and rapidly rising youngsters with a broad if sketchy overview in Britain (*The Economist* December 7, 1991, 70).

20. In the Middle Ages, moneylending (usury) was condemned as the devil's work and largely relegated to Jews, who were excluded from most other professions. The emergence of (Christian) merchant bankers who issued bills of exchange at a discount, rather than charging interest directly, heralded the start of modern banking in the fourteenth century.

21. This was aptly demonstrated by the role of Arthur Lowe in the British television comedy *Dad's Army*. Set in World War II, when military masculinity would have been in the ascendant, he played a bank manager whose position in the Home Guard depended on his high status in the community, but who made an incompetent soldier in practice. His pomposity and incompetence were both subject to ridicule.

22. For example, banking and financial advertisements featuring pictures of chairmen included J. P. Morgan (November 3, 1990, 2–3) (see fig. 5.5) and First Chicago (November 17, 1990, 114). The conglomerate ABB capitalized on this trend with a picture of its chairman, "Bill Coleman [the] banker" (April 28, 1990, 60–61). Meanwhile, extracts from chairmen's statements also proved popular. They appeared, for example, for General Accident (April 28, 1990, 91); Sun Alliance (April 28, 1990, 114–15); and J. F. Fledgling (July 14, 1990, 24; December 15, 1990, 26).

23. Exceptions include Goldman Sachs, with a picture of its founder (September 24, 1994, 24) and Geneva's Private Bankers, with a formal brass and woodwind quintet in venerable surroundings (October 7, 1995, 125).

24. Examples include Kleinwort Benson (January 28, 1995, 89; February 11, 1995, 87 and 89); Price Waterhouse (February 11, 1995, 80; March 18, 1995, 96); Standard London (Asia), Ltd. (September 7, 1996, 59); and Zurich Insurance Group (April 6, 1996, 46–47). Also (although it is not a bank) similar puzzle imagery was used to represent the international arena by Wartsila Diesel Group (February 25, 1995, 124).

25. For example, Merrill Lynch (April 22, 1995, 89) and the ABSA bank (September 7, 1996, survey, 2) offered insight, while Sedgwick compared itself to Leonardo da Vinci (September 21, 1996, 113).

26. Other examples include Sanwa Bank "building a vast network of personal contacts" (March 18, 1995, *survey*, 74); Swiss Bank Corp., with "the key to relationship[s]" (April 22, 1995, 84–85); and ABN-AMRO, "the network bank" (October 5, 1996, 52–53).

27. Compare with the earlier, patriarchal J. P. Morgan advertisement discussed above (fig. 5.5).

28. These advertisements have featured regularly in *The Economist* since 1994. In

1996 they included the following permutations (not an exhaustive list): a white male banker with two white clients, one male and one female (February 17, 1996, back cover); an Asian male (probably the banker) and an Asian female (March 9, 1996, back cover); a black male banker and a white female client (April 13, 1996, back cover) a white female banker and a white male client (May 18, 1996, back cover; June 8, 1996, 149); a Latin male banker with white male and female clients (May 4, 1996, inside back cover); and a white male banker and an Asian female client (October 5, 1996, back cover).

29. On hackneyed images, for example, Swiss Life (May 13, 1995, 28) and Perpetual (May 27, 1995, 67) favored mountain peaks and skyscrapers; Morgan Stanley used a tiger (June 3, 1995, 82–83), and AIG insurance used a gold miner with huge upward-pointing drill (November 12, 1994, back cover).

30. For discussion, see Beck (1992) and Giddens (1991).

31. This rash of risk anxiety was probably related to the general economic downturn at that time.

32. Over the same period, Credit Suisse also ran advertisements with more hackneyed images of masculine virility, such as mountain peaks and skyscrapers (e.g., November 12, 1994, 21).

33. Barthel (1992) argues that commodity fetishism in male business clothing in the 1980s also served this purpose.

34. The contrast with the patriarchal imagery of financial services a few years earlier is striking. Compare the company president in the Chubb insurance advertisement discussed here with the formal patriarchs discussed above.

35. In ads for men's clothes, the poses of the male models also became increasingly coy and homoerotic; Hugo Boss, for example, showed a young man coyly looking up from under his eyelashes/brows (May 6, 1995, 55; March 23, 1996, 51).

36. Although some still persisted. Singapore Airlines was a long-running exception to this rule. It still tended to feature stereotypical "exotic" Asian stewardesses (e.g., March 23, 1996, 2–3). American Airlines also featured a male business passenger and hostess in 1994 (October 22, 1994, 64).

37. The image of the disembodied male "hand of power" has been very common in *The Economist*, advertising everything from wristwatches (e.g., Corum, March 30, 1996, 45) to international telecommunications (Deutsche Telecom, March 30, 1996, 32–33).

38. This New Man father-image contrasts with an earlier Lufthansa advertisement that also featured a businessman-father and little girl image, but in this one the daughter had a "good feeling . . . knowing that someone close to you is in the best hands" (November 3, 1990, 63), emphasizing expertise and safety for daddy, whose place is in the big wide world, rather than him actually wanting to spend time in the domestic realm.

39. As Jackson argues, male bonding as an institution has long been used to regu-

late women and powerless masculinities (Jackson 1990, 170), although the computer "lads" culture seems to be less based on physical bravado than the historical examples he gives. Women are excluded by the content of male bonding banter as much as by time-and-place constraints caused by domestic commitments. As Cockburn argues, "Men bond with each other by using women as symbolic, humour-laden material in their masculine discourse" (Cockburn 1990, 83), with the heavy, heterosexist content preventing misconstruction.

40. Of course, much of this biologism resonates with the arguments of some radical feminists, as does the prospect of a future of artificial reproduction without men (see chapter 2).

41. Japanese business practices, for all their "softness," are not noted for their sympathetic treatment of women's employment aspirations.

42. The economic crisis in East Asian economies since 1998 makes this outcome even less likely.

43. Whether this undermines patriarchy itself, or merely existing patriarchs, is a moot point.

## 6. The *Economist*/IR Intertext

1. This economy is masculine when contrasted with the feminine confusion of "so-called variables [that] proliferate wildly" (Waltz 1986, 52) in the case of Waltz's pluralist rivals.

2. *The Economist Style Guide*—which gives detailed explanation of how to write in Economese—is an in-house booklet that was published by *The Economist* in February 1994.

3. Both *The Economist*'s house style and Waltz's prose strike me as so extreme as to be constantly verging on parody, although I doubt that, in Waltz's case at least, the intention was humorous. This perhaps illustrates the difficulty I have as a female reader in taking any of this hypermasculinity seriously. There is also the question of whether parody—whether intentional or not—can itself undermine hegemony (see Butler 1990a).

4. The patriarchal model of masculinity is fairly muted, both in political realism, where it derives largely from Hobbes's input, and in *The Economist*, where it appears mostly in status-oriented business advertisements. See discussion above. Honor codes of masculinity also make a minor appearance in *The Economist*. See above.

5. Usually featuring successful male sports personalities, although occasionally there is a female star. Examples include Rod Davis, sailor (April 22, 1995, 2–3; June 3, 1995, back cover); Cindy Crawford, model (December 2, 1995, 2–3; December 16, 1995, 2–3); Bryn Terfel, singer (December 9, 1995, back page); and Ernie Els, golfer (May 4, 1996, 2; May 18, 1996, 4; June 1, 1996, 2).

6. That it openly recruits at all is astonishing to a U.K. readership used to extreme government secrecy.

7. For Kissinger's own account of his role in the cold war and detente, see *The White House Years* (Kissinger 1979).

8. *The Economist* acknowledges the influence of environment on the expression of genes—indeed, Matt Ridley, cited above with reference to this point, is himself a former science editor of *The Economist*.

9. A rather more critical analysis is provided by Strange (1990), who also saw globalization as a product of U.S. power, but in a less benign light.

10. As always, there are some exceptions to the general criticism here. For example, in Waever et al (1993), Waever examines the conflicting but twin processes of fragmentation and integration in his discussion of societal security for Europe in the 1990s. This combination of political and cultural fragmentation and integration is widely theorized as connected to globalization (see, for example, Harvey 1989) although the word *globalization* is not specifically referred to by Waever. In his chapter, Buzan (1993b) argues that the current spate of "internationalization" may lead to identity problems. Waever and Kelstrup (1993) also make mention of postsovereignty and postmodernity in their discussion of European identities. This is one fairly mainstream volume (or at least not postpositivist) that does pay attention to subjective questions connected to globalization, however obliquely.

11. Those male postpositivists—such as Jim George, Rob Walker, and Steve Smith—who explicitly acknowledge gender issues have a much better claim to be "speaking from the margins."

12. As mentioned in the introduction, my own writing style is also complicit in that it reproduces many of the codes of hegemonic masculinity.

13. This solution was earlier advocated by liberal feminists such as Betty Friedan (1983) and is in keeping with *The Economist's* editorial commitment to liberal feminism.

### Conclusion

1. This problem parallels my own lapses into Economese, which is also fun to do, and, as mentioned in the introduction, may prove less subversive than intended.

2. For further discussion of this point, see Hooper 1999a.

3. It would no doubt also interfere with their own personal gender identifications and pleasures.

4. For example, continuing the globalization theme, one interesting line of enquiry might be how gender relations and masculinities are responding in developing countries such as China, where, in many cases, traditionally patriarchal rural families are now finding that, through the setting up of manufacturing plants that recruit only young women, teenage daughters are becoming the main or only breadwinners.

Abbott, Franklin, ed. 1987. *New Men, New Minds: Breaking Male Tradition.* Freedom, Calif.: The Crossing Press.

Allison, G. 1971. *Essence of Decision.* Boston: Little, Brown.

Albrow, Martin. 1996. *The Global Age: State and Society beyond Modernity.* Cambridge: Polity.

Alger, Chadwick F. 1991. "Foreign Policies of U.S. Publics." Originally published in *International Studies Quarterly* 21, no. 2 (1977). Reprinted in *Perspectives on World Politics*, ed. Michael Smith, Richard Little, and Michael Shackleton. 2nd ed. London: Routledge.

Althusser, Louis. 1971. *"Lenin and Philosophy" and Other Essays.* Harmondsworth, U.K.: Penguin.

Archer, John, and Barbara Lloyd. 1985. *Sex and Gender.* Cambridge: Cambridge University Press.

Arnot, Madeleine. 1986. "State Education Policy and Girls' Educational Experiences." In *Women in Britain Today*, ed. Veronica Beechey and Elizabeth Whitelegg. Milton Keynes, U.K.: Open University Press.

Ashley, Richard K. 1986. "The Poverty of Neorealism." In *Neorealism and Its Critics*, ed. Robert O. Keohane. New York: Columbia University Press.

——. 1988. "Untying the Sovereign State: A Double Reading of the Anarchy Problematique." *Millennium* 17, no. 3: 227–62.

——. 1989. "Living on Border Lines: Man, Poststructuralism, and War." In *International/Intertextual Relations: Postmodern Readings of World Politics*, ed. James Der Derian and Michael Shapiro. Lexington, Mass.: Lexington.

——. 1996. "The Achievements of Poststructuralism." In *International Theory: Positivism and Beyond*, ed. Steve Smith, Ken Booth, and Marysia Zalewski. Cambridge: Cambridge University Press.

Ashworth, Lucian M., and Larry A. Schwatuk. 1998. "Masculinity and the Fear of Emasculation in International Relations Theory." In *The Man Question in International Relations*, ed. Marysia Zalewski and Jane Parpart. Boulder, Colo.: Westview.

Axelrod, Robert, and Robert O. Keohane. 1986. "Achieving Co-operation under Anarchy." *World Politics* 38, no. 2: 226–54.

Axford, Barry. 1995. *The Global System: Economics, Politics, and Culture.* Cambridge: Polity.

Back, Les. 1994. "The White Negro Revisited." In *Dislocating Masculinity: Comparative Ethnographies*, ed. Andrea Cornwall and Nancy Lindisfarne. London: Routledge.

Bailey, M. E. 1993. "Foucauldian Feminism: Contested Bodies, Sexuality, and Identity." In *Up Against Foucault: Explorations of Some Tensions between Foucault and Feminism*, ed. Caroline Ramazanoglu. London: Routledge.

Banks, Michael. 1984. "The Evolution of International Relations Theory." In *Conflict in World Society: A New perspective on International Relations*, ed. Michael Banks. Brighton, U.K.: Wheatsheaf.

Banks, Olive. 1981. *Faces of Feminism.* Oxford: Basil Blackwell.

Barrett, Michèle. 1980. *Women's Oppression Today.* London: Verso.

——. 1991. *The Politics of Truth: From Marx to Foucault.* Cambridge: Polity.

Barthel, Diane. 1992. "When Men Put on Appearances." In *Men, Masculinity, and the Media*, ed. Stephen Craig. London: Sage.

Barthes, Roland. 1973. *Mythologies.* London: Paladin.

Bartky, Sandra. 1990. *Femininity and Domination: Studies in the Phenomenology of Oppression.* London: Routledge.

Bateson, Mary Catherine. 1990. "Beyond Sovereignty: An Emerging Global Civilisation." In *Contending Sovereignties: Redefining Political Community*, ed. R. B. J. Walker and S. H. Mendlovitz. Boulder, Colo.: Lynne Rienner.

Baudrillard, Jean. 1983. *Simulations.* New York: Semiotext(e).

Beck, Ulrich. 1992. *The Risk Society: Towards a New Modernity.* Trans. M. Ritter. London: Sage.

Belsey, C. 1980. *Critical Practice.* London: Methuen.

Benhabib, Seyla. 1992. *Situating the Self: Gender, Community, and Postmodernism in Contemporary Ethics.* Cambridge: Polity.

Best, Steven, and Douglas Kellner. 1991. *Postmodern Theory: Critical Interrogations.* New York: Guildford.

Betterton, Rosemary. 1987. *Looking On: Images of Femininity in the Visual Arts and Media.* London: Pandora.

Bly, Robert. 1991. *Iron John.* Shaftsbury, U.K.: Element.

———. 1992. *Human Shadow.* Shaftsbury, U.K.: Element.

Boone, Joseph A. 1990. "Of Me(n) and Feminism: Who(se) Is the Sex That Writes?" In *Engendering Men: The Question of Male Feminist Criticism,* ed. Joseph A. Boone and Michael Cadden. London: Routledge.

Booth, Ken, and Steve Smith. 1995. *International Relations Theory Today.* Cambridge: Polity.

Bordo, Susan. 1989. "The Body and the Reproduction of Femininity." In *Gender/ Body/Knowledge,* ed. A. Jaggar and S. Bordo. Piscataway, N.J.: Rutgers University Press.

———. 1990. "Feminism, Postmodernism, and Gender-scepticism." In *Feminism/Postmodernism,* ed. Linda J. Nicholson. London: Routledge.

———. 1993a. "Feminism, Foucault, and the Politics of the Body." In *Up Against Foucault: Explorations of Some Tensions between Foucault and Feminism,* ed. Caroline Ramazanoglu. London: Routledge.

———. 1993b. *Unbearable Weight: Feminism, Western Culture, and The Body.* Berkeley: University of California Press.

———. 1999. *The Male Body: A New Look at Men in Public and Private.* New York: Farrar, Straus, Giroux.

Bourke, Joanna. 1996. *Dismembering the Male: Men's Bodies, Britain, and the Great War.* London: Reaktion.

———. 1999. *An Intimate History of Killing.* New York: Basic.

Bradley, Harriet. 1989. *Men's Work, Women's Work.* Cambridge: Polity.

Braidotti, Rose. 1994. *Nomadic Subjects: Embodiment and Sexual Difference in Contemporary Feminist Theory.* New York: Columbia University Press.

Brennan, Teresa. 1989. *Between Feminism and Psychoanalysis.* London: Routledge.

Brittan, Arthur. 1989. *Masculinity and Power.* Oxford: Blackwell.

Brod, Harry. 1987. "A Case for Men's Studies." In *Changing Men: New Directions in Research on Men and Masculinities,* ed. Michael S. Kimmel. London: Sage-Focus.

———. 1994. "Some Thoughts on Some Histories of Some Masculinities: Jews and Other 'Others.'" In *Theorizing Masculinities,* ed. Harry Brod and Michael Kaufman. London: Sage.

Brod, Harry, and Michael Kaufman, eds. 1994. *Theorizing Masculinities.* London: Sage.

Brown, Chris. 1992. *International Relations Theory: New Normative Approaches.* New York: Columbia University Press.

Brown, Michael E. 1993. *Ethnic Conflict and International Security.* Princeton: Princeton University Press.

Brown, Robin. 1995. "Globalization and the End of the National Project." In *Bound-*

*aries in Question: New Directions in International Relations*, ed. John MacMillan and Andrew Linklater. London: Pinter.

Brown, Sarah. 1988. "Feminism, International Theory, and the International Relations of Gender Inequality." *Millennium* 17, no. 3: 461–75.

Brownmiller, Susan. 1977. *Against Our Will*. Harmondsworth, U.K.: Penguin.

Buchbinder, David. 1994. *Masculinities and Identities*. Melbourne: Melbourne University Press.

Bull, Hedley. 1984. "The Revolt against the West." In *The Expansion of International Society*, ed. Hedley Bull and Adam Watson. Oxford: Clarendon.

Bull, Hedley, and Adam Watson, eds. 1984. *The Expansion of International Society*. Oxford: Clarendon.

Burchill, Scott, and Andrew Linklater, eds. 1996. *Theories of International Relations*. London: Macmillan.

Burris, Beverley H. 1989. "Technocratic Organisation and Gender." *Women's Studies International Forum* 12, no. 4: 447–62.

Burton, Clare. 1985. *Subordination: Feminism and Social Theory*. Sydney: Allen & Unwin.

Butler, Judith. 1990a. *Gender Trouble: Feminism and the Subversion of Identity*. New York: Routledge.

———. 1990b. Gender Trouble, Feminist Theory, and Psychoanalytic Discourse." In *Feminism/Postmodernism*, ed. Linda J. Nicholson. New York: Routledge.

———. 1995. "For a Careful Reading." In *Feminist Contentions*, ed. Seyla Benhabib, Judith Butler, Drucilla Cornell, and Nancy Fraser. London: Routledge.

Buzan, Barry. 1993a. "From International System to International Society: Structural Realism and Regime Theory Meet the English School." *International Organisation* 47, no. 3: 327–52.

———. 1993b. "Societal Security, State Security, and Internationalization." In *Identity, Migration, and the New Security Agenda in Europe*, ed. Ole Waever, Barry Buzan, Morten Kelstrup, and Pierre Lemaitre. London: Pinter.

Buzan, Barry, and B. A. Roberson. 1993. "Europe and the Middle East: Drifting towards Societal Cold War?" In *Identity, Migration, and the New Security Agenda in Europe*, ed. Ole Waever, Barry Buzan, Morton Kelstrup, and Pierre Lemaitre. London: Pinter.

Buzan, Barry, Charles Jones, and Richard Little, eds. 1993. *The Logic of Anarchy: Neorealism to Structural Realism*. New York : Columbia University Press.

Campbell, David. 1992. *Writing Security: United States Foreign Policy and the Politics of Identity*. Manchester: Manchester University Press.

Carlton, David. 1993. "Civil War, 'Terrorism,' and Public Order in Europe." In *Identity, Migration, and the New Security Agenda in Europe*, ed. Ole Waever, Barry Buzan, Morton Kelstrup, and Pierre Lemaitre. London: Pinter.

Carrigan, T., R. W. Connell, and J. Lee. 1985. "Towards a New Sociology of Masculinity." *Theory and Society* 14, no. 5: 551–604.

Carver, Terrell. 1995. *Feminist Theory/Political Theory: Perspectives on Gender*. Boulder, Colo.: Lynne Rienner.

Carver, Terrell, Molly Cochran, and Judith Squires. 1998. "Gendering Jones: Feminisms, IRs, Masculinities." *Review of International Studies* 24, no. 2.

Chapman, Rowena, and Johnathan Rutherford. 1988. *Male Order: Unwrapping Masculinity*. London: Lawrence & Wishart.

Chodorow, Nancy. 1978. *The Reproduction of Mothering: Psychoanalysis and the Sociology of Gender*. Berkeley: University of California Press.

Cockburn, Cynthia. 1990. "Men's Power in Organisations." In *Men, Masculinities, and Social Theory*, ed. Jeff Hearn and David Morgan. London: Unwin Hyman.

Cocks, Joan. 1989. *The Oppositional Imagination: Feminism, Critique, and Political Theory*. London: Routledge.

Cohn, Carol. 1987. "Sex and Death in the Rational World of Defence Intellectuals." *Signs: Journal of Women in Culture and Society* 12, no. 4: 687–728.

——. 1993. "Wars, Wimps, and Women: Talking Gender and Thinking War." In *Gendering War Talk*, ed. M. Cooke and A. Woolacott. Princeton: Princeton University Press.

Collinson, David, and Jeff Hearn. 1994. "Naming Men as Men: Implications for Work, Organisation, and Management." *Gender, Work, and Organisation* 1, no. 1: 2–22.

Coltrane, Scott. 1994. "Theorizing Masculinities in Contemporary Social Science." In *Theorizing Masculinities*, ed. Harry Brod and Michael Kaufman. London: Sage.

Connell, R. W. 1987. *Gender and Power*. Oxford: Polity/Basil Blackwell.

——. 1989. "Masculinity, Violence, and War." In *Men's Lives*, ed. Michael S. Kimmel and Michael A. Messner. New York: Macmillan.

——. 1990. "The State, Gender, and Sexual Politics." *Theory and Society* 19, no. 4: 507–44.

——. 1993. "The Big Picture: Masculinities in Recent World History." *Theory and Society* 22, no. 5: 579–623.

——. 1995. *Masculinities*. Cambridge: Polity.

Connolly, William E. 1989. "Identity and Difference in Global Politics." In *International/Intertextual Relations: Postmodern Readings of World Politics*, ed. James Der Derian and Michael Shapiro. Lexington, Mass.: Lexington.

——. 1991. *Identity/Difference: Democratic Negotiations of Political Paradox*. New York, Cornell University Press.

Connor, Stephen. 1989. *Postmodernist Culture: An Introduction to Theories of the Contemporary*. Oxford: Blackwell.

Coole, Diana. 1993. *Women in Political Theory*. 2nd ed. Hemel Hempstead, U.K.: Harvester Wheatsheaf.

Cornwall, Andrea, and Nancy Lindisfarne. 1994. "Dislocating Masculinity: Gender, Power, and Anthropology." In *Dislocating Masculinity: Comparative Ethnographies*, ed. Andrea Cornwall and Nancy Lindisfarne. London: Routledge.

Court, Marion. 1994. "Removing Macho Management: Lessons from the Field of Education." *Gender, Work, and Organisation* 1, no. 1: 33–49.

Coward, Rosalind. 1984. *Female Desire*. London: Granada.

Cox, Robert W. 1986. "Social Forces, States, and World Orders: Beyond International Relations Theory." In *Neorealism and Its Critics*, ed. Robert O. Keohane. New York: Columbia University Press.

Crystal, Johnathan. 1994. "The Politics of Capital Flight: Exit and Exchange Rates in Latin America." *Review of International Studies* 20, no. 2: 131–48.

Daly, Mary. 1979. *Gyn/Ecology: The Metaethics of Radical Feminism*. London: Women's Press.

Davis, David R., and Will H. Moore. 1997. "Ethnicity Matters: Transnational Ethnic Alliances and Foreign Policy Behaviour." *International Studies Quarterly* 41, no. 1: 171–84.

Dawson, Graham. 1991. "The Blond Bedouin: Lawrence of Arabia, Imperial Adventure, and the Imagining of English-British Masculinity." In *Masculinities in Britain since 1800*, ed. Michael Roper and John Tosh. London: Routledge.

Der Derian, James. 1987. *On Diplomacy: A Genealogy of Western Estrangement*. Oxford: Blackwell.

——. 1989. "Spy versus Spy: The Intertextual Power of International Intrigue." In *International/IntertextualRelations: Postmodern Readings of World Politics*, ed. James Der Derian and Michael J. Shapiro. Lexington, Mass.: Lexington.

——. 1990. "The (S)pace of International Relations: Simulation, Surveillance, and Speed." *International Studies Quarterly* 34, no. 3: 295–310.

——. 1991. *Antidiplomacy: Speed, Spies, and Terror in International Relations*. Oxford: Basil Blackwell.

——. 1995. "Virtual Security: From the Gulf War to Bosnia." Paper given at the Centre for International Studies, University of Southern California. Fall 1995.

Der Derian, James, and Michael Shapiro. 1989. *International/IntertextualRelations: Postmodern Readings of World Politics*. Lexington, Mass.: Lexington.

Dinnerstein, Dorothy. 1976. *The Mermaid and the Minotaur*. New York: Harper & Row.

Donaldson, Mike. 1993. "What Is Hegemonic Masculinity?" *Theory and Society* 22, no. 6: 643–57.

Doty, Roxanne Lynn. 1996. "Immigration and National Identity: Constructing the Nation." *Review of International Studies* 22, no. 3: 235–56.

Dowsett, G. W. 1993. "'I'll Show You Mine, if You Show Me Yours': Gay Men, Masculinity Research, Men's Studies, and Sex." *Theory and Society* 22, no. 6: 697–709.

Dworkin, Andrea. 1981. *Pornography: Men Possessing Women*. London: Women's Press.

Edwards, Tim. 1994. *Erotics and Politics: Gay Male Sexuality, Masculinity, and Feminism*. London: Routledge.

Ehrenreich, Barbara. 1983. *The Hearts of Men: American Dreams and the Flight from Commitment.* London: Pluto.

———. 1987. Foreword to *Male Fantasies,* vol. 1, by Klaus Theweleit. Cambridge: Cambridge University Press.

———. 1995. "The Decline of Patriarchy." In *Constructing Masculinity,* ed. Maurice Berger, Brian Wallis, and Simon Watson. London: Routledge.

———. 1999. "Men Hate War Too." *Foreign Affairs* 78, no. 1: 118–20.

Eisenstein, Zillah. 1979. *Capitalist Patriarchy and the Case for Socialist Feminism.* New York: Monthly Review Press.

———. 1981. *The Radical Future of Liberal Feminism.* New York: Longman.

Elliott, Anthony M. 1995. "Symptoms of Globalization: Or, Mapping Reflexivity in the Postmodern Age." In *The State in Transition: Reimagining Political Space,* ed. Joseph A. Camilleri, Anthony P. Jarvis, and Albert J. Paolini. Boulder, Colo.: Lynne Rienner.

Elshtain, Jean Bethke. 1981. *Public Man, Private Woman: Women in Social and Political Thought.* Princeton: Princeton University Press.

———. 1987. *Women and War.* New York: Basic.

Emmett, Sheila, and Chris Llewellyn. 1995. "Rethinking the Political Imagination: New Companions and New Directions." In *The State of the Academy: New Reflections on Political Studies,* ed. Rohit Lekhi. London: Network/PSA.

Enloe, Cynthia. 1980. *Ethnic Soldiers: State Security in a Divided Society.* Harmondsworth, U.K.: Penguin.

———. 1983. *Does Khaki Become You?: Women and the Armed Forces.* London: Pandora.

———. 1987. "Thinking about War, Militarism, and Peace." In *Analyzing Gender: A Handbook of Social Science Research,* ed. B. Hess and M. Feree. Beverley Hills, Sage.

———. 1990. *Bananas, Beaches, and Bases: Making Feminist Sense of International Relations.* London: Pandora.

———. 1993. *The Morning After: Sexual Politics at the End of the Cold War.* Berkeley: University of California Press.

Evans, David T. 1993. *Sexual Citizenship: The Material Construction of Sexualities.* London: Routledge.

Faludi, Susan. 1991. *Backlash: The Undeclared War against American Women.* New York: Crown.

———. 1999. *Stiffed: The Betrayal of the Modern Man.* London: Chatto & Windus.

Ferguson, Kathy E. 1993. *The Man Question: Visions of Subjectivity in Feminist Theory.* Berkeley: University of California Press.

Filene, Peter. 1987. "The Secrets of Men's History." In *The Making of Masculinities: The New Men's Studies,* ed. Harry Brod. Winchester, U.K.: Allen & Unwin.

Firestone, Shulamith. 1971. *The Dialectic of Sex.* London: Paladin.

Fiske, John. 1982. *Introduction to Communication Studies.* London: Methuen.

———. 1987. *Television Culture*. London: Methuen.

Flannigan-Saint-Aubin, Arthur. 1994. "The Male Body and Literary Metaphors for Masculinity." In *Theorizing Masculinities*, ed. Harry Brod and Michael Kaufman. London: Sage.

Flax, Jane. 1990. *Thinking Fragments*. Berkeley: University of California Press.

Friedan, Betty. 1983. *The Second Stage*. London: Sphere.

Folbre, Nancy. 1994. *Who Pays for the Kids?: Gender and the Structures of Constraint*. London: Routledge.

Forrest, David. 1994. "We're Here, We're Queer, and We're Not Going Shopping: Changing Gay Male Identities in Contemporary Britain." In *Dislocating Masculinity: Comparative Ethnographies*, ed. Andrea Cornwall and Nancy Lindisfarne. London: Routledge.

Foucault, Michel. 1980. *The History of Sexuality*, vol. 1, *An Introduction*. New York: Vintage.

Fregoso, Rosa Linda. 1993. "The Representation of Cultural Identity in Zoot Suit (1981)." *Theory and Society* 22, no. 6: 659–74.

Freud, Sigmund. 1953a. "Three Essays on Sexuality." In *Complete Psychological Works*, standard ed., vol. 7. London: Hogarth.

———. 1953b. "Female Sexuality and Some Psychical Consequences of the Anatomical Distinction between the Sexes." In *Complete Psychological Works*, standard ed., vol. 21. London: Hogarth.

Friedan, Betty. 1963. *The Feminine Mystique*. New York: Norton.

Fukuyama, Francis. 1989. "The End of History?" *The National Interest* (summer): 3–18.

———. 1998. "Women and the Evolution of World Politics." *Foreign Affairs* 77, no. 5: 24–40.

———. 1999. "The Great Disruption: Human Nature and the Reconstitution of Social Order." London: Profile.

Fung, Richard. 1995. "Burdens of Representation, Burdens of Responsibility." In *Constructing Masculinity*, ed. Maurice Berger, Brian Wallis, and Simon Watson. London: Routledge.

Gagnon, V. P., Jr. 1994. "Ethnic Nationalism and International Conflict: The Case of Serbia." *International Security* 19, no. 3: 130–66.

Gamman, Lorraine, and Margaret Marshment, eds. 1988. *The Female Gaze: Women as Viewers of Popular Culture*. London: Women's Press.

Garb, Yaakov Jerome. 1990. "Perspective or Escape? Ecofeminist Musings on Contemporary Earth Imagery." In *Reweaving the World: The Emergence of Ecofeminism*, ed. Irene Diamond and Gloria Feman Orenstein. San Francisco: Sierra Club Books.

Giddens, Anthony. 1990. *The Consequences of Modernity*. Cambridge: Polity.

———. 1991. *Modernity and Self-Identity*. Cambridge: Polity.

Gilman, Sander L. 1995. "Damaged Men: Thoughts on Kafka's Body." In *Constructing Masculinity*, ed. Maurice Berger, Brian Wallis, and Simon Watson. London: Routledge.

Gilmore, David. 1990. *Manhood in the Making*. New Haven: Yale University Press.

Gilpin, Robert. 1986. "The Richness of the Tradition of Political Realism." In *Neorealism and Its Critics*, ed. Robert O. Keohane. New York: Columbia University Press.

———. 1987. *The Political Economy of International Relations*. Princeton: Princeton University Press.

———. 1996. "Economic Evolution of National Systems." *International Studies Quarterly* 40, no. 3: 411–31.

Gourevitch, Peter. 1978. "The Second Image Reversed: The International Sources of Domestic Politics." *International Organization* 32, no. 4: 881–911.

Grant, Rebecca. 1991. "The Sources of Gender Bias in International Relations Theory." In *Gender and International Relations*, ed. Rebecca Grant and Kathleen Newland. Milton Keynes, U.K.: Open University Press.

Grant, Rebecca, and Kathleen Newland. 1991. *Gender and International Relations*. Milton Keynes, U.K.: Open University Press.

Gramsci, Antonio. 1971. *Selections from the Prison Notebooks*. London: Lawrence & Wishart.

Greer, Germaine. 1970. *The Female Eunuch*. New York: McGraw Hill.

Grieco, Joseph M. 1995. "The Maastricht Treaty, Economic and Monetary Union, and the New-Realist Research Programme." *Review of International Studies* 21, no. 1: 21–40.

Grimshaw, Jean. 1991. "Politics, Parody, and Identity." Paper given at Glasgow University, July 12.

Grosz, Elizabeth. 1989. *Sexual Subversions: Three French Feminists*. Sydney: Allen & Unwin.

Hall, Catherine. 1992a. "Missionary Stories: Gender and Ethnicity in England in the 1830s and 1840s." In *Cultural Studies*, ed. Lawrence Grossberg, Cary Nelson, and Paula A. Treichler. London: Routledge.

———. 1992b. *White, Male, and Middle-Class: Explorations in Feminism and History*. Cambridge: Polity.

Hall, Stuart. 1973. "The Determination of News Photographs." In *The Manufacture of the News*, ed. Stanley Cohen and Jock Young. London: Constable.

———. 1992. "New Ethnicities." In *"Race," Culture, and Difference*, ed. James Donald and Ali Rattansi. London: Sage.

Halliday, Fred. 1991. "Hidden from International Relations: Women and the International Relations Arena." In *Gender and International Relations*, ed. Rebecca Grant and Kathleen Newland. Milton Keynes, U.K.: Open University Press.

——. 1994. "The Gulf War, 1990–1991, and the Study of International Relations." *Review of International Studies* 20, no. 2: 109–30.

Halpin, Zuleyma Tang. 1989. "Scientific Objectivity and the Concept of 'the Other.'" *Women's Studies International Forum* 12, no. 3: 285–94.

Hanke, Robert. 1992. "Redesigning Men, Hegemonic Masculinity in Transition." In *Men, Masculinity, and the Media*, ed. Stephen Craig. London: Sage.

Hapnes, Tove, and Knut H. Sorensen. 1995. "Competition and Collaboration in Male Shaping of Computing: A Study of Norwegian Hacker Culture." In *The Gender-Technology Relation: Contemporary Theory and Research*, ed. Keith Grint and Rosalind Gill. London: Taylor & Francis.

Haraway, Donna. 1991. *Simians, Cyborgs, and Women: The Reinvention of Nature.* London: Free Association.

——. 1997. *Modest_Witness@Second_Millennium. FemaleMan_Meets_ Oncomouse_: Feminism and Technoscience.* New York: Routledge.

Harding, Sandra. 1986. *The Science Question in Feminism.* Milton Keynes, U.K.: Open University Press.

Hartley, John. 1982. *Understanding News.* London: Methuen.

Hartstock, Nancy. 1983. *Money, Sex, and Power.* New York: Longman.

——. 1987. "The Feminist Standpoint: Developing the Ground for a Specifically Feminist Historical Materialism." In *Feminism and Methodology*, ed. Sandra Harding. Milton Keynes, U.K.: Open University Press.

Harvey, David. 1989. *The Condition of Postmodernity.* London: Basil Blackwell.

Hearn, Jeff. 1992. *Men in the Public Eye: The Construction and Deconstruction of Public Men and Public Patriarchies.* London: Routledge.

Hearn Jeff, and David L. Collinson. 1994. "Theorizing Unities and Differences between Men and between Masculinities." In *Theorizing Masculinities*, ed. Harry Brod and Michael Kaufman. London: Sage.

Hearn, Jeff, and David Morgan. 1990. *Men, Masculinities, and Social Theory.* London: Unwin Hyman.

Higgs, Robert J. 1987. "Yale and the Heroic Ideal, Gotterdammerung and Palingenesis, 1865–1914." In *Manliness and Morality: Middle Class Masculinity in Britain and America, 1800–1940*, ed. J. A. Mangan and James Walvin. Manchester: Manchester University Press.

Hirst, Paul, and Grahame Thompson. 1995. *Globalization in Question: The International Economy and the Possibilities of Governance.* Cambridge: Polity.

Hodson, Philip. 1984. *Men . . . An Investigation into the Emotional Male.* London: BBC Publications.

Hoffman, Stanley. 1977. "An American Social Science: International Relations." *Daedelus* 106, no. 3: 41–60.

Hoffman, M. 1987. "Critical Theory and the Inter-paradigm Debate." *Millennium* 16, no. 2: 231–49.

Hollis, Martin, and Steve Smith. 1990. *Explaining and Understanding International Relations*. Oxford: Clarendon.

Holm, Hans-Henrik, and Georg Sorenson. 1995. *Whose World Order? Uneven Globalization and the End of the Cold War*. Boulder, Colo.: Westview.

Holsti, K. 1985. *The Dividing Discipline: Hegemony and Diversity in International Theory*. London: Allen & Unwin.

Hondagneu-Sotelo, Pierrette, and Michael A. Messner. 1994. "Gender Displays and Men's Power: The 'New Man' and the Mexican Immigrant Man." In *Theorizing Masculinities*, ed. Harry Brod and Michael Kaufman. London: Sage.

Hooper, Charlotte. 1998. "Masculinist Practices and Gender Politics: Multiple Masculinities in International Relations." In *The Man Question in International Relations*, ed. Marysia Zalewski and Jane Parpart. Boulder, Colo.: Westview.

——. 1999a. "Masculinities, IR, and the 'Gender variable': A Cost-Benefit Analysis for (Sympathetic) Gender Sceptics." *Review of International Studies* 25, no. 3: 475–92.

——. 1999b. "Disembodiment, Embodiment, and the Construction of Hegemonic Masculinity." In *Political Economy, Power, and the Body: Global Perspectives*, ed. Gillian Youngs. London: Macmillan.

——. 2000. "Hegemonic Masculinities in Transition: The Case of Globalization." In *Gender and Global Restructuring: Shifting Sights and Sightings*, ed. Marianne Marchand and Anne Sisson Runyan. London: Routledge.

Huntington, Samuel. 1993. "The Clash of Civilizations?" *Foreign Affairs* 72, no. 2: 22–49.

Hurrell, Andrew. 1995. "Explaining the Resurgence of Regionalism in World Politics." *Review of International Studies* 21, no. 4: 331–58.

Hurrell, Andrew, and Ngaire Woods. 1995. "Globalisation and Inequality." *Millennium* 24, no. 3: 447–70.

Hutton, Will. 1995. *The State We're In*. London: Cape.

Huysmans, Jef. 1997. "James Der Derian: The Unbearable Lightness of Theory." In *The Future of International Relations: Masters in the Making*, ed. Wer B. Neumann and Ole Waever. London: Routledge.

Irigaray, Luce. 1985. *The Sex Which Is Not One*. New York: Cornell University Press.

Jackson, David. 1990. *Unmasking Masculinity*. London: Routledge.

Jardine, Alice, and Paul Smith. 1987. *Men in Feminism*. London: Methuen.

Jeffords, Susan. 1989. "The Remasculinization of America: Gender and the Vietnam War." Bloomington: Indiana University Press.

Jervis, Robert. 1985. Introduction to *Psychology and Deterrence*, ed. Robert Jervis, Richard Ned Lebow, and Janice Stein. Baltimore: Johns Hopkins University Press.

Joffe, J. 1993. "The New Europe: Yesterday's Ghosts." *Foreign Affairs* 72: 29–43.

Jones, Adam. 1996. "Does Gender Make the World Go Round? Feminist Critiques of International Relations." *Review of International Studies* 22, no. 4: 405–30.

Jones, Lynne. 1983. "On Common Ground: The Women's Peace Camp at Greenham Common." In *Keeping the Peace: Women's Peace Handbook*, ed. Lynne Jones. London: Women's Press.

Kandiyoti, Deniz. 1992. "Identity and Its Discontents." *Millennium* 20, no. 3: 429–43.

Kanitkar, Helen. 1994. "Real True Boys": Moulding the Cadets of Imperialism." In *Dislocating Masculinity: Comparative Ethnographies*, ed. Andrea Cornwall and Nancy Lindisfarne. London: Routledge.

Kaufman, Michael. 1994. "Men, Feminism, and Men's Contradictory Experiences of Power." In *Theorizing Masculinities*, ed. Harry Brod and Michael Kaufman. London: Sage.

Kelly, Alison. 1985. "The Construction of Masculine Science." *British Journal of the Sociology of Education* 6, no. 2: 133–54.

Keohane, Robert O. 1984. *After Hegemony: Cooperation and Discord in the World Political Economy*. Princeton: Princeton University Press.

——. 1986. "Realism, Neorealism, and the Study of World Politics." In *Neorealism and Its Critics*, ed. Robert O. Keohane. New York: Columbia University Press.

——. 1991. "International Relations Theory: Contributions of a Feminist Standpoint." In *Gender and International Relations*, ed. Rebecca Grant and Kathleen Newland. Milton Keynes, U.K.: Open University Press.

Kersten, Joachim. 1993. "Crime and Masculinities in Australia, Germany, and Japan." *International Sociology* 8, no. 4: 461–78.

Kimmel, Michael S. 1987a. "The Contemporary Crisis in Masculinity in Historical Perspective." In *The Making of Masculinities: The New Men's Studies*, ed. Harry Brod. Winchester: Allen & Unwin.

——. 1990. "After Fifteen Years: The Impact of the Sociology of Masculinity on the Masculinity of Sociology." In *Men, Masculinities, and Social Theory*, ed. Jeff Hearn and David Morgan. London: Unwin Hyman.

Kimmel, Michael S., ed. 1987b. *Changing Men: New Directions in Research on Men and Masculinity*. London: Sage-Focus.

Kimmel, Michael S., and Michael Kaufman. 1994. "Weekend Warriors: The New Men's Movement." In *Theorizing Masculinities*, ed. Harry Brod and Michael Kaufman. London: Sage.

Kimmel, Michael S., and Michael A. Messner. 1989. *Men's Lives*. New York: Macmillan.

King, Josephine, and Mary Stott. 1977. *Is This Your Life? Images of Women in the Media*. London: Virago.

Kissinger, Henry. 1979. *The White House Years*. London: Weidenfeld & Nicholson.

Kofman, Eleanore, and Gillian Youngs. 1996. *Globalization: Theory and Practice*. London: Cassell.

Kristeva, Julia. 1984. *Revolution in Poetic Language*. Trans. Margaret Walker. New York: Columbia University Press.

Kroker, Arthur, and Marilouise Kroker. 1991. *The Hysterical Male*. London: Macmillan.

Kuhn, Annette, and Anne Marie Wolpe. 1978. *Feminism and Materialism*. London: Routledge.

Kymlicka, Will. 1990. *Contemporary Political Philosophy: An Introduction*. Oxford: Clarendon.

Laclau, Ernest, and Chantal Mouffe. 1985. *Hegemony and Socialist Strategy: Towards a Radical Democratic Politics*. London: Verso.

Lapid, Yosef. 1989. "The Third Debate: On the Prospects of International Theory in a Post-positivist era." *International Studies Quarterly* 33, no. 3: 235–54.

——. 1996. "Culture's Ship: Returns and Departures in International Relations Theory." In *The Return of Culture and Identity in IR Theory*, ed. Yosef Lapid and Friedrich Kratochwil. Boulder, Colo.: Lynne Rienner.

Lapid, Yosef, and Friedrich Kratochwil. 1996. *The Return of Culture and Identity in IR Theory*. Boulder, Colo.: Lynne Rienner.

Lash, Scott, and John Urry. 1994. *Economies of Signs and Space*. London: Sage.

Le Doeff, Michelle. 1993. "Modern Life: Feminism in Hard Times." *New Left Review* 199: 127–139.

Ling, Lily, and Kimberley Chang. 2000. "Globalization and Its Other: Filipina Domestics in Hong Kong." In *Gender and Global Restructuring: Shifting Sights and Sightings*, ed. Marianne Marchand and Anne Sisson Runyan. London: Routledge.

Linklater, Andrew. 1982. *Men and Citizens in the Theory of International Relations*. London: Macmillan.

——. 1990. *Beyond Realism and Marxism: Critical Theory and International Relations*. London: Macmillan.

——. 1996. "Citizenship and Sovereignty in the Post-Westphalian State." *European Journal of International Relations* 2, no. 1: 77–104.

Linklater, Andrew, and John MacMillan. 1995. Introduction to *Boundaries in Question: New Directions in International Relations*, ed. John MacMillan and Andrew Linklater. London: Pinter.

Little, Richard, and Michael Smith. 1991. *Perspectives on World Politics*. 2nd ed. London: Routledge.

Louis, William Roger. 1984. "The Era of the Mandates System and the Non-European World." In *The Expansion of International Society*, ed. Hedley Bull and Adam Watson. Oxford: Clarendon.

Luard, Evan. 1990. *The Globalization of Politics: The Changed Focus of Political Action in the Modern World*. New York: New York University Press.

Mac an Ghaill, Mairtin. 1994. "The Making of Black English Masculinities." In *Theorizing Masculinities*, ed. Harry Brod and Michael Kaufman. London: Sage.

MacCabe, C. 1981. "Realism and Cinema: Notes on Brechtian Theses." In *Popular Television and Film*, ed. T. Bennett, S. Boyd-Bowman, C. Mercer, and J. Woollacott. London: British Film Institute/Open University.

MacKinnon, Catharine. 1987. *Feminism Unmodified: Discourses on Life and Law*. Cambridge: Harvard University Press.

MacInnes, John. 1998. *The End Of Masculinity*. Buckingham, U.K.: Open University Press.

Mangan, J. A., and James Walvin, eds. 1987. *Manliness and Morality: Middle Class Masculinity in Britain and America, 1800–1940*. Manchester: Manchester University Press.

Marchand, Marianne. 1994. "Selling NAFTA: Gendered Metaphors and Silenced Gendered Implications." Paper delivered at Global Politics Conference, Nottingham-Trent University, July 27.

Marchand, Marianne, and Anne Sisson Runyan. 2000. *Gender and Global Restructuring: Shifting Sights and Sightings*. London: Routledge.

Marks, Laura U. 1991. "Tie a Yellow Ribbon Round Me: Masochism, Militarism, and the Gulf War on T.V." *Camera Obscura*. September 27.

Massey, Doreen. 1994. *Space, Place, and Gender*. Cambridge: Polity.

McGrew, A., and P. Lewis, eds. 1992. *Global Politics: Globalization and the Nation State*. Cambridge: Polity.

McDermott, Anthony. 1994. *Ethnic Conflict and International Security*. Oslo: NUPI.

McDowell, Linda. 1991. Life without Father and Ford: The New Gender Order of Post-Fordism. *Transactions of the Institute of British Geographers* 16: 400–419.

McMahon, Anthony. 1993. "Male Readings of Feminist Theory: The Psychologization of Sexual Politics in the Masculinity Literature." *Theory and Society* 22, no. 6: 675–95.

McNeil, Maureen. 1993. "Dancing with Foucault: Feminism and Power-Knowledge." In *Up Against Foucault: Explorations of Some Tensions between Foucault and Feminism*, ed. Caroline Ramazanoglu. London: Routledge.

Mercer, Kobena, and Isaac Julien. 1988. "Race, Sexual Politics, and Black Masculinity: A Dossier." In *Male Order: Unwrapping Masculinity*, ed. Rowena Chapman and Johnathan Rutherford. London: Lawrence & Wishart.

Messner, Michael A. 1993. "'Changing Men' and Feminist Politics in the United States." *Theory and Society* 22, no. 6: 723–37.

Metcalf, Andy, and Martin Humphries. 1985. *The Sexuality of Men*. London: Pluto.

Middleton, Peter. 1992. *The Inward Gaze: Masculinity and Subjectivity in Modern Culture*. London: Routledge.

Mies, Maria, and Vandana Shiva. 1993. *Ecofeminism*. Melbourne: Spinifex.

Millett, Kate. 1970. *Sexual Politics*. London: Abacus.

Mitchell, Juliet. 1971. *Woman's Estate*. London: Penguin.

——. 1974. *Psychoanalysis and Feminism*. London: Allen Lane.

Modelski, George, and Kazimierz Poznanski. 1996. "Evolutionary Paradigms in the Social Sciences." *International Studies Quarterly* 40, no. 3: 315–19.

Mohanty, Chandra Talpade. 1991. Introduction to *Third World Women and the Politics of Feminism*, ed. Chandra Talpade Mohanty, Ann Russo, and Lourdes Torres. Bloomington: Indiana University Press.

Moi, Toril. 1985. *Sexual/Textual Politics: Feminist Literary Theory*. London: Methuen.

Moore, Suzanne. 1988. "Getting a Bit of the Other: The "Pimps" of Postmodernism." In *Male Order: Unwrapping Masculinity*, ed. Rowena Chapman and Johnathan Rutherford. London: Lawrence & Wishart.

Morgan, David H. J. 1992. *Discovering Men*. London: Routledge.

——. 1994. "Theatre of War: Combat, the Military, and Masculinities." In *Theorizing Masculinities*, ed. Harry Brod and Michael Kaufman. London: Sage.

Mort, Frank. 1988. "Boy's Own? Masculinity, Style, and Popular Culture." In *Male Order: Unwrapping Masculinity*, ed. Rowena Chapman and Johnathan Rutherford. London: Lawrence & Wishart.

Mouffe, Chantal. 1994. "For a Politics of Nomadic Identity." In *Traveller's Tales: Narratives of Home and Displacement*, ed. George Robertson, Melinda Mash, Lisa Tickner, Jon Bird, Barry Curtis, and Tim Putnam. London: Routledge.

Mrozek, Donald J. 1987. "The Habit of Victory: The American Military and the Cult of Manliness." In *Manliness and Morality: Middle Class Masculinity in Britain and America, 1800–1940*, ed. J. A. Mangan and James Walvin. Manchester: Manchester University Press.

Mulvey, Laura. 1975. "Visual Pleasure and Narrative Cinema." *Screen* 16, no. 3: 16–18.

Murphy, Craig N. 1998. "Six Masculine Roles in International Relations and Their Interconnections: A Personal Investigation." In *The Man Question in International Relations*, ed. Marysia Zalewski and Jane Parpart. Boulder, Colo.: Westview.

Myers, Kathy. 1986. *Understains: The Sense and Seduction of Advertising*. London: Comedia.

Niva, Steve. 1998. "Tough and Tender: New World Order Masculinity and the Gulf War." In *The Man Question in International Relations*, ed. Marysia Zalewski and Jane Parpart. Boulder, Colo.: Westview.

Nicholson, Linda J. 1990. *Feminism/Postmodernism*. London: Routledge.

Oakley, Ann. 1972. *Sex, Gender, and Society*. London: Temple Smith.

——. 1974. *Housewife*. Harmondsworth, U.K.: Penguin.

Ohmae, Kenichi. 1990. *The Borderless World*. London: Collins.

——. 1995. *The Evolving Global Economy: Making Sense of the New World Order*. Boston: Harvard Business Review.

Olson, W., and A. Groom. 1991. *International Relations Then and Now: Origins and Trends in Interpretation*. London: HarperCollins.

Pateman, Carole. 1988. *The Sexual Contract*. Cambridge: Polity.

Parker, Andrew, Mary Russo, Doris Sommer, and Patricia Yaeger. 1992. *Nationalisms and Sexualities.* London: Routledge.

Peterson, V. Spike. 1992a. Introduction to *Gendered States: Feminist (Re)Visions of International Relations Theory*, V. Spike Peterson. Boulder, Colo.: Lynne Rienner.

——. 1992b. "Transgressing Boundaries: Theories of Knowledge, Gender, and International Relations." *Millennium* 21, no. 2: 183–206.

——. 1994. *(Re)Moving Margins and Sit(uat)ing Relations.* Paper given at the Thirteenth World Congress of Sociology, Bielefield, U.S.A., July.

Peterson, V. Spike, and Anne Sisson Runyan. 1993. *Global Gender Issues.* Oxford: Westview.

——. 1998. *Global Gender Issues.* 2nd ed. Boulder, Colo.: Westview.

Pettman, Jan Jindy. 1996. *Worlding Women: A Feminist International Politics.* London: Routledge.

Pfeil, Fred. 1995. *White Guys: Studies in Postmodern Domination and Difference.* London: Verso.

Phelan, Shane. 1989. *Identity Politics: Lesbian Feminism and the Limits of Community.* Philadelphia: Temple University Press.

Phillips, Anne. 1983. *Hidden Hands: Women and Economic Policies.* London: Pluto.

——. 1987. *Divided Loyalties: Dilemmas of Sex and Class.* London: Virago.

——. 1993. "Dealing with Difference: From a Politics of Ideas to a Politics of Presence." Paper given at Democracy and Difference Conference, Yale, April 16–18.

Phillips, Anne, and Barbara Taylor. 1980. "Sex and Skill: Notes Towards a Feminist Economics." *Feminist Review* 6: 79–88.

Plant, Sadie. 1997. *Zeros and Ones: Women, Cyberspace, and the New Sexual Revolution.* London: Fourth Estate.

Pollock, Griselda. 1977. "What's Wrong with Images of Women?" *Screen Education* 24, no. 3: 25–33.

Ramazanoglu, Caroline. 1993. Introduction to *Up Against Foucault: Explorations of Some Tensions between Foucault and Feminism*, ed. Caroline Ramazanoglu. London: Routledge.

Ramazanoglu, Caroline, and Janet Holland. 1993. "Women's Sexuality and Men's Appropriation of Desire." In *Up Against Foucault: Explorations of Some Tensions between Foucault and Feminism*, ed. Caroline Ramazanoglu. London: Routledge.

Rawls, John. 1972. *A Theory of Justice.* Cambridge: Harvard University Press.

Rengger, Nicholas J. 1989. "Incommensurability, International Theory, and the Fragmentation of Western Political Culture." In *Contemporary Political Culture*, ed. J. Gibbens. London: Sage.

Rich, Adrienne. 1979. *Of Woman Born: Motherhood as Experience and Institution.* London: Virago.

Ridley, Matt. 1999. *Genome: The Autobiography of a Species in Twenty-three Chapters.* London: Fourth Estate.

Riley, Denise. 1988. *"Am I That Name?"*: *Feminism and the Category of "Women" in History*. Minneapolis: University of Minnesota Press.

Robertson, Roland. 1990. "Mapping the Global Condition: Globalisation as the Central Concept." In *Global Culture*, ed. Mike Featherstone. London: Sage.

Rogoff, Irit, and David Van Leer. 1993. "Afterthoughts . . . : A Dossier on Masculinities." *Theory and Society* 22, no. 6: 739–62.

Roper, Michael, and John Tosh. 1991. "Historians and the Politics of Masculinity." Introduction to *Masculinities in Britain since 1800*, ed. Michael Roper and John Tosh. London: Routledge.

Rosenau, J. 1990. *Turbulence in World Politics*. Brighton, U.K.: Harvester Wheatsheaf.

Rosenblatt, Paul C., and Michael R. Cunningham. 1976. "Sex Differences in Cross Cultural Perspective." In *Exploring Sex Differences*, ed. Barbara Lloyd and John Archer. London: Academic.

Rothstein, Robert L. 1991. "On the Costs of Realism." Originally published in *Political Science Quarterly*, 87, no. (1972). Reprinted in *Perspectives on World Politics*, Richard Little and Michael Smith. 2nd ed. London: Routledge.

Rowbotham, Sheila. 1973. *Woman's Consciousness, Man's World*. Harmondsworth, U.K.: Penguin.

Rowe, Michael. 1995. "'Race' and Politics: Broadening the Critical Perspective." In *The State of the Academy: New Reflections on Political Studies*, ed. Rohit Lekhi. London: Network/PSA.

Rubin, Gayle. 1975. "The Traffic in Women: Notes on the Political Economy of Sex." In *Toward an Anthropology of Women*, ed. Rayna Rapp Reiter. New York: Monthly Review.

Runyan, Anne Sisson. 1996. "Trading Places: Globalization, Regionalization, and Internationalized Feminism." In *Globalization: Theory and Practice*, ed. Gillian Youngs and Eleanore Kofman. Cambridge: Polity.

Rutherford, Johnathan. 1992. *Men's Silences: Predicaments in Masculinity*. London: Routledge.

Sahlins, Marshall. 1977. "The Use and Abuse of Biology: An Anthropological Critique of Sociobiology." London: Tavistock.

Said, Edward W. 1978. *Orientalism: Western Conceptions of the Orient*. London: Routledge.

Sandel, Michael. 1984. Introduction to *Liberalism and its Critics*, ed. Michael Sandel. New York: New York University Press.

Saurin, Julian. 1995. "The End of International Relations? The State and International Theory in the Age of Globalization." In *Boundaries in Question: New Directions in International Relations*, ed. John MacMillan and Andrew Linklater. London: Pinter.

Sayers, Janet. 1982. *Biological Politics*. London: Tavistock.

Scott, Joan. 1988. *Gender and the Politics of History.* New York: Columbia University Press.

Segal, Lynne. 1987. *Is the Future Female? Troubled Thoughts on Contemporary Feminism.* London: Virago.

———. 1990. *Slow Motion: Changing Masculinities, Changing Men.* London: Virago.

———. 1994. *Straight Sex: The Politics of Pleasure.* London: Virago.

Seidler, Victor J. 1987. "Reason, Desire, and Male Sexuality." In *The Cultural Construction of Sexuality*, ed. Pat Caplan. London: Tavistock.

———. 1988. "Fathering, Authority, and Masculinity." In *Male Order: Unwrapping Masculinity*, ed. Rowena Chapman and Johnathan Rutherford. London: Lawrence & Wishart.

———. 1989. *Rediscovering Masculinity: Reason, Language, and Sexuality.* London: Routledge.

———. 1990. "Men, Feminism, and Power." In *Men, Masculinities, and Social Theory*, ed. Jeff Hearn and David Morgan. London: Unwin Hyman.

———. 1991. *Recreating Sexual Politics: Men, Feminism, and Politics.* London: Routledge.

Shapiro, Michael J. 1989a. "Textualizing Global Politics." In *International/IntertextualRelations: Postmodern Readings of World Politics*, ed. James Der Derian and Michael J. Shapiro. Lexington, Mass.: Lexington.

———. 1989b. "The Sport/War Intertext." In *International/Intertextual Relations: Postmodern Readings of World Politics*, ed. James Der Derian and Michael J. Shapiro. Lexington, Mass.: Lexington.

———. 1990. "Strategic Discourse/Discursive Strategy: The Representation of "Security Policy" in the Video Age." *International Studies Quarterly* 34, no. 3: 327–40.

Shapiro, Michael, and Dianne Neaubauer. 1990. "Spatiality and Policy Discourse: Reading the Global City." In *Contending Sovereignties: Redefining Political Community*, ed. R. B. J. Walker and Saul H. Mendlovitz. Boulder, Colo.: Lynne Rienner.

Simpson, Mark. 1994. *Male Impersonators.* London: Cassell.

Sinha, Mrinalini. 1987. "Gender and Imperialism: Colonial Policy and the Ideology of Moral Imperialism in Late Nineteenth-Century Bengal." In *Changing Men: New Directions in Research on Men and Masculinity*, ed. Michael S. Kimmel. London: Sage-Focus.

Smart, Barry. 1992. *Modern Conditions, Postmodern Controversies.* London: Routledge.

Smith, Anthony D. 1992. "National Identity and the Idea of European Unity." *International Affairs* 68, no. 1: 55–76.

Smith, Michael, Richard Little, and Michael Shackleton, 1981. *Perspectives on World Politics.* London: Routledge.

Smith, Steve. 1995. "The Self-images of a Discipline: A Genealogy of International Relations Theory." In *International Relations Theory Today*, ed. Ken Booth and Steve Smith. Cambridge: Polity.

———. 1998. "'Unnaceptable Conclusions' and the 'Man' Question: Masculinity, Gender, and International Relations." In *The Man Question in International Relations*, ed. Marysia Zalewski and Jane Parpart. Boulder, Colo.: Westview.

Smith, Steve, Ken Booth, and Marysia Zalewski, 1996. *International Theory: Positivism and Beyond*. Cambridge: Cambridge University Press.

Spybey, Tony. 1995. *Globalization and World Society*. Cambridge: Polity.

Stacey, Judith. 1993. "Towards Kinder, Gentler Uses for Testosterone." *Theory and Society* 22, no. 6: 711–21.

Staples, Robert. 1989. "Masculinity and Race: The Dual Dilemma of Black Men." In *Men's Lives*, ed. Michael S. Kimmel and Michael A. Messner. New York: Macmillan.

Starns, Penny. 1997. *Military Influence on the British Civilian Nursing Profession, 1939–1969*. Unpublished Ph.D. thesis. University of Bristol.

Stearns, Peter N. 1979. *Be a Man: Males in Modern Society*. London: Holmes & Meier.

Steinham, Gloria. 1992. *Revolution From Within: A Book of Self-Esteem*. London: Bloomsbury.

Strange, Susan. 1990. "Finance, Information, and Power." *Review of International Studies* 16, no. 2: 259–74.

———. 1995. "Political Economy and International Relations." In *International Relations Theory Today*, ed. Ken Booth and Steve Smith. Cambridge: Polity.

Sylvester, Christine. 1994. *Feminist Theory and International Relations in a Postmodern Era*. Cambridge: Cambridge University Press.

———. 1996. "The Contributions of Feminist Theory to International Relations." In *International Theory: Positivism and Beyond*, ed. Steve Smith, Ken Booth, and Marysia Zalewski. Cambridge: Cambridge University Press.

Taylor, Charles. 1989. "Cross Purposes: The Liberal Communitarian Debate." In *Liberalism and the Moral Life*, ed. N. Rosenblum. Cambridge: Harvard University Press.

Theweleit, Klaus. 1987. *Male Fantasies*, vols. 1 and 2. Cambridge: Cambridge University Press.

Thrift, Nigel. 1994. "On the Social and Cultural Determinants of International Financial Centres: The Case of the City of London." In *Money, Power, and Space*, ed. Stuart Corbridge, Nigel Thrift, and Ron Martin. Oxford: Basil Blackwell.

Tickner, J. Ann. 1991. "Hans Morgenthau's Principles of Political Realism: A Feminist Reformulation." In *Gender and International Relations*, ed. Rebecca Grant and Kathleen Newland. Milton Keynes, U.K.: Open University Press.

———. 1992. *Gender in International Relations*. Oxford: Columbia University Press.

——. 1996a. "Identity in International Relations Theory: Feminist Perspectives." In *The Return of Culture and Identity in IR Theory*, ed. Yosef Lapid and Friedrich Kratochwil. Boulder, Colo.: Lynne Rienner.

——. 1996b. "You Just Don't Understand: Troubled Engagements between Feminists and IR Theorists." Paper given at the School of International Relations, University of Southern California, August.

Tierney, Margaret. 1995. "Negotiating a Software Career: Informal Work Practices and 'The Lads' in a Software Installation." In *The Gender-Technology Relation: Contemporary Theory and Research*, ed. Keith Grint and Rosalind Gill. London: Taylor & Francis.

Tolson, Andrew. 1977. *The Limits of Masculinity*. London, Tavistock.

Tomlinson, John. 1997. "Global Modernity: The Cultural Implications of Globalization." Cambridge: Polity.

Tosh, John. 1991. "Domesticity and Manliness in the Victorian Middle Class: The Family of Edward White Benson." In *Masculinities in Britain Since 1800*, ed. Michael Roper and John Tosh. London: Routledge.

True, Jaqui. 1996. "Feminism." In *Theories of International Relations*, ed. Scott Burchill and Andrew Linklater. London: Macmillan.

Viotti, P., and M. Kauppi. 1993. *International Relations Theory: Realism, Pluralism, Globalism*. 2nd ed. New York: Macmillan.

Waever, Ole, and Morten Kelstrup. 1993. "Europe and Its Nations: Political and Cultural Identities." In *Identity, Migration, and the New Security Agenda in Europe*, ed. Ole Waever, Barry Buzan, Morten Kelstrup, and Pierre Lemaitre. London: Pinter.

Waever, Ole, Barry Buzan, Morten Kelstrup, and Pierre Lemaitre. 1993. *Identity, Migration, and the New Security Agenda in Europe*. London: Pinter.

Walby, Sylvia. 1990. *Theorizing Patriarchy*. Oxford: Blackwell.

Walker, R. B. J. 1992. "Gender and Critique in the Theory of International Relations." In *Gendered States: Feminist (Re)Visions of International Relations Theory*, ed. V. Spike Peterson. Boulder, Colo.: Lynne Rienner.

——. 1993. *Inside/Outside: International Relations as Political Theory*. Cambridge: Cambridge University Press.

Walker, R. B. J., and S. H. Mendlovitz. 1990. "Sovereignty, Identity, Community." In *Contending Sovereignties: Redefining Political Community*, ed. R. B. J. Walker and S. H. Mendlovitz. Boulder, Colo.: Lynne Rienner.

Waltz, Kenneth. 1979. *Theory of International Politics*. Reading, Mass.: Addison-Wesley.

——. 1986. "Laws and Theories and Reductionist and Systemic Theories." In *Neorealism and Its Critics*, ed. Robert O. Keohane. New York: Columbia University Press.

Ware, Vron. 1992. *Beyond the Pale: White Women, Racism, and History.* London: Verso.

Watt, I. 1957. *The Rise of the Novel.* Harmondsworth, U.K.: Penguin.

Weber, Cynthia. 1990. "Representing Debt: Peruvian Presidents Belaúnde's and García's Reading/Writing of Peruvian Debt." *International Studies Quarterly* 34, no. 3: 353–65.

——. 1993. "Something's Missing: Male Hysteria and the U.S. Invasion of Panama." *Genders* 19.

——. 1994. "Good Girls, Little Girls, and Bad Girls: Male Paranoia in Robert Keohane's Critique of Feminist International Relations." *Millennium* 23, no. 2: 337–49.

——. 1995. *Simulating Sovereignty: Intervention, the State, and Symbolic Exchange.* Cambridge: Cambridge University Press.

Weeks, Jeffrey. 1987. "Questions of Identity." In *The Cultural Construction of Sexuality,* ed. Pat Caplan. London: Tavistock.

——. 1989. *Sex, Politics, and Society: The Regulation of Sexuality Since 1800.* 2nd ed. London: Longman.

Whitworth, Sandra. 1989. "Gender in the Inter-paradigm Debate." *Millennium* 18, no. 2: 265–72.

Whyld, J. 1983. *Sexism in the Secondary Curriculum.* London: Harper & Row.

Wight, Martin. 1966. "Why Is There No International Theory?" In *Diplomatic Investigations,* ed. Herbert Butterfield and Martin Wight. Winchester, U.K.: Allen & Unwin.

——. 1991. *International Theory: The Three Traditions.* Leicester: Leicester University Press.

Williams, Raymond. 1977a. "Marxism and Literature." Oxford: Oxford University Press.

——. 1977b. "A Lecture on Realism." *Screen* 18, no. 1: 61–74.

Williamson, Judith. 1978. *Decoding Advertisements.* London: Marion Boyars.

Wilson, Elizabeth. 1977. *Women and the Welfare State.* London: Tavistock.

Winship, Janice. 1981. "Handling Sex." *Media Culture Society* 3, no. 1: 25–42.

Wollestonecraft, Mary. 1929. *A Vindication of the Rights of Women.* London: Everyman.

Young, Iris. 1981. "Beyond the Unhappy Marriage: A Critique of Dual Systems Theory." In *Women and Revolution,* ed. L. Sargent. Boston, Mass.: South End.

Yudice, George. 1995. "What's a Straight White Man to Do?" In *Constructing Masculinity,* ed. Maurice Berger, Brian Wallis, and Simon Watson. London: Routledge.

Zalewski, Marysia. 1996. "'All These Theories yet the Bodies Keep Piling Up': Theory, Theorists, Theorising." In *International Theory: Positivism and Beyond,* ed. Steve

Smith, Ken Booth, and Marysia Zalewski. Cambridge: Cambridge University Press.

Zalewski, Marysia, and Cynthia Enloe. 1995. "Questions about Identity in International Relations." In *International Relations Theory Today*, ed. Ken Booth and Steve Smith. Cambridge: Polity.

Zalewski, Marysia, and Jane Parpart, eds. 1998. *The Man Question in International Relations.* Boulder, Colo.: Westview.

Zinn, Maxine Baca. 1989. "Chicano Men and Masculinity." In *Men's Lives*, ed. Michael S. Kimmel and Michael A. Messner. New York: Macmillan.